T0334660

Philosophy of Nature

The concept of naturalness has largely disappeared from the academic discourse in general but also the particular field of environmental studies. This book is about naturalness in general – about why the idea of naturalness has been abandoned in modern academic discourse, why it is important to explicitly re-establish some meaning for the concept and what that meaning ought to be.

Arguing that naturalness can and should be understood in light of a dispositional ontology, the book offers a point of view where the gap between instrumental and ethical perspectives can be bridged. Reaching a new foundation for the concept of 'naturalness' and it's viability will help raise and inform further discussions within environmental philosophy and issues occurring in the crossroads between science, technology and society.

This topical book will be of great interest to researchers and students in Environmental Studies, Environmental Philosophy, Science and Technology Studies, Conservation Studies as well as all those generally engaged in debates about the place of 'man in nature'.

Svein Anders Noer Lie is Associate Professor at The Arctic University of Norway in Tromsø.

Routledge Explorations in Environmental Studies

Philosophy of Nature
Rethinking naturalness

Svein Anders Noer Lie

LONDON AND NEW YORK

from Routledge

First published 2016
by Routledge

2 Park Square, Milton Park, Abingdon, Oxfordshire OX14 4RN
711 Third Avenue, New York, NY 10017

Routledge is an imprint of the Taylor & Francis Group, an informa business

First issued in paperback 2017

British Library Cataloguing-in-Publication Data
A catalogue record for this book is available from the British Library

Library of Congress Cataloging-in-Publication Data
Lie, Svein Anders Noer, 1969-
Philosophy of nature : rethinking naturalness / Svein Anders Noer Lie.
pages cm
Includes bibliographical references and index.
ISBN 978-1-138-79288-3 (hardback) -- ISBN 978-1-315-76169-5 (ebook)
1. Philosophy of nature. I. Title.
BD581.L495 2015
113--dc23
2014031952

ISBN: 978-1-138-79288-3 (hbk)
ISBN: 978-0-8153-5556-4 (pbk)

Typeset in Goudy
by Saxon Graphics Ltd, Derby

Dedicated to the memory of my beloved father, my dear friend
Marianne Iversen and her daughter Ravdna Iversen Schei

Contents

Figures

Preface

The person to whom this book is a rejoinder is the one who says implicitly or explicitly, and without any qualification, 'Man has always manipulated nature, so why should he not continue to do so?' When this is said without qualification we completely take for granted that any manipulation of nature is as good as any other. A similar way to express this view is to say that man cannot help to change nature and the environment, or that it lies in our nature to do so. 'Without qualification' here means that the proponent of this view often seems to take no interest in the question of *how* we should change nature or the environment. To overlook this question is not wrong mainly because of unfortunate consequences (e.g. environmental problems), but because of the position, which I will develop in this book, that things *have natures*. When things are seen to have natures, there are good and bad ways to manipulate them – and *because* things have natures, it *eventually* becomes clear that there are good and bad consequences. Finally, it is because things have a nature that we can have an ethics regarding those things or beings in the first place.

It is utterly easy to tear down the idea of naturalness, but without a conception of naturalness we are left with a social constructivist approach or an *ontological* approach where we would have to say that any type of change is *really* as good as any other. Both of these approaches are built on the claim that there is no nature in nature – inferring implicitly or explicitly that the beings and properties that we find in nature are discrete and fully compossible,[1] and therefore can, within some physical and practical limits, be taken apart and rearranged anew in any way that we humans prefer. This is the *ontology* that this book is meant to counter.

What I argue for in this book is that there *are* good ways to manipulate nature. This means that I also disagree with the position assuming that the (really) good way to manipulate nature would be to leave nature entirely alone (as many conservationists would claim). In my view, there is an ignored space between leaving nature completely alone and manipulating nature with the assumption that everything is fully compossible. Humans are a part of nature, but that does not mean that every type of manipulation is "right". We should manipulate nature with the background assumption that there are some dispositional properties to which we should relate in *specific* ways.

However, saying what we 'should or should not do' already exceeds the scope of this book. The present goal is not to work out an ethically viable position, but rather to show how and why naturalness belongs to the descriptive side of the is/ought distinction. I aim to show that with the right ontology we may, without too much pain, welcome naturalness into our descriptions – and also, in fact, *acknowledge* that naturalness is *there* already.

Including naturalness on the descriptive side, the *is-side*, where propositions can ideally be said to be true or not true, will move it further away from the *ought-side*, the side belonging to ethics. This is fortunate because whenever the scientist rejects naturalness in his or her descriptions (on the grounds that naturalness "belongs to ethics"), the ethicist is confronted by a question that s/he cannot handle, ontologically. In its short form, the issue is as follows. Ethics is about values and normative actions. It is assumed that naturalness entails normative statements about the world, but that is in my view not correct. The ascription of naturalness can be true or untrue, but naturalness in itself is neither good nor bad. When I say that there is a bad and a good way to manipulate nature, one may still argue that it is morally good to manipulate nature in a bad way. Nevertheless, ascriptions of value depend upon whether the being in question *has* a certain nature or not. Perception therefore precedes ethics, in that the way that we choose to describe things has a bearing on what kind of values we may eventually choose to ascribe to these things. The strong distinction between 'is' and 'ought', science and ethics tells us however that ethicists have no authority to challenge or contest the descriptions that are scientifically produced since s/he is not a scientist. The result of this line of reasoning is a free-floating ethics. An ethics that tries to say something about nature (presumably) without any preconception of what nature really is. This insurmountable situation characterizes many of the debates taking place today over environmental issues and at the intersection between ethics and (bio)technology, one that is "solved" by retreating into various positions of utilitarian ethics.

What prevents us from taking the natures of things into consideration? The obvious answer to this is that we don't think that they have natures. In the main, the ontology that underpins such a belief is reductionism – or, more broadly, what I call passivism.[2] My treatment of this issue is by far the most comprehensive analysis in this book. Massive effort is required to explain why reductionism *works*, despite the rejection of naturalness that it involves.

In this preface, I would also like to say something about what kind of debate I place this book within. I have already mentioned the general debate within environmental ethics, but I also see the book as contributing to the discussion that is taking place at the juncture between ethics and modern technology in a more general sense. One might say that the divide that occurred in the fifteenth century between the human world and the natural world is now starting to be "reconciled". But in my mind this "reconciliation" is happening the wrong way around. Rather than rethinking the ontology that created this divide in the first place, we are protecting the ontology while it floods into the so-called autonomous sphere of humanity. Today we see a progressing small-step-naturalization of the human sphere which is not a problem in itself, but becomes a problem as long as it happens on the terms of passivist ontologies. Human behaviour is increasingly explained in passivist terms, while technology progressively answers an expanding range of problems with which we as humans are confronted. The way that we explain ourselves has wide-ranging implications for how we explain non-human nature (and vice versa), and it seems as though there are no limits to what science and technology can do! To understand that there *are* limits is a very delicate and complex matter, because the limits that are relevant are neither "physical" nor ethical. What they are is the major issue of this book.

It has not been an easy task to picture an 'ideal reader' while writing this book. While I am a philosopher, and this is in many aspects a philosophical book, the intended audience extends beyond philosophers. At the same time, the aim has not been to write a book that is accessible to all. Rather, it is directed to a range of specialists: ecologists, biologists, STS-researchers, social scientists, environmental scientists and scientifically trained managers within the "environmental field" (as well as to philosophers and environmental ethicists, of course). I have also – not to forget – had the well-informed environmentalist in the back of my mind. The most difficult segment of the book for those who are not trained in philosophy is chapters 4 and 5. I considered writing a lighter version of these chapters, but I quickly left that idea, because a lighter version is not possible. Either I had to share the whole picture with the reader or just leave these chapters out altogether, which was not an option.

The most "difficult" parts for the philosophers, meanwhile, are those parts where I make broad claims that are not safeguarded by references and vindications in all corners. I have in mind claims about social constructivism, epistemology, philosophy of science, etc., which are needed for the general argument in the book, but which are not fully treated in their own right as philosophical issues. My confidence is in The Argument in these cases. I have tried to expose my thinking as far as possible, leaving it up to the reader to agree or disagree with the line of reasoning that is put forward.

The most "difficult" parts for the scientists, I imagine, are where I claim something about science or a particular scientific field that does not pay enough attention to disagreements and debates within science in general, and/or within given fields. I claim, for instance, that science has a particular view of the welfare of animals (salmon), although I know that the view that I present is not fully agreed upon. I hope that readers will be flexible enough to see that I cannot present the full picture in such cases, and will trust that I have caught the consensus within the field in question.

How to understand naturalness is not a question that can be addressed in a well-defined way where each point of the story and argument depends neatly on the other. The complexity of the issue makes it difficult to present a perfectly linear story. Many of the early arguments depend upon later ones, so that what seems to be an unsatisfying justification in the first instance will only appear more solid when later parts are read and understood. The issue itself is, in other words, not one that lends itself to being approached in the way in which philosophy is generally done today. It is simply not possible to establish an adequate account of naturalness in the form of articles that can stand more or less on their own – if only because there are too many assumptions involved, many of which are not well established in the literature. However, if everything were clear and fully justified at the outset, there would be little reason to write a book in the first place.

Notes

1 The term 'compossible' comes from Armstrong (1989). See introduction to Part II of this book.
2 The expressions 'passivism'/'passivist ontology' will be used throughout this book. The main reference for this concept is Brian Ellis (2002), and can generally be taken to signify the view that the behaviour of beings is determined by external forces and objects.

References

Armstrong, David (1989) *A Combinatorial Theory of Possibility*, Cambridge University Press.
Ellis, Brian (2002) *The Philosophy of Nature*, Acumen.

Acknowledgements

There are many people whom I would like to thank for their various contributions. Finn Johannessen, my father in philosophy, has let me into the details of his overarching philosophical point of view in a way that made it possible to go down the road resulting in this volume. The best parts of this book are dedicated to him. Arnt Myrstad has commented and worked his way through this manuscript at an earlier stage. Rani Lill Anjum is a dear friend and a "dispositional partner" in crime, and has helped me with the manuscript at different stages. Fern Wickson took the time to read and comment on the whole manuscript at an earlier time in this process. That was an immense contribution!

Lisa Thompson was the linguistic saviour of this manuscript at an earlier stage. I thank her for her self-sacrificing effort and for her friendship. I also thank her husband Ignacio Chapela at Berkeley for his facilitating presence, his friendship, and for his help and relentless belief in this project.

Stephen Mumford's philosophy has a central place in this book. During the years he has also become a good friend and a collaborator. I want to thank him for all the things he has taught me about dispositions and other things, through both his books and his spoken words.

My thanks also to Vito De Lucia, Jonas Jensen, Raul Primicerio, and Michael Morrau for their smaller and bigger contributions to the process of completing this manuscript. I also want to thank my closest friends whom I have discussed these things with over many years: Thomas Bøhn, Stein Erik Gillund, Gunnar Kristiansen and Per Schrader.

Other people whom I would like to thank are Halvor and Rigmor Noer, Terje Traavik, Johannes Persson, Øyvind Stokke, Torje Mikalsen, Uwe Petersen, Valerie Kerruish, Matthias Kaiser, Sigurd Tønnessen, Kåre Nolde Nielsen, Ann I Myhr, Frøydis Gillund, Simon Mills, Owe Steen Hansen, Melina Duarte, the University of Nottingham, the University of Tromsø, Institute of Philosophy and First semester studies in Tromsø, GENOK - Center for Biosafety, *Altonaer Stiftung für Philosophische Grundlagenforschung* in Hamburg and the participants in the "disposition-group" in Nottingham 2007/2008. I also thank those who have commented on parts of this manuscript at different conferences and seminars during the last ten years.

A very special thank you goes to Ruth Groff, who has worked her way through this final version of the manuscript. Her general comments and the work she has done with the syntactic and philosophical clarity of the book have been of utmost importance for the final result. Her way of carefully balancing between intervening and "letting be" is more than admirable. Readers who may find the writing style or parts of the content philosophically problematic should not hold her responsible. I would also like to thank the two anonymous readers at Routledge, and my editors Khanam Virjee and Helen Bell for their important assistance and smooth patience.

Last but not least, I would like to thank my wife Marte and my children Severin, Ragne and Solan for their support and curiosity. There have been sacrifices along the way, especially for my wife. Thank you a thousand times! I will also use this opportunity to thank my mother and father for their relentless love and support, and finally my brothers – for their brotherhood.

Part I
Disputable natures

1 Naturalness

1.0 Introduction: the dubious status of naturalness

Queries into the question of naturalness do not occur frequently in contemporary philosophical literature. In fact, only a few articles and some book chapters in a few books treat this topic as a theme in its own right, and for good reason, many would say. The word 'nature' is one of the most complex words in our language (R. Williams 1976, 184), and the word 'naturalness' is barely less complex. What *'naturalness'* signifies is ambiguous, and many would say that in the end it refers to *nothing*.

Various paradoxes come to the surface when we approach and try to understand naturalness as a term in its own right. Here are some, helter-skelter:

- If unnaturalness is taken to mean those things brought about by human agency, how can we at the same time assume that we are a part of nature? (Environmentalists usually take both claims to be true at the same time.)
- Can we differentiate between natural and unnatural actions in terms of voluntary/involuntary actions? And if we can, would the destruction of our environment, which might be seen as involuntary, be seen as a 'natural action'?
- If natural means pristine or 'untouched by human hands', is there anything today that can be called natural at all? And if not, is there is no naturalness "left" in nature? And if there isn't, can anything formed by the human hand and mind be called unnatural?
- What is the real difference between those things that we regard as natural and those that we regard as artificial? For example, what is the defining difference between an athlete who uses EPO and an athlete who stays in an altitude chamber?
- If nature develops historically and changes all the time, how can one type of change be more or less natural than another state or type of change?
- Could something be coincidental or contingent and natural at the same time? If nature obeys the laws of nature, how can we be able to perform anything deemed unnatural if our actions and technologies are based on the same laws?

The following are some of the typical and possible ways 'natural' is used: 'Being a homosexual is unnatural'; 'Being a homosexual is perfectly natural'; 'Natural water'; 'Containing completely natural components'; 'The energy coming from an atomic plant is completely natural'; 'I resent eating genetically modified organisms (GMOs) because I think they are unnatural'; 'Naturally, I will do that'; 'I only eat natural foods'; 'That baby does not look natural'; 'The breasts are natural all the way through'; 'He died from natural causes'. The antonyms are also interesting: 'The whole thing was done in an artificial way'; 'People from Oslo are so unnatural'; 'I think he is the guilty one, his behaviour seemed so artificial'; 'No artificial flavours added'.

I share these examples of paradoxes and daily usage in order to underline what the non-specialist reader would expect: 'Naturalness' is a frequently used word, but it is used in different ways, with different meanings and without consistency. Strikingly, however, when it is *used* it is often used with a relatively precise meaning. People do (often) have a particular understanding of the concept when they use it, although they might know in the back of their mind that its meaning is both contentious and widely disputed. This is, of course, not exceptional in any way; many words are like this. But the problem that I meet in discussions about the concept of naturalness is that I am often confronted with the situation where people want to have it both ways. They would like to be "critical" (about the meaning of the concept), while at the same time they are not critical about the concept that they want to criticize (that is: not aware of the fact that the "intuitive" concept they are criticizing might refer to a *special* understanding of naturalness and not 'naturalness' as such). That is, of course, again not an ideal starting point for a deeper analysis of naturalness as being a property in its own right.

What comes in addition to the range of uses and paradoxical meanings and connotations of the word is that 'naturalness' is not *comme il faut* in either science or social sciences. 'Naturalness' is a term that might be used in our mundane conversations, but not in scientific discourse. For a scientist, there are no such things as unnatural atoms or unnatural ecosystems, for example. If the Amazon jungle is cut down and transformed into a desert, there are hardly any scientists who stand ready to defend the claim that the desert is an unnatural ecosystem. Rather, the presumption amongst scientists is that nature has no state of being that is more natural than any other state of being.

For a social scientist the word 'natural' often has repressive connotations, and is sometimes associated with so-called reactionary movements (Soper 1995, 119ff.). A social scientist will typically point to examples that show how 'natural' is used to defend what an interest group deems to be normal. Even more important, the prevalent view within social sciences is that meaning and action are constituted by language and social practices, which means that words in our language refer to *other words* rather than to 'reality'. In this context, the whole concept of naturalness seems incongruous. "Natural" is a word that critically depends upon its reference to *something* beyond what is or can be socially constructed, and is therefore at odds with a core idea that makes social science social science.

This connects further to a debate within environmental ethics in which environmentalists are accused of being "naïve realists". What is the environmentalist really defending? Is it nature? What kind of nature? Asking these questions, it seems obvious that the environmentalist is really defending a socially constructed and interest-based concept of nature and naturalness, not nature itself. Paul Wapner speaks of this position in the following way:

> Anti-environmentalists such as Charles Rubin and Alstone Chase, for example, now claim that, if there is no such thing as "real" nature, we need not treat the nonhuman world with unqualified respect. If we think it is in our interest, we can truly choose to pave the rainforest, wipe out the last panda bear, or pump high levels of carbon dioxide into the atmosphere. What is critical to notice in both cases is that criticism of "nature", whether they come from the left or are co-opted by the right, are playing an increasing role in structuring the confrontation between anti and pro-environmentalists. And they are resetting the fault lines within the environmental movement itself.
>
> (Wapner 2003, 2)

Wapner's description applies to the concept of 'naturalness' as well as to the concept of 'nature'. His point is that the social sciences and Left thinking have come together on the basis of the ontological claim "What is, could have been different", and that assumptions about something being specifically natural, or not, easily come down to reactionary politics.[1]

If this is not enough, there is also a fast-growing scepticism towards this concept amongst environmentalists and environmental thinkers themselves. In Chapter 6 we will encounter some of the reasons for this controversy, but more generally we may speak of a group of environmental thinkers who argue that we should manage the planet in accordance with human interests (in agreement with so-called scientific principles), and leave the idea of naturalness as a guiding principle for management and orientation. (See e.g. Wuerthner et al. 2014 for an elaboration and criticism of this view.) The main argument is that there is no way to define 'nature' or 'naturalness' and that we therefore, by this negative argument, might as well resign ourselves to an "environmental account of a postnatural world" (e.g. Vogel 2002).

Finally, the word 'naturalness' also has a dubious standing within philosophy itself, and any attempt to re-establish it will immediately make most philosophers think that someone is trying to re-actualize Aristotelian metaphysics. This, at least, has been my experience. And such a reflex has its philosophical merits (as we will see later in Chapter 2). For many philosophers, the layperson's use of the concept is therefore regarded as a case where "enlightenment has failed". This may partly explain why there has been literally no philosophical work devoted to this issue for the last 300–400 years.

The primary aim in this book is not first and foremost to identify the *right* concept of naturalness, but to defend the philosophical *viability* of the concept. Others have addressed the issue of naturalness by way of mapping what philosophers, scientists and others directly or indirectly *mean* when they use this concept, or when a certain concept of naturalness is implied in an argument (Siipi 2005). This is not the method that I adopt, because we should not take it as a given that the concept is viable (and that a mapping of definitions would therefore make any difference for a defence of the concept). Instead, I am engaged in a fundamental reconsideration of the concept. I have taken this approach because it is only through such an effort that the viability of the concept can be established. You will therefore find a tension in this book between the pursuit of a general account of the "possibility of naturalness" and a more goal-oriented search for a specific concept that I myself would support.

1.1 General motivation

Given all the difficulties listed above, it may seem that we should just abandon this ship and seek one that is able to find dry land. However, I believe that it is possible to illuminate the concept of naturalness in a way that will make us willing to acknowledge that it has a real referent. The reason for this is fivefold.

§1   The way that we philosophically and scientifically understand naturalness today is the result of *flawed but hegemonic* ontology. The many conceptual difficulties that we find in the relation between science and ethics are, in my view, partly due to this ontology. I argue: (a) that a *disposition-ontology* can do much to establish that the current ontological regime is not the only one; and (b) that the concept of naturalness will gain a new meaning through this ontology.

§2   The environmental debate presupposes a concept of naturalness. Without a concept of naturalness, words like contamination, environmental sustainability, animal welfare, biodiversity, pollution, etc., will *only* yield meaning as something socially constructed, something that is matter out of – or matter in – place (Douglas 1966). What are environmentally degrading activities if not simply change of some arbitrary order? How can someone talk about anthropogenic emissions of climate gasses and therefore be engaged in the climate issue at all if a certain concept of naturalness is not presupposed?

It is not fully understood that the alternative to naturalness has to lean on some kind of Humean or necessitarian idea of how things are related in nature; an idea that would have to render any change (made by humans) as good as any other. One does not therefore understand clearly that without a concept of naturalness, fighting pollution, defending a species from extinction or a forest from "destruction" are just meaningless phrases produced by a social group that wants to defend a particular constructed idea about how that group wants nature to be. Without a concept of naturalness we are completely right in asking "What kind of nature do we want?" In a democracy, we would be right to ask for a nature that is fully formed and constructed in accordance with democratic decisions. Talk about welfare problems in fish farming would be completely based on the premise that the different views only represent subjective projections from different interest groups. The salmon itself would have "nothing to say", and those who would claim such a thing would be *ventriloquists* (Vogel forthcoming, ch. 6).

The environmental debate needs or even presupposes a concept of naturalness. But it is one thing to implicitly appreciate this "harbour"; it is another thing to argue for it explicitly. Because of the complexity of the problem, one might give up before getting started, and resign oneself to the less laborious utilitarian debates – which is typically what has happened in the GMO debate. This is not to say that environmental issues are not in part dependent upon socio-cultural aspects. It is rather to claim that such aspects may rest upon further assumptions, which are themselves part of the argument. The assumptions that I am talking about concern what reality really is, i.e. they are *ontological assumptions*. A relevant and pertinent concern here is, as we have seen, that many environmentalists have started to draw the conclusion that since human impact is increasingly all-pervasive we should just give up any reference that goes beyond a *functional idea of nature* (see e.g. Cole and Yung 2010, and Chapter 6). This is also what is indirectly advocated by those who "embrace the Anthropocene" (e.g. Peter Kareiva, Stewart Brand, Emma Marris and others). The explicit idea for those who "embrace the Anthropocene" is that we humans should, for a number of reasons, decide what kind of nature we want. I think this is a conclusion that is not only based on false premises; it is also an extremely dangerous shift in our attitude towards nature. Even though I do not take direct part in the discussion of the Anthropocene in this book it is my aim to show why even the 'embracement strategy' stands in the need of a concept like naturalness and cannot base itself on a 'functional approach towards nature' (Chapter 6).

§3 The role that science plays in the invention, development and production of new and sometimes contested technologies has initiated a debate about what science really is and whether it is appropriate to continue to operate with distinctions like subject/object, fact/value, experts/politicians, etc. (Latour 1991 and 1998; Wynne 1992; Beck 1988; Funtowicz and Ravetz 1993; Gibbons et al. 1994). What kind of role do and should scientists play in these debates? Do scientists already hold a fixed view that dictates how discussions that potentially may involve 'naturalness' will go? Often we see that naturalness is brushed off as misplaced axiology by the scientist, something that inevitably leads to intractable and confusing debate (Deckers 2005; Heffernan 2003; Kwieciński 2009; Wynne 2001; Verhoog 2003; Lie 2008; Nuttfield Council of Bioethics 1999). The broadly accepted fact/value distinction is never questioned in such discussions. It is assumed that facts cannot tell us *anything* about how we should act towards nature, leaving "free-floating ethics" to be our sole guide (see section 1.4). This in turn raises the question of how ethics can possibly be biocentric if the *bios* can tell us nothing about how to handle concrete situations. How can we *really* assess the consequences for nature, if nature consists only of contingent states and contingent changes in those states?

The main point for me in this regard is to tease out what it really means to say or assume that "nature has no nature", and to show the implications of this view. Is the claim that concepts such as 'naturalness' and 'nature' "belong to the trash bin" an ontologically innocent assertion? Does it contain a claim about the reality of things that has to be defended in its own right? If so, then we should also be able to ask for a positive account of what it means to say that the vocabulary of naturalness belongs to those who are less enlightened.

An example of what I am talking about is the following. In the book *What Scientists Think* there is an article in which the famous professor in mathematics Norman Levitt is interviewed. Levitt suggests that the European resistance to GMOs can be understood by looking at "their particular cultural dogmas of *purity and danger*". Levitt makes use of the anthropologist Mary Douglas to analyse the situation.[2] It is true that through the lens of Douglas's approach we may view the GMO issue as a disagreement between two different *cultural* stances. In this case, however, Levitt thinks that there is a realist position and a cultured position. As *a scientist* Levitt seems to be in a position that enables him to disavow the European arguments against GMOs simply by calling attention to the fact that they represent a cultural interpretation – by which he logically implies that there is an 'uncultured realist interpretation' of genetic engineering (GE). This realist interpretation based in molecular genetics takes as its starting point that there is no naturalness/non-naturalness that can be ascribed to genes, and therefore nothing that could be unclean, pure, dangerous, monstrous, or what have you. Reference to naturalness here is therefore simply a category mistake, according to Levitt. In Levitt's view, what has happened when, for example, a plant is genetically modified is simply a (deeply contingent) molecular *event*. This amounts to nothing more than moving a grain of sand from one place to another: change has occurred – nothing more, nothing less. Saying that this change is unnatural is to misunderstand what nature really is. It is similar to saying for instance, that 'this bush is unclean'. Thus, every intrinsic or principled critique of GE will be deemed to be a matter of 'culture', while the opposite will not be. In other words, any reaction that transcends the scientific ontology of Levitt will be cultured, and thus by definition will also be biased. There is something, a deeply entrenched way to view nature, which allows Levitt to say this without many questions being asked (see also Kwieciński 2009).

On the one hand, Levitt's view seems to be in line with some of our intuitions. On the other hand, his view seems to contradict other intuitions that tell us that naturalness has a place. For instance, if you want to teach a dog to find chanterelles, you are right if you expect that there are better or worse ways to do that; if you want to make ice from water there will of course be better and worse ways to do that as well. What does it mean that there is a way to do things – that we cannot really sit down and rearrange things without knowing how 'things behave'? Leaving this question out will leave the molecular biologist alone with his expectation that he can change the genome of an organism in any way he wants. If there is a restricted potentiality in the world, however, we cannot really decompose and recompose the world in a way that is consistent only with human interests. It must also be done in accordance with something that goes beyond what we want to do. What is this if not 'the nature of things'? If we cannot agree upon this in general, or on a specific way to understand this nature, science and scientists would be right to continue their enlightenment project, one that, all in all, amounts to showing that the attribution of naturalness is mere anthropomorphic projection. The scientist versus layman debate will continue in the way that it has, with the scientist patiently explaining to the layman how the world really works.

This debate between laymen and scientists is interesting, and makes up some of the background that has motivated me to write a book about 'naturalness'. However, the essence of the debate is even more interesting. If there were no restrictions on the way that we can manipulate nature other than those that come with the contingent necessities of the world, there would be nothing other than ethics to restrict our actions. And what kind of ethics? An ethics that can be applied to facts or to some kind of difference-making realm? No, that is of course already ruled out by the ontology itself, and by the fact–value regime that reigns between science and ethics (see section 1.4). So, what kind of ethics, again? Ethics that is accepted as being fundamentally subjective (e.g. Putnam 2002, 1; McInerny 1982, 53).

My claim in this book that the 'autonomy of ethics', which is cherished by many, has ultimately come about as a *reaction* to a specific ontology. It is a mistaken ontology that has designated the role that we think is viable for ethics to play today – a role that in my opinion is an utterly powerless one; despite the fact that it is enjoying its heyday in ethical committees throughout the western world.

What difference does it make in the debate between science and society when scientists refuse to accept naturalness as a viable concept for the participants to appeal to? A scientist would normally agree to participate in a risk debate, but not in a debate about naturalness since that would be regarded as taking part in a value debate (Wynne 2001; Midgley 2000). The result of this is that the participants have to channel all their arguments into a debate about consequences, i.e. risk assessments (e.g. Verhoog 2003). What we see is that environmental ethicists and others have tried to establish arguments for the intrinsic value of different entities in nature, but that any communication with scientists is only possible through the frame of utilitarianism or other types of consequentialist ethics. This leads to a schizophrenic situation. Since the question about naturalness is disputable and our concepts of nature and naturalness are deployed differently in different situations, we often find ourselves in the situation where the unreflecting laymen's concept of naturalness is rejected by the scientist (Meyer and Sandøe 2001; Marris 2001), but is defended by the environmentalist with the argument of intrinsic value (Verhoog 2003). That is, we get a breakdown in communication between laymen, who do not accept utilitarian calculations as the only way to discuss these issues, and scientists who are trying to engage in debates such as this.

In "Having an Ethical Discussion about the Objects of Natural Science: The Is and Ought Distinction" (Lie 2008), I tried to show that the standard risk debate in fact presupposes an implicit concept of naturalness, and that scientists should be consistent and either stay away from the risk debate or accept naturalness into the discussion. In any case, the point is that even though naturalness is a dubious concept philosophically and scientifically, it plays an important role in our everyday lives, including our political lives. This renders an elaboration of the concept welcome, even necessary. Of course, the fact that the environmental debate is in *need* of a concept of naturalness is no reason whatsoever to assume that such a concept refers to something real. That must be argued for independently.

§4   My fourth motivation is connected to the way in which current technology develops. Modern technologies like (modern) biotechnology, nanotechnology, synthetic biology, so-called converging technologies, etc., challenge our ethical views and our layman's concepts of naturalness in different ways. The number of controversial technologies and future scenarios connected to these technologies is literally exploding these days.

Take the hypothetical example, where we imagine that a bio-tech company made a hen (let's call her *pol-ly*) who was square, without legs, with a novel and feed-functional beak, without any hierarchical pecking or herd instincts, laying square eggs (for rational packing) – and all this we would get with the true warranty that there would be no risks or hazards involved – what would be wrong with that? Are we violating something that the hen *has*?

These questions also arise in the human sphere. What is wrong with human clones? What is wrong with technologies that can extend our lives by 700 years? What is wrong with genetically or chemically manipulated athletes? The technology itself would probably (but not surely) allow for a future where athletes are specially designed for running, for football, for cross-country skiing, etc. There seems to be something about naturalness – the spontaneity, and possibly the coincidental, or non-constructedness that is "provided by nature" – that should be added to our notion of autonomy.[3] We are impressed by the self-made man, but not by the (self)-constructed man. 'Self-made' seems to be based on some aspects that are "not fully constructed", although not completely arbitrary either. Can we say something about naturalness that can play an enlightening role here?

At present I am not aiming at a concept of naturalness that can address and answer these questions directly. The account with which I end will have *some* implications, though, for issues such as integrity and intrinsic value, etc., and I will try to give my opinion on how far this account can be employed in this debate (section 5.6). It is my hope that this will be enough to help clarify important aspects of the discussion in these areas. To go further would require an additional, explicitly ethical argument, which would lead us far astray from the narrow path that I want to chart in this book. I will, however, use the GMO debate and cases from biochemistry and biotechnology as my primary examples throughout the text, both because they are directly philosophically relevant and because they point to important issues and debates outside the text itself – as I have indicated here.

§5 A more positive motivation for trying to establish the viability of the concept of naturalness is the prospect of providing an operational account of how to *utilize* nature. I will pursue a way of describing the relationship between humans and nature according to which humans are a part of nature, and in light of which humans might become a *better* part of nature by trying to act in keeping with what we believe to be the nature of things. There are many aspects of the environmental issue and there is truly a wild-running plethora of suggestions on how to "solve the problem". My fundamental belief is that none of these solutions will work if they are in conflict with the way things work naturally. If we could, in small and bigger steps, move on this fundamental level in the right direction I have great hopes for the future (though maybe not for a hundred years or so).

An important part of this movement will be to pull the question of naturalness out of the realm of ethical discourse and back into that of ontology – and eventually into a scientific description of the world. Modern science partly came into being as a result of the settlement with Aristotelian teleology, and since the Aristotelian teleology was, and still is, considered to be the 'philosophy of naturalness', it is also considered unscientific to talk about naturalness. I maintain that there is no necessary connection between teleology and naturalness, and that science can safely adopt the ontology that, in my view, supports a viable concept of naturalness.

These different points, five in number, demand a fully developed philosophical defence. But I want to underscore that this book is motivated by the belief that naturalness is a "real-world phenomenon", albeit one that stands in need of being properly conceptualized. The issues that I have touched upon in this chapter will be treated in more depth in the chapters to come. The reader should not fear that claims made above will be left to stand alone without further exposition.

1.2 'Naturalness': the semantic job

The wide and sometimes paradoxical use of the word 'natural' suggests that we should carry out a semantic clean-up job. Clearly this concept has different meanings that live parallel and sometimes intersecting lives. I will present and discuss twelve different ways to understand this concept. This presentation will be followed by a discussion of what we should regard as essential aspects in the argument over these different meanings.

#1. Natural as pristine

The word 'pristine' means in this context 'untouched by man'. This concept of naturalness therefore fully depends on the idea that man and nature belong to different worlds, where fundamentally different principles rule. Areas protected from human impact allow us to see what nature would have done on her own if man had not interfered. The most clear-cut proponent of such a view is Bill

McKibben (1989), along with other preservation and conservation environmentalists. Mark Michaels (2001) is one of several opponents of this view, and he shows how difficult it is to find a criterion with which to distinguish between human interference and "natural" interference. His conclusion is that such criteria are impossible to obtain and that the only viable determinant to "measure" whether a certain type of interference is of the right sort is whether or not it serves our own purposes and interests. More generally he states that 'interference' should be left out of the analysis altogether.

The discussion in the 1980s and 1990s between proponents of the classical paradigm in ecology established by Odum and Clements and opponents trying to establish the "ecology of disturbance and patch dynamics" (Pickett and White 1985) had similar implications for the effort to understand naturalness as pristineness (for more on this see Chapter 6). The tendency to distinguish between human interference and interference from other non-human factors, i.e. between man and nature, is a fundamental feature of modernity (e.g. see Latour 1991), and we should not be surprised by the fact that a particular definition of naturalness has emerged from this vital distinction.

#2. Natural as normal

'Natural' can sometimes be used as a synonym for 'normal'. "It is not natural to be gay". "It is not natural to behave like you are 25, when you are really 50", etc. To say that something is normal by saying that it is natural is to claim indirectly that a current situation cannot be changed. Naturalness is used as a way to tell oneself or others that there is no choice but to follow a particular rule of conduct. Naturalness is associated with inevitability and necessity, and the use of the concept might be seen as a way to take away responsibility or the possible space for agency. If you think that 'naturalness' comes down to *no more* than a way to talk about what we take to be normal, it might be that you are a social constructivist, according to whom any attempt to refer to a natural state directly is a kind of 'naturalization of the culture'. It is often the aim of social reformists to criticize what might be called misplaced naturalizations. But we should note that this characterization partly rests on an (ontological) idea about nature, framing it as the 'kingdom of necessity'.[4]

#3. Natural as principle, essence and being

I have already used the expression 'the nature of nature'. One may interpret this expression as referring to a 'principle' of nature, which on many occasions can be seen as what we mean when we speak of a nature of nature. For instance, the Ionic philosophers took it as given that nature had a principle, and quarrelled over what this principle might be. Today we come across principles like the competition principle in biology (i.e. 'It lies in our *nature* to compete') or the 'principle of succession' in ecology. One might also portray the quest for finding the Theory of Everything as a struggle to find a principle underlying everything else. There are, of course, other types of principles like Pierre Teilhard de Chardin's law of complexity, which concedes that the history of the universe "strives" towards complexity and consciousness. A principle like this says that it is natural for the universe to develop in a certain direction. Such principles describe the inevitable being of things or processes; principles we cannot choose to evade or override.

Another and obvious way to understand the expression 'the nature of nature' is to interpret it as an alternative way to talk about the essence of things, and the further idea that 'naturalness' necessarily must be embedded in a certain type of essentialist ontology. (This issue is discussed throughout this book.)

A more modest claim would be to say that things have a certain *being* (essential or not). Such things can have their being in virtue of many things – in virtue of laws, in virtue of dispositions, in virtue of decrees from a deity, in virtue of their proper parts, etc. – some of which presuppose that the being in question is irreducible and some of which render their being only derivative or supervenient. As we will see throughout this book, I argue that we must take as fact that whenever we talk about the natural being of a certain thing or a process we must assume that this is not a phenomenon that can be fully reduced to other and assumingly more primordial 'natural beings or entities'. A general concept of naturalness presupposes irreducibility, and an argument for the naturalness of certain beings therefore requires a defence of this irreducibility (see esp. Chapter 4). A weakness of modern versions of essentialism is that they are often aligned with reductionism, which I take to be problematic. Aristotelian essentialism, meanwhile, is neither a viable nor compelling way to rescue an essentialist understanding of naturalness (Chapter 2).

#4. Natural as opposed to monstrous

The meaning of this association is not too far removed from #2. When naturalness is seen as the norm of some phenomenon, the deviation from this norm will be seen as unnatural, or if the deviation is comprehensive: monstrous. This is a common idea for all those who think that nature has some kind of *telos*, or who think that there is some kind of striving towards an ideal being in nature. Children born with various physical disabilities will, in such a view, be deemed more or less monstrous. They defy the "necessity" that is embedded in the development of their nature. Monstrosity also has to do with aesthetics and the proportions of nature – principles designed to turn chaos into an ordered world and to keep chaos at arm's length, when at play. The view that something can be deemed monstrous may also have its source in non-teleological accounts, but not accounts that see nature as either completely contingently related or as related by necessity. If there is a sense in which one thinks that certain things belong together and others not, one might permit calling some human-caused combinations monstrous. Frankenstein's monster is an example of this. Flounder-genes in potatoes are another more contemporary example (see Midgley 2000, and discussion in sections 2.3 and 5.6).

#5. *Natural as opposed to the supernatural*

If we define naturalness as that which is *not* supernatural, then our concept of naturalness will strongly depend upon our religious beliefs. As O'Neill et al. note after reading Hume on this topic: "Once one rejects the idea of the miraculous, then '*every* event which has ever happened in the world' is natural" (2008, 127). In this view, everything has a natural explanation. Such explanations are what science provides. This is the soil wherein the *scientific* concept of 'naturalness' lies buried. For science there is nothing in nature itself that can be unnatural or more or less natural. If something could have been called unnatural at all, it would be supernatural. A flying stone would be regarded as unnatural in this sense. The important point here is, however, that a concept of naturalness according to which everything (except the supernatural) is natural, is not, in fact, a concept of naturalness. It is trivial or vacuous. Naturalness then comes to be looked upon as something that is *projected from our human minds onto our descriptions of nature*. Natural/unnatural is expression without meaning. Nature is all natural and therefore a-natural. For example, in an editorial in *Nature* (10 April 2008), we are told that our reactions to what seems unnatural are a kind of evolutionary response that had fitness-effects in the past. Thus, even though modern biotechnology allows "humans to manipulate their biological make-up in an ever-increasing degree … *the game has not been fundamentally changed*" (my emphasis). When we assume that something has to be supernatural to be unnatural, we already presuppose that the word 'unnatural' could never be a part of the scientific vocabulary. Accordingly, there is no way that the game could have ever been fundamentally changed in the first place. Moreover, any reactions that employ the concept of naturalness would be *a priori* 'visceral reactions' (see #2). If the scientist had stumbled upon something unnatural in his laboratories he would have found something supernatural, which as it happens is highly unlikely given the methodological constraints of science (e.g. a miracle is by definition a singular event making reproducible experimental testing impossible). This issue, that of 'no naturalness in nature', is treated in Chapter 2.

#6. *Naturalness in the sense of biologically equipped*

This rests on the suggestion that humans have a primordial biologically furnished nature, and that this nature can be further moulded through technology and social practices (sometimes called second nature). Hair can be coloured, a woman's breasts can be "fixed" and athletes may add drugs to their diet. The word 'enhancing' in the discussion about enhancing technologies needs a reference, some kind of "natural condition" as defined here. Something can only be enhanced on the basis of some given (natural) state of affairs. Natural, then, is equated with the idea of being unadulterated. This looks a bit like position #1, but natural in the present sense does not exactly mean pristine. Rather, it is the biologically *original* that defines what we regard as natural. This way of defining natural also has its pitfalls. Evolution by natural selection might work on conditions that are previously established by learning and "culture" (Lindholm 2012; West-Eberhardt 2003). What is first as opposed to second nature, if first nature (in a dispositional manner) stretches into second nature (e.g. the learning of language)? It is difficult to define precisely what should be regarded as a normal addition (there is always some addition) to what is biologically original and what should be regarded as having brought about *too much change* in cases where we talk about unnaturalness. What is the difference between eating a special type of food (e.g. protein powder) and injecting a steroid such as nandrolon? Some may say that since there is no way to draw this line in an exact way we are better off abandoning the whole definition (see e.g. Harraway 1991, 152, or Harris 2007, ch. 7). The problems that occur under this definition are problems that will follow us all the way through this book.

#7. Natural as in the sense of "historically established"

When things develop over time they merge into each other locally and globally in a way that may be called natural. This concept of naturalness is a concept that is supported by John O'Neill et al.

> The concept of Naturalness is a spatiotemporal concept. There is no such thing as a state or a condition of something which constitutes its "being natural", or an identifiable set of characteristics which make any item or event "natural". Being natural is, and is only, determined by origin and by history: it is a spatiotemporal concept, not a descriptive one.
>
> (2008, 148)

In this way of defining naturalness we are able to see humans as a part of nature and what we deem to be natural (ibid., 149). However, the definition as it stands is not very operational. Later you will see that a similar view of naturalness can be developed in terms of what I call HEDFs (historically evolved dispositional facts). The latter definition is hopefully more operational than the one at hand. Robert Elliot in his *Faking Nature* argues that it is precisely the unique historical creation that lies behind a certain item or state of affairs that makes it natural. A copy of a Vermeer painting has almost no value compared to the original exactly for this reason.

Natural in terms of "historically established" may also mean normal: "This is the way we have done it – so this is the way it *should* be done." Some may call a culture or parts of a culture natural in virtue of being historically established, on such an account.

#8. Natural in the sense of 'intrinsic'

There is a sense in which we think that things are natural when they are self-contained. Naturalness viewed as *something intrinsic* about the natural beings has at least two implications. When environmental ethicists use the expression 'intrinsic value', they refer to a kind of being that the entity in question has – namely, a kind such that it ought not be reduced to being a means for our ends.

We can make it into such a means, but intrinsically it has a way of being that is violated by our anthropocentrically oriented manipulations. This ethical argument points towards an independent/intrinsic nature of the being in question, although the implicit ontology is often not made clear (see subsection 1.4.2).

The other way that natural in the sense of intrinsic is used has more to do with the capacity to resist change. A rubber band might be stretched, but then attain its 'natural shape' if we leave it alone. The early pioneers of ecology like Frederic Clements and Eugene Odum thought that an ecosystem had an original state that it would seek to maintain and come back to if disturbed.

This idea of naturalness often leads to the question of what we should regard as "really intrinsic". What is intrinsic, really, about the natural shape of the rubber band? Is not the intrinsic shape of the rubber band really *dependent* upon various conditions, such as the bonding between molecules, the temperature in the air around it, etc? Would we not change the intrinsic shape of the rubber band if we changed these conditions? This shape is, in other words, not independent after all. We might then ask whether or not there are any natural units that have the ability to resist being changed under changing conditions. If that was our thinking would we not be *inclined to think* that such units/entities/properties would somehow have to be fundamental? To get to what is "natural" would thus mean to somehow brush away all the layers of "contamination", so that things in their purity will be able to catch the light. Everything else would be seen as being a composition of these original and natural independent units (atoms, subatomic particles, strings, etc.). This seems to be the thinking behind what David Lewis calls *perfectly natural properties* (1983, 344). Any mereological fundamentalist approach will find its suitable place under this heading, although the term 'naturalness' might not be fancied to express this belief by all of those who hold that position (see section 3.2).

#9. Natural as opposed to forced action

We can use the following expression of 'natural' about *human behaviour*. We can say: "it came naturally" or "naturally, I will do that" (i.e. that's the way I am …). Or we may say: "She was so strange and artificial". This probably has to do with the way we are tuned to the general situation in virtue of the way we (think) we are. Things may sometimes be forced and over-determined, so that our actions lack flow. We don't go *with*, but *against*, what is already there as a precondition for our actions. People who have worked with physical elements (e.g. a mechanic working with cars) over time will often (but not always) learn from those elements how they should adjust their use of energy in relation to the existing "energy" of the objects. (One may be helped by the heaviness of certain objects, etc.)

This distinction has some similarities to the distinction between authentic and inauthentic, although we may regard the latter as involving a broader concept. Forced movement may, of course, also be applied to the relationship between human agency and nature's agency. Given that we grant nature such agency we may use this phrase whenever our agency crosses nature's agency. Aristotle called this forced movement the concept of naturalness (see section 2.1).

#10. *Natural as opposed to intended*

Martin Krieger once (1973) wrote a famous article called "What is Wrong with Plastic Trees?", where he basically argues along the lines found in #2. Partly in response to this, Eric Katz developed the view, saying that there is a substantial difference between "things made from nature" and things "made by humans" in that things made from nature are made without intention (1996). Things made by humans are by definition made for a certain purpose or goal. A restored ecosystem or a de-distinct species can therefore never be natural since these beings originate from a (human) purpose. It does not help that the intended being mimics the natural well. The restoration of an area or an ecosystem already entails a designated purpose for which the restoration can succeed or not. Similarity is not the crucial point. What marks off something as being natural is therefore those things, processes or states of affairs that just exist – beyond human purpose. This is why we call something a fake, no matter how similar the fake version appears.

#11. *Natural as opposed to synthetic*

In the 1950s (in Norway at least) things 'made from nature' were cheap and low-value, while plastic things made in a factory by humans were considered more attractive. Today we often see the opposite. Plastic is low-value: 'synthetic and artificial'. It is difficult, however, to argue that the distinction has anything to do with 'made from nature', since everything inevitably is 'made from nature'. The distinction probably trades on our intuitions about the degree of processing involved, and probably also even on our intuitions about level-specificity (see subsection 4.5.1). It seems that the term 'synthetic' is almost always used where the product mimics nature. Synthetic fur, synthetic grass, synthetic substances, synthetic biology or "synth-music" are deemed so because they somehow don't appear in nature without the aid of human efforts and conduct, but are at the same time mimicking what is 'directly made from nature' – which may explain why they are called synthetic (rather than unnatural). A Wikipedia article on the topic *Synthetic fibres* expresses a similar idea: "Rayon and acetate are both artificial fibers, but not truly synthetic, being made from wood. Nylon, the first synthetic fiber, made its debut in the USA, as a *replacement* for silk" (last accessed: 20 June 2014, my emphasis).

This is the category where we distinguish between chemical and organic fertilizer or between synthetic and organically processed vitamins, etc. The synthetic item mimics the product but not the *process* through which it comes about. It seems that 'synthetic' alludes to the fact that the phenomenon in question has been *produced* in a different way. Human agency has selected certain naturally occurring substances, decomposed them, and then recomposed (synthesized) them in new ways.

There is a deeper meaning to this as well, at least in the area of health and environmental issues. If humans are made from 'natural selection' then natural ingredients will have a better chance of being good for our health than ingredients and compositions of ingredients that we have never met on our historical pathway created through evolution. The reason why synthetic substances in certain cases can be fatal for certain groups of animals and plants is not that they are poisonous *in themselves*, but rather that the animals and plants for whom they are toxic have never been subjected to those substances during their evolutionary history. We may today produce substances and whole *environments* that are alien to us in an "evolutionary sense" (see Chapter 5). We see this when we hear about studies showing that children's playrooms are full of 'synthetic contaminants' from toys and other sources (e.g. Tønning et al. 2009). This fact may underlie the uneasiness that many people today ascribe to the proliferation of synthetic materials, and the fact that the word 'synthetic' has a negative standing.

The idea underlying the phrase 'made from nature' is the same idea that underlies Charles Darwin's phrase 'natural selection'. Artificial selection of domesticated animals has human need as its purpose. Today we are debating whether GMOs are artificial in the second degree or whether the technique is the same as "normal" artificial selection.

#12. Natural as opposed to cultural

Where 'cultural' is seen as an antonym of 'natural' we are already implying that cultural means something *more* than "human". Conversely we do not call any type of humpback whale behaviour cultural. There is some certain type of property that can be ascribed to humans which makes us think that our behaviour is "more than human". The consequence is that on this account the *whole* category of *non-human* entities is deemed natural. We may ask ourselves: If humpback whales were able to say something about "their culture", would they put all *non*-humpback-whales into one category? They might talk about what was herring-like, saltwater-like, seagull-like, etc., instead of simply calling all of non-humpback-culture the natural behaviour of the natural world.

Natural construed as the domain of the non-cultural presupposes that there is a categorical difference between what is cultural and what is not, that to be human-like is something more and different from being, for instance, humpback-whale-like. The type of categorical distinction that we are talking about here has its philosophical heritage in the metaphysics that occurred in the fifteenth century. Describing nature as law governed challenged the conventional ideas about where humans belonged in the universe. Where nature is described as law governed and/or chancy and human action as essentially *free* in some sense, it becomes problematic to call human action natural. Given this categorical distinction it is not surprising that many would see human action as being *a priori* unnatural, reaching beyond the postulated necessitarian and chancy behaviour of nature. There are many good reasons to reject this categorical dichotomy, which has also been challenged *unsuccessfully* ever since Rousseau and the German Romantics.

1.2.1 Further delineations

It normally becomes clear, upon having examined diverse meanings of a given concept, which definition one prefers to pursue. That is not the case here. The meanings I have reviewed are interconnected, and I do not want to exclude any of them from further scrutiny. Nevertheless, #3 serves as a starting point for the analysis, in the sense that I come to the question of naturalness in virtue of analysing the being of beings (viz. substances, processes, systems, etc.). It is clear that naturalness is a property and not an object, a property that may or may not be ascribed in different degrees to objects and processes. The way in which we characterize being and beings is fundamental in that all of the other meanings listed above are influenced by our views on this question. Dispositional properties say something about how we should characterize beings. When I criticize different ontologies I am motivated by the fact that certain ontologies characterize the being of things in a way that ultimately makes it *impossible* to designate something as being more natural or less natural. This means first of all that I am not, as pointed out previously, looking for what kind of human *activity* would be natural or unnatural. That would already invoke circularity and (Cartesian) dualist assumptions in the first place. I am not trying to decide whether nappies or whether side-effects of intentional human actions are natural or not. To say that naturalness *is* about human activity is to create a straw man that is too easy to shoot down. What I am searching for is rather a position from which we can say that there is a natural "course" *in* nature, which we can deviate from in different degrees. The question is not whether our actions are natural or not, but whether there *is* something "there" which can be said to have a nature at all.

Given the multiplicity of meanings to be pursued, I will try to excavate some general features about naturalness that will demand enduring attention in this book. One of the major conclusions stemming from this examination is that we need a *concept that refers to a reality that would allow us both to fail and to succeed in our efforts to treat something in accordance with it.*

I will try to explain this as I examine five features that could stand in the way if we were to develop this concept further.

(1) *Humeanism.* In a Humean world, everything is *contingently connected*, each "thing" and property having its identity independently of everything else. But since everything can cause everything else, it is difficult to see what these identities really are (see section 2.5). And if every change is contingent, it will also be impossible to operate with a vocabulary of naturalness and unnaturalness. If the way that the world is related is fundamentally contingent, then my rearrangement of that ("natural") world would result in something that is equally contingent. I could therefore neither fail nor succeed in treating something in accordance with its nature. (A Humean view would certainly be able to give full ontological support to the social constructivist in #2.)

(2) *Determinism.* In the case of (full) determinism we would of course not be able to *fail* to act in accordance with the nature of some given entity (the entity being an ecosystem, an atom, a particular animal, etc.) (see Chapter 2).

(3) *Reductionism.* The possibility that there is no other real being other than the real constituents of things is preliminarily mentioned in #6. If the hen is not really a hen, but a contingent aggregate of the basic parts "constituting" the

hen, we would not be able to act in accordance with the hen's nature, since there is no hen-nature (see Chapter 2).

(4) *Understanding of being.* At issue here is whether or not humans can relate to other beings in their being. Stones and trees exist, but what if they are not able to relate to their being, in their being. Martin Heidegger makes a considerable effort in *Sein und Zeit* to expose how and why it is possible for us not just to note that something exists, but also to relate to the fact that a certain being has this or that being (*Seinsverständnis*). This, he says has to do with the fact that we ourselves can relate to ourselves in our own being.[5] It is a fact that I am a man, but my being is not given by this fact; rather, my being is given by the *way* (mode) I am a man (Heidegger 1927, 117). This is why Heidegger declared: "Our essence lies (*liegt*) in our existence" (ibid., 42). Without this special kind of being it would quite meaningless to talk about *failing and succeeding* in treating something in accordance with something we call its nature, because we would just do what we do without considering whether it was more or less in keeping with something (i.e. something that we would be able to call natural). I mention this issue here, though I will not pursue it further. It is important to bear it in mind, however, so that the precondition to which it directs our attention is not totally left out of the exposition.

(5) *Social constructivism.* If every concept of naturalness was just another narrative, we would be seeking blindly for a concept that refers to the being of things and processes.

There is also a supplement to the fourth point, which must be mentioned. Above, in #5, I said that science, broadly speaking, presumes that the concept of naturalness is an anthropocentrically ascribed feature (viz., "any reactions that employ the concept of naturalness would therefore be *a priori* 'visceral reactions'"). The idea is that nature exists "out there", while naturalness exists only conceptually, in our minds. I reject this idea even though I do allow that *Seinsverständnis* (see #4) is a condition for the possibility of acting in accordance with what is natural. I take the view that I do because I think that naturalness captures a *relational property*. Since I believe that the nature of things is relational,[6] I also believe that acting in accordance with what is natural *also* involves acting in accordance with oneself, or a relational net that includes oneself. A hen does not simply have a nature in itself. The nature that we can say that the hen has, is what it is in virtue of the dispositional net of properties that the hen's dispositions were developed under. Natural food obviously means that it is natural for a being that has undergone a certain evolutionary process etc. Eating 'the right food' is a relational issue. This is a specific relation that should not be interpreted as subjective or projected onto the "reality itself". The food is not natural 'independently of everything else'. The way to understand this relationality is that it is not different from the relationality that exists between e.g. the sun and photosynthesis or between the tree and soil that sustains and supports the roots, or between the hydrogen molecule and the oxygen molecule, etc. However, we *can*, according to Heidegger, relate to this *relation* itself, and we can "freely" make amendments in virtue of our ability to so relate. Without this freedom it would be meaningless to call for our actions to comply with an understanding of the natural way to do things.

Other features of the foregoing that we should keep in mind include the following. We are talking about the possibility of naturalness as such, not a particular type of naturalness. The claim coming from the scientific concept of naturalness (#5) is that it states that everything is (equally) natural, and that to try to determine or fix something as (more) natural would be arbitrary or inconsistent, and thus cultured. However, a scientist who holds the view that everything is natural will also have to defend this position positively. That is, he or she will also have to defend the ontological foundation for the thesis that there is no nature in nature (as opposed to the negative claim saying that "naturalness is a misconception"). The only views that without any further complication would allow one who held them to defend this positive thesis are Humeanism and certain types of necessiterian ontologies. In other words: to defend the positive notion "that things have no nature" might seem to be broadly correct in the first instance, but on a second look it really requires a defence of specific, and to my mind demanding metaphysical models. This whole topic, with its many implied claims, will be handled in greater detail later.

What, then, of the focus of this book – namely the potential viability of a *positive* concept of naturalness? For now I can only give a sketch. Consider point #7. If there is something that is positively natural, then "synthetic" will refer to those ways of dissembling and reassembling things that are not in compliance with the natural ways of doing so, e.g. ways that are established through evolution. Holding that not everything is compossible is thus a precondition of talking about a nature in nature. Conversely, maintaining that everything is, in principle, freely compossible is the same as saying that there is no nature in nature. It also amounts to saying that the things to which we attend have no (real) being (#3). If the claim that everything is compossible were true, our discussion would be over before it started. However, the claim that not everything is compossible must be defended. I will need to argue *why*, and *how*, and in *what way* everything is *not* (fully) compossible![7] That is what I try to do in this book.

The focus on ontology in this book is, as I have said, related to the assumption that certain ontologies allow for a concept of naturalness while others do not. This does not mean that we can *deduce* a given concept of naturalness from given ontologies, only that given ontologies *allow* for given concepts to be used without committing any kind of conceptual fallacy. *Allowance* is the central issue (see subsection 1.4.2).

Now, there is a kind of asymmetry between ontologies in this respect. Proponents of necessitarian and Humean ontologies alike need not bother with how things are connected, as the nature of the connection is more or less settled in advance. By contrast, if one believes that things are connected in *certain* ways, which are neither necessitarian nor contingent, then one is faced with a much more complicated task. This task is the subject matter of chapters 3, 4 and 5.

1.3 Nature: constructivism, epistemology and ontology

What about 'nature'? Won't any effort to resurrect a viable concept of naturalness break down on the assumption that we cannot "access" nature itself? Won't our epistemological limitations make it impossible to take an ontological approach to this question?

There is an enormous literature reminding us that the word 'nature' has many meanings and that there are always separate and several stories or narratives implicit in our use of the word (R. Williams 1976; Rothenberg 1992, 85; Soper 1995; Hansen 2006; Vogel 2002; Wickson 2008; Castree 2014). I take it as a given that the word 'nature' can mean many things, but we should ask ourselves again whether this means that the word has no extra-linguistic referent. I take theorists who are satisfied when the variety of meanings is *categorized* to hold a constructivist position to the effect that, "Scientists hold one narrative, environmentalists a different one".[8] In some cases this might be a wise strategy, designed to challenge the widely acknowledged privileged access to true beliefs that scientists are supposed to have. In environmental debates, for instance, we see that environmentalists have been squeezed into accepting that their views are *only* cultured and/or that they are engaged in ethically driven wishful thinking about reality (in the way designated above, e.g. by Norman Levitt). Sometimes, a way to get out of this corner is to show how and why scientists cannot really claim to be less "cultured", by demonstrating that their understanding of nature is 'just a narrative like any other'. This is, in my mind, what motivates sympathy for (social) constructivism, although few like to defend this position theoretically.[9] However, the cost of defending this move is high for the environmentalist if it means that s/he loses the reference to what s/he wants to defend; at least this is the case for the declared "bio-centrist" (Palmer 2003, 33; See also Chapter 5 and Soule and Lease, 1995). After all, it is unsatisfying to wind up arguing in a circle: i.e. for a supposed narrative-constituted nature rather than for nature itself.[10]

I will expand on this issue throughout this book, but I will briefly state the argument that makes me convinced that the social constructivist position is an unwarranted and defensive strategy, rather than a progressive strategy, as often alleged.

1.3.1 Constructivism

The immediate problem we encounter when we want to say something about *reality itself* is the widely accepted idea that we cannot really say anything about reality before we know the conditions for how knowledge about the reality of the world can be obtained. This is why we generally accept that '*epistemology precedes ontology*', implying that to do ontology would be a waste of effort and time in the first place. The question, however, is whether this dogma itself depends upon a certain ontology.

If we presuppose that reality is something that in each and every case must be accessed as something 'in itself' – *independently of everything else* – we have already stated something *ontological* about the being in question, something that might have a crucial influence on our epistemology and the role that we think that epistemology should play. When Locke stated that we need to distinguish between primary and secondary qualities, he also stated that what we should consider to be real are those properties that belong to the being in question *independently* of everything else. This requirement does not only apply to the relationship between objects, but also to the relationship between the object and the knowing subject. In other words, it is a principle that does not differentiate between: (1) describing the world 'as it really is'; and (2) describing the world 'independently of us and everything else'. To describe the world 'as it is' just is, from this perspective, to describe it 'independently of us', i.e. *as if the real properties of the world are indeed those that exist "independently of everything else"*.

It follows from this principle that the most interesting epistemological question would be: "How can we *possibly* access the distinct independent being of the being, without distorting this very being with our human cognitive capacities?" Worries about, and extreme interests in how, such things as our transcendental properties (Kant), our language, our sense perception, our cultural backgrounds and our 'being-in-the-world-immersed-beings' impinge upon our cognition of the object 'as it is in itself' all follow from this question. Hence, large parts of the philosophically trained community have been dealing with these questions ever since the fifteenth century, and even more so in the wake of the works of René Descartes, John Locke, David Hume and Immanuel Kant. One may therefore ask if the core problem of epistemology for the last 500 years is due to a universal epistemological relation between the subject and the object, or whether it arose as a problem because everyone accepted the (basically Aristotelian!!) idea that *to be* is to exist *independently* of everything else. Is it perhaps true then, that the 'thing in itself' is principally impossible to know anything about, and that the reason for this might be because *there is nothing that exists in itself*, and therefore that notably Kant's paradigmatic framing of and solution to the problem is based on a problem that did not exist in the first place? In any case it is safe to say that the idea about "the thing in itself" led Locke, Kant and many others to see themselves as confronted with riddles staged by the distinction between the phenomenal and noumenal world, where the (naïve) realist thought we could reach into the noumenal sphere (empiricists), while the constructivists could raise clever and principal questions about this possibility. For instance: Heidegger could say "we are always-already-in-the-world" and somehow believe that the problem was solved. What I am asking is whether this is a solution to a problem created by a certain ontological tradition, which the "problem-solver" was not aware that he had accepted by taking its fundamental ideas for granted.

To sum up: the claim is that the concern that philosophers have had with epistemological issues originates from a specific ontology. This ontology raises the question of how to *access* reality. Philosophical theories suggesting how it can be done have focused on the supposed imposition or intrusion of subjective capacities, which in turn has led parts of the philosophical community to "surrender" by saying that such access cannot be obtained (constructivists). Is there a way out of this? I think that there is, but the road is closed if we cannot take a step back to see the circular argument we are caught in if we take for granted that 'there is no use in doing ontology before we have solved our epistemological problems'. The only way out is (again) an *ontological* reorientation. (See (sub)sections 2.4.1, 4.5.3, 4.7, 5.4 and 6.1.1.)

What we must do is to state baldly that we do not believe in the ontology that creates the feeding ground for (social) constructivism in the first place. If we affirm instead that beings are active in a dispositional sense,[11] we will not first and foremost ask ourselves how to access them, because we will know that we are *in medias res* already. A non-passivist ontology, where beings are understood as fundamentally active, ushers in the view that beings have their being *in relation* to other beings, and not independently of everything else. On one such dispositional account, for instance, the claim is that particular dispositions are *manifested* in keeping with the relational situation in which they exist (which one as a spectator, would be a part of) (see Chapter 4). This means that what we see is the *same* thing displaying different dispositional properties depending on the situational context (see sections 4.4 and 5.7). A photon can manifest itself as a wave in one situation and as a particle in another situation *and still be the same photon*. There is nothing peculiar about this if you accept *de re* (real) potentiality. The real potentialities (dispositions) of the being in question (photon) interacts with the spectator and her measurement devices – in the same way as it interacts with other beings!

Since the world, on this ontological view, does not consist of a *set of given facts*[12] waiting passively to be discovered, it leaves us in an epistemological position in which our engagement with the world does not *automatically* render the knowledge borne of such engagement subjective, constructed, or untrue. Instead, our beliefs are a manifestation of a relational situation in which humans are one of the partners. That humans are one of the partners does not mean that the object does not truly have the property (disposition) in question!

That there exists such an alternative ontology, and therefore also a different understanding of the role of epistemology, shows that there is a possible alternative to the position described above. If we are unaware of this, however, we will take it for granted that any ontological question must be subordinate to the analysis of different epistemological accounts. If realism is the position that takes the *intrinsic* being of things as a starting point, social constructivism depends upon this ontological claim even to be a position at all. (See also subsection 2.4.1.)

We may agree that scientific realism and social constructivism are different positions, but only in the sense that realists think that we can access those "intrinsic" beings, while social constructivists deny this. If the *premise for access* was not the assumption that things are what they are *in themselves*, but rather that things are what they are in *relation* to other things, we would not have to regard *social constructivism* as a position in its own right. Social constructivism stands out as a full alternative to "realism" only so long as we are not willing to consider relationalism as a viable option. Paradoxically, the fact that social constructivism seems to be the only alternative to "realism" appears to be the strongest argument for *clinging* to a non-relational "realism" in the first place.

For the social constructivist there is no way out of this configuration, because the alternative requires a particular ontological reconsideration. This is an option that social constructivists must deny themselves, since taking the necessary steps would only mean the construction of yet another (illusory) narrative. To reiterate: the main and severe problem with social constructivism is that it stands out as a meaningful alternative to "realism" because its proponents indirectly accept the non-relational ontology of "realism". Social constructivism is the idea that we cannot access the beings in nature in themselves, *on the assumption* that there are, in fact, beings that exist in themselves. By confirming this non-relational ontology (through the denial of our possible access to this reality and by *presenting itself* as an alternative to the ontologically loaded "realism"), social constructivism becomes a part of the whole picture, which makes it next to impossible to see that a more radical alternative is even thinkable. The fly is trapped when walking on the window. The question is why.

Wilfred Sellars's critique of the idea of the *given* mainly focuses on the naïve empiricist idea that the outer world lies ready to be harvested as non-inferential facts that are *eventually* accessible via the inferential processes that go on in theory-making (1956). The critique that is raised *here* is broader. It concerns first of all the idea of *intrinsic-ness*: the idea that things exist as such, in themselves – or, in other words, the idea that there is a *given* world out there where the being of things is not relationally constituted. It is *this* kind of givenness that underlies the givenness sought for in empiricism and later doubted by Sellars and many others. Before Sellars and others could regard "The Given" as a meaningful entity, they would accordingly have to assume that the world has a non-relational being.

The main idea here is to rouse and maybe provoke the reader to see that the "epistemology-precedes-ontology-dogma" can be questioned to the extent that it might be fruitful to ask ontological questions and expect fruitful answers. If the reader is not willing to consider this possibility, it will be little use in approaching a concept like 'nature' or 'naturalness' further.

There is also a second reason to resist the ideas of social constructivism on this issue. As I said above, a social constructivist would consider an attempt to outline a concept of nature and the natural futile; we would not end up with anything more than a new narrative, at best, which is not what we want. A social constructivist is satisfied with a *presentation* of different narratives, which circulate in the semantic sphere (see e.g. Castree 2014, 16).[13] A more general "critique" of the social constructionist position comes from a tradition that goes all the way back to antiquity, one in which it is assumed that it is, indeed, possible to *philosophically* understand and discuss what nature really is. Aristotle developed a teleological ontology; Galileo, Descartes and Boyle developed a mechanistic ontology; Locke developed a reductionist ontology; Whitehead developed a process ontology; and even though Hume would deny it, I would say that Hume developed a Humean ontology; etc. (cf. section 2.5). This is of course a dominant tradition in philosophy, although social constructivists and Humean empiricists have for a long time declared the death of metaphysics. Some might agree with their criticism for certain reasons, but the problem is that one cannot help but think that metaphysics and ontology will always reappear in all kinds of knowledge systems *in any case*! If we deem the concept of nature meaningless, as the social constructivist does, s/he will in the second round be influenced by ideas that s/he denies the existence of. If you, on the other hand, think that ontology and metaphysics are *inevitable*, even though you may also think that the ambition of describing the world *as it really is* is beyond our abilities or the scope of philosophy, you might also think that it is better to be aware of your own ontology and even defend it, than to hold an ontology while naively rejecting that you have one. If, in addition, you think that many problems occurring in philosophy, science and society can be traced back to ontological issues and misconceptions, then you will be in a much stronger position than the social constructivist who has thrown away the beliefs and tools that could have made an ontological rethinking in the designated areas possible.

1.4 Following nature?

Assuming that we are willing to grant naturalness a place within the sphere of conduct, what is thereby implied for what we will have to say about human behaviour? If there is a natural path/way of something that we also believe that we should follow, what do we mean by follow? Is there any force or necessitation involved? Can we totally neglect to follow what is found natural? Does the natural ways of things give guidance to what we ought to do? Can naturalness be discovered and understood by science, or is it a normative concept? These are questions that will be focused upon in the forthcoming sections.

1.4.1 Is and ought

What is and what ought to be are clearly distinct matters. That something *is* the case does not entail that something *ought* to be the case, and vice versa. Science deals with facts and ethics deals with values. The debate on how and if our descriptions are under the influence of norms has a long-standing history of debate. At the heart of this controversy is the idea that we generally think that ethics and ontology do, and should, exist as two separate areas of discourse. In forthcoming sections it will become clear that I am not so interested in how norms and values perpetrate our (scientific) descriptions (the epistemic debate), but rather in how our descriptions influence our norms and values, or more generally how *ontology influences ethics*. While the epistemic debate is challenging the autonomy and realist aspirations of science, the ontological debate – which is the focus of these sections – is challenging the autonomy of ethics and the role that 'the normative' does and can play in relation to 'the descriptive'.

What difference can ontology make for ethics? Quite a few philosophers and others would reject the very question – one in which I seem to overlook the basic and long-standing agreement of keeping 'is' and 'ought' apart. It is said that the distinction is unbridgeable, and that Hume's guillotine will fall upon all those who transgress this boundary line (see e.g. Graham 1981; Hudson 1969; Heffner 1981; Brink 1989, 145). If it is unbridgeable, what difference would it make if we were able to argue for a viable concept of naturalness? Nothing, it seems – since what 'is' would have nothing to contribute to our various 'oughts'. This is why we should carefully examine the relationship between the is/ought issue and naturalness further.

As Hume noted, we are not on safe ground when we *logically* infer from the 'is' to the 'ought' (1739–1740, 469).[14] J. S. Mill who might also be regarded as an influential source for the way in which the is/ought distinction has been viewed, has the same thing in mind when he says that "they do so because they have a notion, either clearly or confusedly, that what is, constitutes the rule or standard for what ought to be" (1863, 13). Mill seems to have the enlightenment hat on when he wants to educate people to simply see that 'is' dictates no imperatives for how we should act. There is a good reason for Mill to put on this pleasant hat since we (laymen as well as scientists) often appear to infer 'ought' from 'is'. Some examples that might illustrate this are: "Poor people do not want to work. We *should* therefore not bother to engage in their problems." (Even in cases where this would be correct, the reason to engage in their problems could be charitable, etc.) Or: "If we release more greenhouse gasses equivalent to 450 ppm CO_2, we might face irreversible cascading adverse effects. Thus we *should* not let out more than 450 ppm." (Some might in fact think that we *ought to* favour a happy and carefree life now, in spite of the long-term consequences for later generations.) It is truly difficult for many, if not everyone, to resist the temptation of jumping to conclusions about how we should behave, given how the world is. Despite this tendency, we might say that philosophers and others have succeeded in their enlightenment project, at least in the dominion where intellectual life takes place. The is/ought distinction is today seen to be self-evidently true, and often we see this distinction employed as a favoured tool in heated debates where scientists want to say something about ethics and where ethicists want to say something about technology and science.[15]

The is/ought distinction has a weakness, however, at the point at which it seems to be at its strongest. When we want to logically *infer* something from something else we are already implying that there is a *necessary* relation between the premises and the conclusion. One might therefore ask whether there is *anything* that could ever necessitate an 'ought' in any case. Could an 'ought' ever be inferred from other 'oughts', in any case? Would not even the most solid commitment to the most "solid value" in the world still raise the question "Why ought I to do Y?". The problem might not lie in the inference from 'is' to 'ought' therefore, but in the nature of logically valid inferences, i.e. in this case: the fact that we are looking for premises that would eventually lead to a claim where we *necessarily* ought to do Y.

Say we have a set of premises $p_1 \ldots p_n$ containing at least one normative statement p_y. This is sufficient to derive the normative conclusion Y. So now the 'ought' conclusion Y is justified by $p_1 \ldots p_n$. But what about the normative premise p_y? This too will need to be derived from a set of premises containing at least one normative statement. Unless one could find an ultimate normative principle P, we would be caught in a vicious regress, where every 'ought' requires a further 'ought'. Why do we end up here? I think the reason is that we are looking for something that will require that we *necessarily* ought to do Y; i.e. the very meaning of "ought" is at odds with the meaning of "necessity". It is a contradiction in terms to say that I *necessarily* ought to do Y. If logical inference is what we are looking for it does not only exclude inferences from 'is' to 'ought', but also inferences from values to 'oughts'.

This suggests that 'the unbridgeable gap between "is" and "ought"' is based on a truism where the criteria that are contained in the word 'inference' simply have very little to do with the subject matter of the issue (normativity). (See also Anjum et al. 2013.) The truism is useful for reminding ourselves that we cannot assume that any 'ought' *necessarily* follows from anything else (either from what 'is' or from other 'oughts'), but it is not useful for evaluating or understanding which modal relations (i.e. other than necessity) can or cannot be established between 'is' and 'ought'. We should therefore leave behind our trust in the idea that there is *always* a fallacy involved in the *conversion* from 'is' to 'ought', and devote ourselves to the *content* of the subject matter instead. The content that I am interested in here is ontology. I will argue that it is mainly *ontological reasons* that lead us tacitly to accept the strong is/ought divide. This means that those who want to defend the strong is/ought distinction will need to do more than to defend the "placeholder-truism" of the strong is/ought distinction. They will also have to defend a specific ontological theory about how the world works.

Some philosophers, such as Hans Jonas, have argued that Hume's *logical point* has prevented the strong is/ought distinction from being seriously contested (Jonas 1979/1984, 44. See also Tullberg and Tullberg 2001, 173; MacIntyre 1969, 36ff.). Hans Jonas argues that our willingness to accept the strong is/ought distinction is really due to the fact that we accept a *particular* ontology as "the true complete concept of being" (ibid.). Peter Geach's criticism of G.E. Moore's argument in *Principia Ethica* can be interpreted as expressing the same view (1956). If I say "he was a good football player", the primordial question is not "what do you mean by 'good'", but rather "what do you mean by 'football player?'" To investigate what a football player *is* (even though we might not be able to *agree* on what a football player is) would in this case *answer* what I mean by 'good'. To investigate what a tree is, on the other hand, would allegedly not tell me what 'a good tree' means, if we have already ontologically stated that a tree cannot be possibly good or bad. In one case the ontology plays a role: in the other case it presumably does not. If the description plays a role for what we mean by good in the first case, why does it not play a role in the second case? It should be obvious that there is an *ontological reason* for this and that ontology plays a role in both cases. To deny this you would have to (at least implicitly) appeal to an ontological statement about the world, which of course would be self-defeating.

If this is correct then there will be nothing left in Hume's formulation other than the trivial truth that very few things, if anything, outside of logic and mathematics, can be inferred (by necessity) from anything else. If we agree that we are not looking for a logically waterproof argument but rather for some real coherence/incoherence based on the *content of 'is' and 'ought'*, it should be acceptable to investigate what it would mean to make weaker connections between is and ought.

1.4.2 Three ontologies

The reason that I distinguish between the following three ontologies is that I believe, in keeping with what I said in the previous section, that ontological considerations influence not only our understanding of what we ought to do, but also the whole relationship between 'is' and 'ought' as such. It follows from this that I will argue that the current is/ought agreement is not ontologically neutral. To discuss the relationship between 'is' and 'ought' further we therefore need to delve deeper into some concrete features about certain ontologies to uncover the important aspects that govern the is/ought relation in general.

The following three ontologies are not arbitrarily chosen, but the choice does not entail that other ontologies could not have been chosen as candidates to illustrate this principal issue.

A. The disallowance-relation

I have previously talked about passivism as a general ontology, and I have referred to Brian Ellis as the coiner of this concept (2002, see also Bunge 1963, 173). Passivism is also the main subject in Chapter 2, and I have written about this concept elsewhere (Lie and Wickson 2011). In general I take 'passivism' to signify the idea that the behaviour of beings is determined by some kind of external agent, force or "agency" stemming from some type of contingent source. In contradistinction to Ellis, I do not reserve this term for only Humean ontologies, but also certain types of essentialism, reductionism, social constructivism, as well as certain law-ontologies and structuralist ontologies, (Lie and Wickson 2011, and Chapter 2). Ontologies that challenge passivism are ontologies that are able to describe the being of beings as being active. (See C. below.)

Historically Immanuel Kant, among others, realized that a (passivist) ontology like the 'law-governing regime' would necessarily lead to a redefinition of the *role* that ethics could and should play (Kant 1997, 52/4: 446. See also e.g. *Stanford Encyclopaedia of Philosophy*: 'Kant': ch. 5.2 and Schneewind 1998, 518ff.). Kant's particular answer to law-ontological descriptions of nature is to posit the transcendental ego. In virtue of being transcendental egos, it is effectively possible for humans to side-step the cause and effect-determined necessities that create the heteronomous "actions" that take place in us and elsewhere in nature. This ego is needed to make space for the possibility of "our oughts", and hence for the autonomy of ethics and the possibility of human freedom as such. Even though Kant argues directly that this is the only way that humans can escape the necessity of nature (*Naturnotwendigkeit*), little points to the fact that he thereby *rests* his system of ethics on taking a certain ontology as a given starting point for his ethical theory (Bunge 1963, ch. 7 and Schneewind 1998). That humans are free in contradistinction to nature is not a Kantian invention, however. In *The Invention of Autonomy* (1998) Jerome Schneewind argues that even though Kant coined the notion 'autonomy', the idea about self-determination is not Kantian as such. 'Self-determination' is nothing but a fundamental supposition that regulates our identities and our moral visions in "western liberal societies" (ibid., 5).[16]

The contrasting idea that generates the need to develop a concept like 'self-determination' is not that of, e.g. 'natural law', 'divine natural laws' (Aquinas), or 'reductionism', but the *broader* and more unspecified idea that beings of nature are *externally determined*. This is what passivism, and inversely what autonomy, is about. If the behaviour of some particular natural being is totally determined by laws or the contingent congregation of properties, or a mixture of these two modalities, a strong is/ought divide seems to be sensible. What could possibly make me infer anything from what 'is' to what ought to be if what happens in the world happens by necessity or by total contingency? There is nothing *in* nature that has any type of relevance for how I ought to act, assuming such an ontology. 'Ought' must be generated from somewhere else, and the ethics that would come from this other source would also be an autonomous sphere (*Reich der Zwecke*) that we would need to protect in order to guard us against the *a-moral* reality that we find in nature.

In social sciences there is a tradition starting with Weber that insists upon taking the postulated difference between social and natural science to be a kind of issue in itself. The antipositivists of the last century argued strongly that the natural sciences and its methods do not apply in social sciences (e.g. Rhoads 1991). This position, which is a part of the basic intuition of Critical Theory, is a denial of the thesis that the passivist ontology of nature applies to the human sciences. To say this is not to deny that it is the business of natural science to uncover the laws of nature; it is only to say that this is not the right starting point for social sciences. It is to accept that nature is passive, while maintaining that humans are active and self-governed. Is it a happy agreement?

What we see in Jürgen Habermas's grand philosophy, for instance, is that he develops a comprehensive theory to show that instrumental rationality is not threatening, as Adorno and Horkheimer had claimed, *as long as we are able to keep our discourse-ethical institutions live and fresh*. The problem for Habermas is not the ontology of science and the methods that we trust in our ambition to gain knowledge of nature, but rather the attempt to employ them in a different realm, Habermas says (Vogel 1996, 108). What he does not question then is the passivist ontology that creates the problem in the first place.[17] Although his philosophical accomplishment is valuable in many ways, we may therefore see it as a pure *reaction* to something that he mistakenly takes for granted, rather than a philosophical theory that stands on its own feet. This means that the strategy motivating his meta-ethical theory will not be relevant (or at least fully relevant) *unless we all agree to a passivist ontology*. What seems to entice both Habermas and us as readers is his *de facto* and indirect agreement with the passivist ontology despite his obligatory criticism of scientism. Without the anticipation of a passivist ontology one must ask whether his whole theory is redundant.

In the nature versus nurture debate we see the same phenomenon on full display. A socio-biologist such as Richard Dawkins, for instance, claims that all living creatures, including humans, are just *vehicles* for genes that somehow work as selfish agents (Dawkins 1976). Social scientists react to claims such as this because it is assumed that if they were true, human freedom, social science and ethical conduct would be impossible. Their reaction towards Dawkins and other similar accounts strikes us as being critical, but what all of the parties in this debate agree to is the *passivist ontology* that created the *threat* in the first place.[18] In this case this is also displayed indirectly when we see that social scientists rarely argue that social and natural sciences should collaborate more *if or when* the natural sciences understand their objects differently (in a non-passivist way), when – consequently – the expansion of the "nature-side" would no longer pose a threat to the descriptions of humans *as such*.

Again we see that it is preconditions buried in the *ontology* of nature that create the guiding relation between 'is' and 'ought', not a universal meta-argument covering the relationship between 'is' and 'ought' in itself. In other words: it is because we agree to the passivist ontology that we also accept the is/ought distinction. However, if we think that the is/ought distinction yields meaning universally (independently of ontology) we will not be *able to question* and reconsider this distinction since the distinction itself tells us that ontology could not make a difference for ethics in the first place! According to the is/ought distinction a different ontology *cannot* make a difference for the normative field. It would therefore be irrational to argue that alternative ontologies *could* make a difference for the distinction in the first place. A specific ontology makes it futile to allow a certain exchange between is and ought, while at the same time making this ontological argument ('Thou shall not infer from is to ought') look like a purely logical argument; deeming every attempt to break out of this ontological trap an act of fallacious thinking. We are therefore *imprisoned* in a forceful circular argument unless we *decide* to break out of it by investigating further whether it *is* the case that alternative ontologies could not possibly change the relationship between is and ought.

B. *The embeddedness-relation: teleology and environmental ethics*

Everyone familiar with some basic philosophy will know that there are certain ontologies where value and normativity seem virtually already built into the 'is' and that Aristotelian teleology is typically a type of ontology where we would say that values and normativity are already embedded in reality (see section 2.1). In this embeddedness-view, we are not confronted with a situation where we are asked to *infer* from is to ought, since there is no fundamental distinction between what is and what ought to be in the first place. One who holds an embeddedness-view may even go as far as to say that "a bad knife" corresponds to "not a knife", and expand this reasoning to yield meaning for all levels of reality. Moreover, the way Aristotle defined the fact that a particular unit (a substance) was real and not just an arbitrary compilation of other substances was that it had a *telos* of its own. A bed (made by humans) is as such not a real substance, since the bed itself does not have a telos in the sense of "an inner principle of rest and change" (see section 2.1). In this view, ethics is not something that originates in, or concerns only, the human sphere. Humans value things because the world is already valuable.

One may argue that modern passivist ontologies are virtually defined by the fact that they are *not* teleological. One may in some cases even call them anti-telos ontologies, which means that we have the variety of ontologies we have *today* because they are *not teleological*, and not necessarily because they are good or strong in their own right.[19] Modern science began when there was a historical break with Aristotelian teleology (Bunge 1963). In addition to Galileo's, Kepler's and Newton's efforts to describe inanimate nature in a non-teleological fashion, the Darwinian breakthrough was so stunning precisely because his theory was able to explain the current (biological) situation, as well as the origin of this situation, without making an appeal to a telos or telos-mimicking explanation.

However, and this is important, even though Aristotelian teleology has been generally[20] abandoned as an overarching theory, the approach still enjoys a great deal of influence in the sense that we agree that if something did have a telos, its value would be embedded in the being in question. Even more important, where there is no such telos, there is no value to the being in question *except* the value that we humans subjectively project upon it, instrumentally or otherwise. This sets the premise of the debate: in order to argue that something has value beyond our subjective projection, we need to be convinced that the being in question can be described in a way that is consistent with a "telos-orientation" (e.g. when Kant in his own eyes was able to grant that humans are *ends in themselves*, he did not think that he *additionally* had to argue that we are valuable).

In the extreme version of a teleological world view we would picture a God-artisan who endowed each and every being in his constructed world of natural kinds with a purpose (see McInerny 1982). One may call this external teleology (Lee 1999, 33). A tree would have an embedded value in relation to its ability to fulfil its hierarchically ordered purpose set by God. On this extreme version of a teleological world view we would not be able to defend the view that trees have an embedded value unless we believe in this type of great-chain-of-being created by God. Scientists and others who think that this is what it takes for something to have an "objective value", and who don't believe in a God such as this, would therefore see an unbridgeable gap between description and value.

When a teleological account is considered, the question has often been whether or not we can have embedded value with something less than Aristotelian or external teleology. What about the species and relations and the flow of energy and matter making up an ecosystem that *works*? Can we say that the rainy season has been (objectively) good? Can we say that wolves are good, and that therefore no wolves are bad in Yellowstone National Park? (See Chapter 6.)

Unrelated to the specific is/ought issue, Ernst Mayr (1965) recommended that we distinguish between teleology and teleonomy in the case of biological entities.[21] Teleonomy signifies a capacity to be goal directed without there being any purpose to be fulfilled (in this type of directedness as such). Among other things, this allows biology to operate with functional explanations in addition to causal explanations (Mayr 1996). This is useful since it seems insufficient to explain the change of colour in the feathers of the grouse when autumn turns to winter by referring to the increased production of certain hormones (causal explanation), and since it also seems unsatisfactory to explain this by saying that the grouse changes its colour because it intends to do so (realizing that it will increase its ability to survive predators better). Does this mean, however, that the grouse is valuable in virtue of its teleonomical activity?

Many environmental ethicists have referred explicitly or implicitly to the fact that certain biological entities display some kind of goal-directed behaviour, and that this calls directly for the ascription of values, since being goal directed shows that the entity is or can be 'an end in itself' (implying embeddedness). The argument is, as we may recognize in this case, anchored by an ontological claim! What we see here is an anticipation of the idea that a different description of the being in question would more or less automatically grant value to it. This idea creates certain problems for the environmental ethicist, however, which are not easy to spot and solve.

Environmental ethics has gained its predominant identity from its various ways of standing in opposition to 'traditional human-centred ethics' (Leopold 1987; O'Neill et al. 2008, 91ff; Sylvan 2003; Curry 2006, 6). In the disallowance-relation described above we saw that non-humans are regarded as "passive beings" that – because they are so – cannot belong to the axiological or normative sphere. Related to this, environmental ethics is dominated by the distinction between biocentric versus anthropocentric ethics. Should we argue for the moral status of non-human beings *via* some asserted moral status of humans (anthropocentric), or should we argue for this status independently of the embedded value that we ascribe to humans (biocentric)? The most prominent approach within environmental ethics is the latter. Here one tries to transcend human-centred ethics by reassessing what falls inside and what falls outside *the morally considerable* – and one does this by pointing to some kind of "teleological activity". This is implicitly an ontological argument, of course. Environmental ethics is thus seated in the great liberation movement where slaves, non-aristocratic men, women, children, etc., have step by step gained a seat at the table of equal rights. (See Light and Rolston 2003, 7; Næss, 1976, 18.) This "inclusion strategy" requires the establishment of a certain *criterion of distinction*; a criterion that defines what may or may not fall inside of the area of what we find morally considerable (Light and Rolston 2003, 5 and Part II). Holding certain properties that indicate goal-directed behaviour grants a being the status of being an end in itself, and this 'end in itself' is, as we have seen, what constitutes intrinsic (embedded) value (Callicott 1995; O'Neill 2003, 131). What does this mean? It means that whether something has the *property* of reason, the property of being sentient, the property of having interests, the property of having life, the property of being self-organized, the property of being self-conscious, etc., must all be based on *descriptions*. And the descriptions ultimately depend upon certain ontological commitments. We would, in other words, not be able to establish these *ethically* relevant criteria without giving a certain *descriptive* account of the being in question. Although in expanding from the tradition of natural rights we would again be violating current received belief with respect to the is/ought distinction.[22]

One may argue that this is a problem as such and that this approach is self-defeating, but understandably I don't consider this a problem. The real problem with this strategy is that the environmental ethicist has not established an argument that is able to make us take his or her descriptions seriously. For at the outset the environmental ethicist *has no special authority when it comes to the art of giving descriptions*. On the contrary, their descriptions is likely to be seen as value laden. In contemporary western societies, it is scientists who have been granted the authority to describe reality as it is (in itself). The environmental ethicist is therefore caught in a dilemma. The only way to include non-human beings into the family of ethically relevant subjects is by changing our perception of them by giving them a different *description*. (Much in the same way as a new *description* changed the ethical status of women, slaves, Jews, etc.) The ethicist, however, does not have any authority when it comes to descriptions. Reaching for the embeddedness view therefore seems to be a detour, where the premises are already laid down by the special relationship between teleology and passivism. (A scientist will only accept an ontology that is non-teleological, cf. subsection 1.4.2.A and Chapter 2.)

We may here make the following clarifying remarks. Above we sought to establish the following complicated reasoning: the first claim was that the 'is/ought distinction' has nothing to it over and above an uninteresting statement that is generated from logic itself. The reason why we think that 'is' and 'ought' must be (strictly) separated is because we implicitly accept and subscribe to the passivist *ontology*. If the object in question is described in a way that carries the mark of some type of passivism, we would under normal circumstances not think that the object in question has an objective value or that it would be valuable to choose to somehow "follow" the behaviour of the being in question. Something happening by necessity or total contingency cannot give rise to normativity. Now, the reason why we think that this is the case is in turn due to the implicit claims imbedded in *Aristotelian* teleology. Things need to have or display some type of goal-directed behaviour to be granted embedded value. On this embeddedness view, we do not even have to make an inference, in contradistinction to the passivist view where this inference is ontologically (and logically) unsound. To try to change the value of something by trying to change the description would therefore be fallacious in any case. The problem is that this is fallacious only as long as we are blind to the fact that it is fallacious only when we implicitly or explicitly accept that passivism is the *only* real alternative to teleology. For the environmental ethicist this amounts to an insurmountable problem. S/he will have to accept passivism in order to accept that a new description has broken the long-standing agreement that is and ought should be kept apart – unless s/he is able to see through the riddle and come up with a realist alternative to the interlocked relationship between passivist and teleological ontologies. This alternative cannot of course be a teleological alternative, since such an alternative is considered unscientific by definition. The environmental ethicist would therefore have to give a description that is ontologically passivist to be taken seriously, a description that in turn excludes embedded value, which was the aim of the whole endeavour! I will provide an example to make this situation even clearer.

The scientific advice underlying the regulation of the welfare of the salmon in salmon fish-farms focuses mainly on density and water quality. How can I trust that science delivers the facts here – facts that the professional ethicists and the politicians must take for granted? In this case the EU organs have accepted that this stimulus–response-based research (where stress hormones and brain states, etc., are measured against different stimuli) is neutral. On what grounds have they done that? How can we postulate that stimulus–response-based research is relevant for describing the properties of the salmon, properties that are relevant for the criterion of distinction that has (ideally) been agreed upon?

In this case, it is already *assumed* that a salmon *is* a stimulus–response type of entity, behaviourally, while giving the description. (By contrast, research on humans and human behaviour that was based on a stimulus–response paradigm would in most cases be regarded as insufficient to understand human welfare.[23]) In the case of the salmon, the bio-centrist risks the accusation "You are projecting your own values into the description" if s/he were to attempt an alternative description of the salmon. In the case of humans we would see that a similar accusation would be thrown at research that *was* based on stimulus–response experiments to answer welfare questions. The difference between the two cases is ontological: what is a salmon, and what is a human being? In both cases, these descriptions are highly relevant for what we would think that we *ought* to do with fellow humans and non-humans like the salmon. Would there be a way to determine which description would also be the right description?

If both the scientist and the bio-centrist were asked to explicate their views of what the salmon *is*, they would have equal standing in any debate, because they would both have to argue for their views in terms of *ontological* (and not only scientific) justifications. If you think that the salmon can be described fully as a stimulus–response working unit, then you would possibly have to argue for an ontological view where the *being* of the behaviour of the salmon is entirely determined by – (let us say) its biochemical parts. To argue for this would be a philosophical task for the scientist, and it is therefore (?) something that we rarely see.

When the role that ontology plays in the intersection between science and value is neither discussed nor acknowledged, the scientist will always get the upper hand in the sense that he can always brush off the talk about alternative descriptions as being subjective. The relationship between science and society can therefore remain relatively harmonious as long as we all agree that scientists go by the right ontology in their descriptions in the first place. If we can agree on that, we can happily disagree over ethical issues. However, if the disagreement over ethical issues really is, in many cases, ontological disagreement – covered up as being ethical – then we need to reconsider the relationship between ethics, ontology and scientific descriptions.

This is why, in addition to all the reasons given above, I will suggest a third, already well-announced option that goes beyond the traditional option of choosing between 1 and 2.

C. *The allowance-relation*

In line with the main argument thus far, we will have to present a third ontology in order to see if an alternative to the disallowance- and embeddedness-relation is possible and viable. A different ontology might give rise to a different understanding of the relationship between 'is' and 'ought'. Major parts of this book (chapters 3 and 4) are devoted to an in-depth exploration of the disposition-based ontology. I will therefore only point to some features characterizing this ontology in relation to the issue we are dealing with in this chapter.

"Dispositionality" is a type of modality that allows for real (*de re*) potentiality. It allows for a description of behaviour and relations that does not implicitly require them to be necessary or contingent (or both in certain combinations). Properties are such that they tend towards their manifestation, a modal condition that is less than necessity and more than contingency (Mumford and Anjum 2011; Lie 2010). Objects are identified in virtue of what they are able to do and what things are able to do is to be understood as neither contingent nor necessitated. This is an ontology that describes nature in a way that is compatible with normativity, autonomy, intentionality and ethics in general, and where the idea of naturalism in ethics does not automatically confront us to take a stance on *compatibilism* (Anjum et al. 2013). In "Dispositions and Ethics" (Anjum et al. 2013) I and others argue that a dispositional ontology, broadly construed, might be seen as a (neglected) "precondition for some of the key debates and concepts within ethics" (p. 231). It does not follow from this, however, that a particular ethical attitude, theory or stance follows from the ontology itself.

It would therefore be a clear misunderstanding if we took this as an invitation to argue for an embeddedness-relation. A dispositional ontology is an ontology that renders all beings of nature active, but without requiring that 'active' means, or should mean, goal directed. It is the beings themselves that are the main source of their activity, but this activity is not had in virtue of a specific striving towards the realization of a goal. Implied in the allowance-view is the idea that the valuer would neither have to presuppose that 'is' *entails* normative valuations or that 'is' *prohibits* normative valuations.

A concept of naturalness based on an "allowance-ontology" like this does not imply that value or normativity is embedded in nature or what we find to be natural. That does not, however, exclude the possibility that we can describe certain processes or states of affair as being natural. More importantly, and in contradistinction to passivist ontologies, it does not *a priori* exclude us from searching for a viable and compelling concept of naturalness. Moreover, on this version of an allowance account we may accept that the question about the naturalness of a certain being can be answered by science, without implying at the same time that our descriptions *are* valuations.

Various more specific implications of the dispositional ontology concerning the is/ought relation will become clearer as we go through the chapters of this book. We will therefore have more to say about this question in Chapter 6 and, at least indirectly, in Chapter 7.

1.4.3 To amend or not to amend is not the question

John Stuart Mill concludes in the essay "Nature":

> If the natural course of things were perfectly right and satisfactory, to act at all would be a gratuitous meddling, which as it could not make things better,

must make them worse ... To do anything with forethought and purpose would be a violation of that perfect order.

(1923, 19–20)

Mill argues that since we logically cannot help but change the course of nature with our actions, every action would cross this order in any case: therefore *every* action that corrects and mitigates nature cannot be wrong. The question of amending and manipulating nature is for Mill an either/or question. Mill's argument has some similarities to the disallowance-relation discussed in subsection 1.4.2.A. If nature is seen as totally contingent, totally determined or a combination of these two modalities, there will be *no use* in contemplating whether one way of manipulating nature is better than another way. However (and fortunately), there is an alternative. We can define a concept of naturalness (and operate in the world in relation to the understanding underlying such a definition) such that we will be able to see our amendments as being more or less in agreement with "nature" and not just either in agreement or not in agreement. The question is not "amend or not amend?", but "amend yes – but in what way?"

The aim of this book is to show that naturalness is not something that we ethically project upon nature, but neither is it something that is *in* nature in the sense that it more or less "forces" us to act in accordance with it. The concept of naturalness that we require here is, as I said in subsection 1.2.1, a *concept that refers to a reality that would allow us both to fail and to succeed in our efforts to treat something in accordance with it.* This means that it should be possible for science to point out roughly what the natural behaviour of a system, a process or a being is, without implying that this description necessarily prescribes what we ought to do. What we ought to do is *connected* to, but not *determined* by, what we describe as being real in such cases.

An increasingly popular argument against naturalness is, as we saw in section 1.0 and in Mill's understanding above, to say that the concept itself presupposes a distinction between man and nature, i.e. man has to be something categorically different from nature if we anticipate that human actions are or can be unnatural. Conversely, we would have to say that if we are a part of nature it would follow that all the things we do "is natural". But something can, at least principally, be a part of something, and not be "in line" with the whole it is a part of. And if a case can be made for the fact that we can plausibly talk about "naturalness in nature" we could also talk about a part that is or is not "in line" with the whole which the part is a part of. The question of naturalness does not therefore depend on whether we are a part of nature or not but on the question "Is there a nature in nature in the first place?" This is the order of things in this case and in similar cases such as in the case of un-Christian acts. To establish a case for un-Christian acts we would have to establish the fact that there exists a Christian religion in the first place. And furthermore: an un-Christian act presupposes an agent that is a *part of* Christian religion. To say that we can only act "unnaturally" when we are *not* a part of nature is to say that an agent can only act in an un-Christian way if he or she is *not* a part of Christianity, which is an absurd claim. In other words, there is no conflict between being a part of nature and the very concept of 'naturalness' or 'unnaturalness'. When we see the notion of 'naturalness' as being intractable and deceptive it is *not* because we see ourselves as being a part of nature, but rather because our *ontological* understanding of nature is such that it would be meaningless to ascribe any naturalness to it in the first place (cf. passivism).

It should be obvious by now that I want to change the perceptions that lead to different behaviours towards non-human nature, and to do so by framing the issue as an ontological one. I have suggested that it is a hopeless project to argue for a new ethics towards nature, while keeping or overlooking the ontology that, in my mind, guided us in the wrong direction in the first place. But what is the alternative to the prevailing ontology? To many it would be (as we have seen) Aristotelianism, simply because the ontology that prevails today is seen as a dialectical reaction to the ontology of Aristotle. Aristotelianism is not the only alternative, however, and I have therefore suggested a disposition ontology, which I take to be a worthy replacement for Aristotelianism, as the main contender. For those who are familiar with the ontology that I endorse, it is undoubtedly obvious that there are certain continuities between the two. As the reader will see, however, I will argue that those aspects of Aristotelian ontology that seem untenable to us today are either not a part of the disposition ontology or they are handled differently. The disposition ontology therefore gives us the opportunity to transcend the passivist ontologies without having to accept Aristotelianism as the only, but unfeasible, alternative.

I hope that this chapter has helped the reader to take a step back to see the issue of naturalness from a fresh point of view. Now, however, we need to take a closer look at the two deficient alternatives (Aristotelianism and passivism), and also to see how our concept of naturalness might look, according to the two accounts.

Notes

1　This issue will be treated more carefully in (sub)sections 1.3.1, 2.5.1, 5.4 and 6.1 and other places.

2　Levitt says:

> Why should this [GMO] have promoted so much concern? ... Mary Douglas in her book *Purity and Danger*, puts forward the idea that cultures assume that there are "natural " categories, the transgression of which will bring about retribution. This obviously underlies much of the uneasiness concerning GM foods.
>
> (in Stangeroom 2005, 148)

3　This is an idea going back to the Greeks (see Johnson 2005: 105, n. 28). It's also interesting that *The President's Council on Bioethics* (2002, 19–20), and the commission to *Bundestag of the federal republic of Germany* have similar argumentation. E.g. in the latter report we can read: "The fact that human beings are not the project and the planned experiment of their parents, but are the product of chance of nature, secures the independence of the human beings from each other, their individual worth" (quoted in Siipi 2005). See also Sandel (2004).

4　When naturalness is immediately associated with the *ontological* idea of necessitation, we often see that social constructivists typically therefore reject *naturalness*, and not the underlying "ontology of necessitation". The social constructivist therefore sees the debunking of people's "naturalized" perceptions as an advanced and elevated part of the *emancipation* project. Ian Hacking suggests representing this idea in the following way:

> Social constructionists about X tend to hold that:
> "1. X need not have existed, or need not be at all as it is. X, or X as it is at present, is not determined by the nature of things; it is not inevitable.
> Very often they go further and urge that:
> 2. X is quite bad as it is.
> 3. We would be much better off if X were done away with, or at least radically transformed". More about this later.
>
> (Hacking 1999, 6)

5 Or as Kierkegaard would have said, "A human being is a relation (forhold) that relates to itself as a relationship" (1994, 73 [1AA]). Cf. also Charles Taylor on 'strong evaluations' and Harry Frankfurt on 'second order desires'.

6 See chapters 3 and 4.

7 Things and properties might be compossible in many ways, but that's not the same as saying that all those ways would be naturally compossible. This is the difference between what I later call possible-I and possible-N in Chapter 5.

8 Environmental theorists who hold what one might call a social constructivist view are e.g. Macnaghten and Urry (1998), Luke (1997) and Vogel (2002).

9 E.g. Hacking and Latour, who have been accused of being constructivists, typically deny that they are.

10 There has been a comprehensive debate over this issue in e.g. *Environmental Ethics* (e.g. winter 1999; see also Kidner 2000, Crist 2004).

11 Since I will have to leave closer descriptions of the meaning of terms and expressions such as 'dispositions', 'manifestations of dispositions', 'relationalism', 'passivism', etc. to later chapters, I will have to trust that the reader can grasp the more intuitive and rudimentary meaning of these terms and expressions at this point.

12 See sections 2.6 and 3.2.

13 The view that Castree presents in his interesting and noteworthy book *Making Sense of Nature* illustrates the point that I am trying to make about the restrictions that social constructivists have put on the capacity to do ontology. He identifies four main ontological meanings of the word 'nature' (p. 10). His constructivist position tells him not to investigate whether one of these four meanings is better or truer than any other. For him to embark on that would be meaningless – or, rather, self-defeating – of course.

14 Max Black casts doubts on even this assertion (in Hudson 1969, 100). What Hume really meant by this famous phrase is debated by MacIntyre, Arkinson, Hunter, Flew and Hudson in the same book.

15 Above I gave the example where we saw that Levitt argued for the view that the European resistance against GMOs mixes values into science. Typically, an argument like Levitt's would be countered by saying that science itself represents a value system and that scientific results or technologies should never be presented as value-free in the first place – indicating that the perceived role of science, namely to *deliver* pure knowledge into the social sphere of politics and ethics, should not naively be presented as a trouble-free zone (see e.g. Wynne 2005).

16 See also Schneewind 2003; he argues that this is not a trait distinctive to Kantian ethics but applies to the general development of ethics in the eighteenth century.

17 For instance, he calls Herbert Marcuse's *open* idea about a "different science in the future" "a very romantic idea" (Frankel 1974, 46). See also Outhwaite 1994, 21.

18 There are several social scientists and others who challenge the role that Dawkins gives the genome, e.g. Svendsen 2001, but this criticism is rarely a principal criticism of passivism as a mode of thinking in science, but rather that biologism does not apply to social science.

19 Schelling's ontology is typically one of the ontologies that did not survive the test of being "not teleological".
20 Although there are philosophers, such as Ralph McInerny, who defend modern versions of Aristotelianism (1982).
21 He refers to Collin Pittendrigh, who four years earlier suggested the term, which goes back to Kant and his idea of "*Zweckmässigkeit ohne Zweck*" (1790). One may also question whether Aristotle really would agree with the classical mediaeval interpretation of teleology that was highly influenced by the Christian philosophers of the time, or whether he would be more satisfied with something similar to the definition of teleonomy.
22 There is a strange inconsistency here. Human rights are secured by referring to these rights as being natural, while the rights of other non-human beings cannot be argued for along the same lines (naturalistic fallacy). Although the tradition of "natural rights" is disputed, this goes to show again that non-human beings are seen as a completely different ontological category before anything else is considered.
23 There are of course some theorists who would like to see behaviourist or positivist research programmes applied to humans, but such ontological views are regarded as highly controversial, something that is not true in most cases regarding non-human ethology.

References

Anjum, R.L., Mumford, S., and Lie, S.A. (2013) "Dispositions and Ethics", in Groff, R. and Greco, J. (eds.) *Powers and Capacities in Philosophy: The New Aristotelianism*. Routledge.

Aristotle (1996) *Physics* (trans. R. Waterfield), Oxford University Press.

—— (1998) *The Metaphysics* (trans. Lawson-Tancred) Penguin.

Armstrong, D. (1989) *A Combinatorial Theory of Possibility*, Cambridge University Press.

Beck, U. (1988) *The Risk Society: Towards a New Modernity*, Sage.

Black, M. (1969) "The Gap Between Is and Should", in Hudson, W.D. (ed.) *The Is and Ought Question*, Macmillan.

Brink, D. (1989) *Moral Realism and the Foundations of Ethics*, Cambridge University Press.

Bunge, M. (1959/1963) *Causality*, Meridian Books.

Callicott, B. (1995) "Intrinsic Value in Nature: A Metaethical Analysis", *Electronic Journal of Analytic Philosophy* 3.

Castree, N. (2014) *Making Sense of Nature*, Routledge.

Cole, D. N. and Yung, L. (2010) *Beyond Naturalness: Rethinking Park and Wilderness Stewardship in an Era of Rapid Change*, Island Press.

Crist, Eileen (2004) "Against the Social Construction of Nature and Wilderness", *Environmental Ethics*, Spring.

Curry, P. (2006) *Ecological Ethics*, Polity.

Dawkins, R. (1976) *The Selfish Gene*, Oxford University Press.

Deckers, J. (2005) "Are Scientists Right and Non-scientists Wrong? Reflections on discussions of GM", *Journal of Agriculture and Environmental Ethics* 18.

Douglas, M. (1966) *Purity and Danger: An Analysis of Concepts of Pollution and Taboo*, Routledge.

Ellis, Brian (2002) *The Philosophy of Nature*, Acumen.

Frankel, B. (1974) "Habermas talking: An Interview", *Theory and Society* 46.

Funtowicz, S. and Ravetz, J. (1993) "Science for the Post-Normal Age", *Futures*, September.

Geach, P. (1956) "Good and Evil", *Analysis*, vol. 17, pp. 32–42.

Gibbons, M. et al. (1994) *The New Production of Knowledge: The Dynamics of Science and Research in Contemporary Societies*, Sage.

Graham, L. (1981) *Between Science and Values*, Columbia University Press.

Hacking, I. (1999) *The Social Construction of What?*, Harvard University Press.

Hansen, A. (2006) "Tampering with Nature: Nature and the Natural in Media Coverage of Genetics and Biotechnology", *Media, Culture & Society* 28.

Harraway, D. (1991) *Simians, Cyborgs and Women*, Free Association Books.

Harris, J. (2007) *The Enhancing Evolution*, Princeton University Press.

Heffernan, T. (2003) "Bovine Anxieties, Virgin Births and the Secret of Life", *Cultural Critique* 53.

Heffner, P. (1981) "Is/Ought: A Risky Relationship between Theology and Science", in A. R. Peacocke (ed.) *The Sciences and Theology in the Twentieth Century*, Oriel Press.

Heidegger, M. (1927/1992) *Being and Time*, Blackwell.

Hudson, H. (1969) "Introduction", in W.D. Hudson (ed.) *The Is and Ought Question*, Macmillan.

Hume, D. (1739–1740/1978) *Treatise on Human Nature* (trans. L.A. Selby-Bigge and P.H. Nidditch), Oxford University Press.

Johnson, M. (2005) *Aristotle on Teleology*, Oxford University Press.

Jonas, H. (1979/1984) *The Imperative of Responsibility*, University of Chicago Press.

Kant, I. (1785/1997) *Groundwork for the Metaphysics of Morals* (trans. Mary Gregor), Cambridge University Press.

—— (1790/1987) *Critique of Judgment*, Hackett Publishing.

Kass, L. R. et al. (2002) *Human Cloning and Human Dignity*, The President's Council on Bioethics, July.

Katz, E. (1996) *Nature as Subject: Essays in Environmental Ethics and Policy*, Roman and Littlefield.

Kidner, David W. (2000) "Fabricating Nature: A Critique of the Social Construction of Nature", *Environmental Ethics*, Winter.

Kierkegaard, S. (1849/1994) *Sykdommen til døden*, Samlede verker, Gyldendal.

Krieger, M. (1973) "What is Wrong with Plastic Trees?" *Science* 179, pp. 446–455.

Kwieciński, J. (2009) "Genetically modified Abominations", *EMBO reports*, vol 10.

Latour, B. (1991) *We have Never been Modern*, Harvard University Press.

—— (1998) "From the World of Science to the World of Research?", *Science* 280: 208–209.

Lee, K. (1999) *The Natural and The Artefactual*, Lexington Books.

Leopold, A. (1949/1987) *A Sand County Almanac*, Oxford University Press.

Lewis, D. (1983) *Collected Papers*, vol. I, Oxford University Press.

Lie, S. (2008) "Having an Ethical Discussion About the Objects of Natural Science: The is and Ought Distinction", *Jahrbuch der ASFPG 3*, Der Andere Verlag.

—— (2010) "Naturalness Reconsidered: Dispositions Ethics and Ontology", (PhD Dissertation), University of Tromsø.

Lie, S.A.N. and Wickson, F. (2011) "The Relational Ontology of Deep Ecology: A Dispositional Alternative to Intrinsic Value?", in A. Aaro and J. Servan (eds.) Environment, Embodiment & History, Hermes Texts.

Light, A. and Rolston III, H. (2003) "Introduction", in A. Light and H. Rolston III (eds.) *Environmental Ethics – An Anthology*, Blackwell.

Lindholm, M. (2012) *Evolusjon, naturens kulturhistorie*, Spartacus forlag.

Luke, T. (1997) *Ecocritique: Contesting the Politics of Nature, Economy and Culture*, University of Minnesota Press.

McInerny, R. (1982) *Ethica Thomistica*, University of Notre Dame Press.

MacIntyre, A. (1969) "Hume on Is and Ought", in W.D. Hudson (ed.) *The Is and Ought Question*, Macmillan.

McKibben, B. (1989) *The End of Nature*, Random House.

Macnaghten, P. and Urry, J. (1998) *Contested Natures*, Sage.

Marris, C. (2001) "Public Views on GMOs: Deconstructing the Myths", *EMBO Reports* 2(7).

Mayr, E. (1965) "Cause and Effect in Biology", in D. Lerner (ed.) *Cause and Effect*. New York: Free Press.

—— (1996) "What Makes Biology Autonomous: The Position of Biology Among Sciences", *The Quarterly Review of Biology* 7(1).

Meyer, G. and Sandøe, P. (2001) "Public Debate and Scientific Ignorance", *EurSafe 2001 Third Congress of the European Society for Agricultural and Food Ethics*, October 3–5.

Michaels, Mark A. (2001) "How to Interfere with Nature", *Environmental Ethics*, Spring.

Midgley, M. (2000) "Biotechnology and Monstrosity", *Hastings Center Report 2000*.

Mill, J.S. (1863/1923) *Nature: The Utility of Religion and Theism*, Longmans Green.

Moore, G.E. (1903) *Principia Ethica*, Dover Publications, 2004.

Mumford, S. and Anjum, R. L. (2011) *Getting Causes from Powers*, Oxford University Press.

Næss A. (1976) *Økologi, Samfunn og Livsstil*, Universitetsforlaget, 1991.

Nuttfield Council of Bioethics (1999) "Genetically modified Crops", April.

O'Neill, J. (2003) "The Varieties of Intrinsic Value", in A. Light and H. Rolston III (eds.) *Environmental Ethics – An Anthology*, Blackwell.

O'Neill, J., Holland, A. and Light, A. (2008) *Environmental Values*, Routledge.

Outhwaite, W. (1994) *Habermas: A Critical Introduction*, Stanford University Press.

Palmer, C. (2003) "An Overview of Environmental Ethics", in A. Light and H. Rolston III (eds.) *Environmental Ethics – An Anthology*, Blackwell.

Pickett, Steward T.A., and White, P.S. (eds.) (1985) *The Ecology of Natural Disturbance and Patch Dynamics*, Academic Press.

Putnam, H. (2002) *The Collapse of the Fact/Value Dichotomy*, Harvard University Press.

Rhoads, J. (1991) *Critical Issues in Social Theory*, Pennsylvania State University.

Rothenberg, D. (1992) *Hands End*, University of California Press.

Sandel, M. (2004) "The Case Against Perfection", *The Atlantic*, April.

Schneewind, J.B. (1998) *The Invention of Autonomy: A History of Modern Moral Philosophy*, Cambridge University Press.

—— (2003) *Moral Philosophy from Montaigne to Kant*, Cambridge University Press.

Sellars, W. (1956) "Empiricism and the Philosophy of Mind," in H. Feigl and M. Scriven (eds.), *Minnesota Studies in the Philosophy of Science*, vol. I, University of Minnesota Press, 253–329.

Siipi, H. (2005) "Naturalness, Unnaturalness and Artificiality in Bioethical Argumentation" (unpublished doctoral thesis), University of Turku.

Soper, K. (1995) *What is Nature*, Wiley-Blackwell.

Soule, M. and Lease, G. (eds.) (1995) *Reinventing Nature: Responses to Postmodern Deconstruction*, Island Press.

Stangeroom, J. (2005) *What Scientists Think*, Routledge.

Svendsen, L.F. (2001) *Mennesket, moralen og genene*, Universitetsforlaget.

Sylvan, R. (2003) "Is there a Need for a New Environmental, Ethic?", in A. Light and H. Rolston III (eds.) *Environmental Ethics – An Anthology*, Blackwell.

Tønning, K. et al. (2009) "Kortlægning af kemiske stoffer i forbrugerprodukter" Nr. 103.

Tullberg, B. and Tullberg, J. (2001) "A Critique of the Naturalistic Fallacy Thesis", *Facts and Values*, September.

Verhoog, H. (2003) "Naturalness and the Genetic Modification of Animals", *Trends in Biotechnology*, July.

Vogel, S. (1996) *Against Nature: The Concept of Nature in Critical Theory*, SUNY Press.

—— (2002) "Environmental Philosophy after the End of Nature", *Environmental Ethics*, Spring.

—— (forthcoming) *Thinking Like a Mall*, MIT Press.

Wapner, P. (2003) "Leftist Criticism of Nature", *Dissent Magazine*, Winter.

West-Eberhardt, M.J. (2003) *Developmental Plasticity and Evolution*, Oxford University Press.

Wickson, F. (2008) "Narratives of Nature and Nanotechnology", *Nature Nanotechnology* 3(6), pp. 313–315.

Williams, R. (1976) *Keywords: A Vocabulary of Culture and Society*, Oxford University Press.

Wuerthner, G. et al. (2014) *Keeping the Wild: Against the Domestication of Earth*, Island Press.

Wynne, B. (1992) "Uncertainty and Environmental Learning: Reconceiving Science Preventing Paradigm", *Global Environmental Change* (June 111–127).

—— (2001). "Creating Public Alienation: Expert Cultures of Risks and Ethics of GMO", *Science as Culture* 10.

—— (2005) "Reflexing Complexity: Post-genomic Knowledge and Reductionist Returns in Public Science", *Theory, Culture & Society* 22(5).

2 'No Naturalness, only Nature'

2.0 Introduction

'Nature *is* nature. Nature is just everything there is. Everything is natural.' How did this view become our view on 'nature'. The term that I think brings us a long way in answering this question is 'passivism'. Passivism gives us a world where everything is ontologically contingent and fully *compossible*, and at the same time possible to handle and manipulate in a way that does not invoke or depend on a 'natural way'.

In this chapter I will present the ontological background picture that has come to dominate the present-day concept of naturalness, and how this picture is reinforced as an operable passivist ontology in science. The big bad wolves in environmental philosophy have traditionally been René Descartes and Francis Bacon. I have chosen to focus on John Locke and David Hume, not because they are big bad wolves, but because I focus on passivism and how this ontological regime is related to scientific practice. I have found that the way Lockean essentialism and the way Hume thinks the world is related is able to effectively wrestle the "activity of things" and make them 'passive' in a far more effective and comprehensive way than Bacon and Descartes did.

In chapter 3 I introduce "a third alternative" that is neither Aristotelian nor passivist. We need to understand Aristotelian teleology to see how this ontology is related to passivism, but also to realize why the third alternative is *not* susceptible to the same problems that made 'Aristotelianism' unfit for the development of today's scientific culture.

To recognize how passivism operates in science we cannot avoid focusing on the inferential relationship between *in-vitro* and *in-vivo*. I claim that it is our ability to study and understand the being of things *in-vitro* and later misinterpret what is going on when we infer from *in-vitro* to *in-vivo* cases that makes it possible for us to overlook the massive anomalies of passivism. The reader should keep in mind that the general claims made in this chapter will be followed up throughout this book, especially in Chapter 5.

2.1 Aristotle: 'existing by nature'

We saw in section 1.3 #3 that one common use of the word 'natural' assumes that it is *things* that have natures. Although Wittgenstein thinks that it is fallacious to think this way, it nevertheless seems intuitive to think that if something is a thing, it must also be a particular kind of being. It is *this* thing and not *that* thing. When we speak about naturalness, we tend to mean that the nature of a thing must be something that persists through both time and space. If the nature of a thing does not remain the same through change, but changes in response to changing conditions, we will be unwilling to say that the thing in question has a nature in the first place.

The concept of a substance, essentialism and the notion of intrinsicality have origins going back to Aristotle and further. When Aristotle was partly thrown overboard as *comme il faut* in the seventeenth century, naturalness was in many respects thrown out with him. Even though many may agree that we still have a lot to learn from him, the suggestion is often that Aristotle's ontology as a whole does not apply to our contemporary scientific world view. The project of re-establishing the concept of naturalness may therefore seem to be an anachronistic one. In this chapter, we see how the destiny of naturalness turned from being a central concept in Aristotelian metaphysics to the situation we face today where 'naturalness has nowhere to hide'.

In *Metaphysics* (Δ IV), Aristotle asserts: "The discussion should have established that primary **nature**, in the fundamental account, is the substance of those things with a principle of process *within themselves qua themselves*" (1015a, my emphasis). Natural things inhere within themselves a principle (of rest and change). Whenever this principle is "followed", we see the instantiation of a natural process.

> Some things exist by nature, others are due to other causes. Natural objects include animals and their parts, plants and simple bodies like earth, fire, air and water; at any rate, we do say that these kinds of things exist naturally. The obvious difference between all these things and things which are not natural is that each of the natural ones contains within itself a source of change and of stability, in respect of their movement or increase and decrease or alteration. On the other hand something like a bed or a cloak has no intrinsic impulse for change – at least they do not under any particular description and to the extent that they are a result of human skill, but they do in so far as and to the extent they are coincidently made out of stone or earth or some combination of the two.
>
> (192 b8–b19)[1]

That which really exists is substances. A substance ('thing') consists of *matter* and *form*. The nature of a substance is determined by its *form* (*eidos/morphē*). We describe the form of a substance when we describe its essential and universal properties. These universal properties, which are shared by the same kind of substances, are what make the substance the substance it is. When we know the form of a substance we know what it is; its identity. In picking out substances, we have to discern between necessary and contingent properties. By doing this we arrive at the *essential* properties of the substance, properties it could not be without, without ceasing to be what it is (see *Metaphysics* Δ VII, Z X). This is mainly what makes Aristotle an *essentialist* and which will make us think that we know the nature of a thing when we know 'its essence'.

The essential properties making up the form are what makes the substance *behave* in a certain way. An electron behaves in a certain way that is essential to being an electron. What something is, is defined by its *activity*. Identity and activity can be distinguished but not separated. The being of a thing is defined by what it does or has the capacity to do; its *way* of being. Aristotle believed that every substance that can rightly be called substance has an essence.

Identities can also be ascribed when the behaviour of a substance depends upon the intervention of an external source (ibid., b30). However, things with such identities 'exist by *technē*' not by nature, and in such cases the behaviour and thus the identity are *coincidental* or contingent and not natural. A chair does not have the identity of being a chair by its nature; even though a chair works as a chair or has the capacity to work as a chair, it has this capacity accidentally (see below). The chair is not a chair because it strives towards the realization of being a chair. "If shipbuilding were intrinsic to wood, then wood would naturally produce the same results as shipbuilding does" (ibid., 199 b29). Substances without natures are therefore, strictly speaking, not substances (Johnson 2005, 133).[2] Rather they are artefacts.

The central issue for Aristotle seems to be that we can observe processes wherein certain behaviours are not determined by contingent forces, but instead seem to have their own course. A dropped stone will spontaneously fall to the ground; fire and heat will spontaneously go upwards, and despite the changing forces of wind, drought, rain, etc. (excepting severe conditions), the acorn will grow into an oak tree. There is nothing in the world that spontaneously turns into a bed. That the bed has become a bed depends on causes that are external to being a bed. For the same reason, the decay of the bed does not happen in a *bedlike* way, since it is an *assembly of parts* ("accidentally") put together by humans, and those parts can be made of "anything", whereas we on the other hand *would* say that wood decays in a wood-like way.

Aristotle asks the question: "Is the nature of a thing its matter or its form?" (ibid., 193 a8ff), and conveys his arguments via engagement with the *materialists* of his time. The materialists say that the form (in Aristotle's example of "the design and functional arrangement of the bed") is just made up of coincidental attributes of the wood (e.g. in the bed). Earth, air, fire and water (in this context: 'matter') "have been named by various things as the *nature* of things" (ibid., a23). Aristotle counters that according to this view everything is an "affection, state or disposition of this" (nature), or as we may say today: 'is supervenient on that' (nature) (see also Johnson 2005, section 6.4).

Aristotle's general answer to the matter-is-the-source-of-identity position is to show that what he calls form is not just an *affection* of the "material" elements, but is rather an integral aspect of the real being of things. What we single out as matter, according to Aristotle (a singling out that is only possible conceptually), is only *potentially* a specific being. When we say that clay is the matter of a pot, we are able to talk about *matter* in this way only because the clay has already *acquired a form* as a pot. Form is therefore not just a coincidental "product" of the material base. Without the pot we would not see clay as matter, simply because clay is not *matter in itself* but only matter in relation to the pot. To pick out the matter requires *ex post facto* reasoning.

The same goes for Aristotle's 'simple elements' such as earth, fire, air and water: pure matter does not have *being*. Without form, matter is nothing. And vice versa (ibid., 200 a5). To be something at all, the one aspect needs the other. Given that 'each needs the other' we cannot say that either supervenes on or is an affection of the other. The only thing that can exist by itself is a composition of *form* and *matter*: a substance. This combined view where neither form nor matter is seen as more real than the other is often referred to as the *hylomorphic* view (i.e. form (*morphē*) and matter (*hylē*)). Aristotle's hylomorphic view entails the assumption that you need to understand substances from the "perspective" of the substance. If we want to understand humans for instance, we need to understand humans as (*qua*) humans and not humans *qua* genes for instance. If we want to understand an ecosystem (if there is such a thing, which is a different question), we need to understand it *qua* ecosystem. This is given by the fact that Aristotle thinks that the form of a being is real.[3]

Being a thing/substance means being in a continuous state of alteration that is directed towards fulfilment. This fulfilment is made possible by the continuous display of the essential behaviours of the thing in question. The behaviour of the being in question can therefore be described as goal directed, and this is why we use the expression 'teleological' to describe Aristotle's ontology. As should be clear by now, continuous change is not arbitrary change from one state to another. Change has the character of accomplishment and "completability" – a fulfilment which Aristotle considers to be *good in itself*: "Goodness is a kind of completion: it is when something becomes as good as it may be that we say that it is complete, because that is when it pre-eminently conforms with its nature" (ibid., 246 a11; O'Neill 2003, 137). In other words: everything has a nature, which culminates in the thing's fulfilment of itself – its nature, its end. This nature is "seen" in full when completion is reached. However, form is not the *product* itself, the product is the *hylomorphic* substance (see *Met.* Z 9). Further: completion is *good*; deviation from completion is bad: "Not every final stage has a claim to be called an end, only the best is an end" (*Phy.* 194 a32; see also *Met.* Δ XVI and XXII). Here, the Platonist in Aristotle comes to the fore, although it must be admitted that 'as good as it may' (*aretē*/virtue), is not the same as perfect. The finalized stage has a particular Aristotelian way of being ideal.

So even though Aristotle and the Greeks had not established a deep cleft between human and non-human nature, they might still maintain that to disturb or alter this process of fulfilment would be morally wrong. It would disturb a process that is *good in itself*. On this account, therefore, crossing or not crossing natural behaviour should be considered as an axiological question, which is the reason why we say that normative statements follow from Aristotle's ontology (see chapter 1.4.2.B).

To conclude: "The point is that those things are natural which undergo continuous change, starting from an intrinsic source of change and concluding at a particular end" (*Phy.* II. 8. 199b 15–16). This means that the *telos* is immanent (as opposed to some kind of extrinsic teleology such as theological teleology, or human-imposed teleology) (see Lee 1999, 49). It is this teleology that we need to take into consideration when we want to know whether we act in accordance with nature or not, and to consider this is also to consider whether our actions can be called good or bad.

2.2 Fixed beings

There is a major difference between causal factors that make a difference for the *realization process* (e.g. of the plant), and causal factors which make a difference for the *telos* (of e.g. the plant).

Something (external) that changes the *telos* and the form of a plant would be both *external and accidental* to the plant. Or, to put it differently: when some substance (having matter and form) is made into 'just *matter*' for an alien form, we would have a case of unnaturalness. 'Alien' would mean: not in compliance with its original realization potential.

A tree is a substance that in accordance with Aristotle is constituted by matter and form. A tree might become "just matter" in a chair, and a chair is of course not the form of wood. Causing the substance to acquire a new form demands external efficient causes for both the production and the maintenance of the new "substance" (i.e. artefact). This is different from instances where we see that a natural substance is only externally *influenced*, since in the latter case the being in question will "naturally" return to its place or state when the influence is subtracted. A chair left alone will not grow into something that is chair-like or something else that follows from being a chair; it will not decay or develop in a chair-like manner. Therefore, according to this position, a chair would be considered unnatural (*Phy.* II 1.A. See also Johnson 2005, 133f.). The form in this case depends on other beings maintaining its form. The form is thus accidental; the substance therefore lacks an "intrinsic source".

Aristotle thinks that the form of a natural substance is fixed. This makes it difficult to allow graduation of artifice. Something is either a (natural) substance or an artefact. This is not in compliance with for instance, a Darwinian view, where living creatures are seen as being in constant change – change that is basically accidental (cf. Reiss and Straughan 1996). What is a fixed species, but a snapshot of the ever-changing river of evolution? What, in turn, could the "fixed" nature of such a phenomenon be, and what would be a substantial change of such a nature? On the Darwinian view there seems to be no principled difference between accidental changes that are imposed by humans and changes that the organisms have undergone due to other sources of change.

Take the taming of an animal for example. Over many generations we might be able to domesticate a given species of animal by selection, changing their "inner source of change and rest" in a human-favoured direction. But is this change a complete change? Is it now an artefact?

In this case we would say that the tamed animal would need some, but (of course) not full, external support for its development and maintenance. In other cases, however, one may observe that the animal would need full and vital support for its maintenance and the change would be substantial (*Phy.* 201 a6, see also next paragraph). In many cases we see that some animals are not easily "tameable",[4] and must for instance be fenced in order to serve the wanted purpose (e.g. fur production or recreation). In most cases we would say that such animals have preserved a large proportion of their "inner source of change and rest", even though it may be impeded in its process of realization. Humans may obstruct the natural movements of such creatures (i.e. via forced movement), but the animals' "inner source of change and rest" is fairly unchanged. For example, their offspring may be fully capable of living without support in the wild.

With new techniques that make it possible to alter the organism or species on a genetic level (such as recombinant DNA technology), we are perhaps seeing a more radical change in the relation between form and matter however, where the original substance can potentially become "just matter" for a man-made form. It is interesting to see that reminiscences of the Aristotelian concept of naturalness are used in an attempt to grasp what are perceived as radical intervention techniques (cf. Meyer and Sandøe 2001; Marris 2001; Fox 1990; Verhoog 2003; Lee 1999, 53; Deckers 2005). Many people react against GMOs because they think that the to-be-modified organism has some kind of *integrity*, a self-sufficient ability to flourish and maintain its own life. This is a so-called intrinsic argument against genetic engineering, meaning that the technology itself (and not only its consequences) is unacceptable (Verhoog 2003). Changes made to the organism/species on a genetic level are seen as *too radical*; one is not only impeding the realization but enforcing a change that can be characterized a change of the organism or species' "inner source of change and rest" (a *substantial* change in Aristotelian terms). We are changing its nature. Normal breeding would just be a *forced movement* in terms of selection pressure, while genetic engineering would be a case of changing the source itself, its being. It is this being that secures the ascribed integrity, and therefore the possibility of violating this integrity. Without the idea of "an inner source", we would not be troubled by considerations like this.[5]

Naturalness, according to Aristotle, may be summed up in the following way: whenever a given substance is subjected to external change that is accidental and substantial (i.e. change of "the inner source"), and where the outcome of that change is a substance that has a form that requires external maintenance to persist as it is, then we can refer to that substance as an artefact. This is an operational concept since it does not assume that unnaturalness follows from *any* human act, but it does allow that some of our actions might lead to the production of "unnatural change". To illustrate: from this perspective it would be acceptable to have hens in a cage, but it would not be acceptable to change the inner source (*telos*) of the hen.

Even though such a view might be easily accepted by laypeople, it will not be accepted by those philosophers and scientists who are not willing to accept Aristotelian teleology (which amounts to quite a lot. See e.g. Ashby 1978, 83). This is not a problem in itself. The problem is rather that 'naturalness' is perceived as an "Aristotelian concept". And as long as naturalness is identified with Aristotle, the rejection of Aristotelian concepts such as teleology, essence and form will lead those who are theorizing naturalness to regard it as a subjective construct.

2.3 Understanding today's concept of naturalness

The emergence of our scientifically oriented societies came, as we have noted, partly as a result of a philosophical repudiation of the teleology of Aristotle; more specifically as an attack on the final and formal causes that Aristotle had introduced 2,000 years earlier (Losee 1980, 52; Lee 1999, 19; Bunge 1963, 32; Schmaltz 2014, 5).[6] There was a certain exhaustion connected with seemingly interminable debates within scholastic philosophy, and therefore also a striving towards a more empirical orientation (e.g. Funkenstein 2005, 51). This orientation was ignited by the nominalists of the fourteenth century (e.g. William of Ockham), who denied the real existence of universals (and therefore also the syllogistically based reasoning that underscored the scholastic disputes), and who therefore *had to* emphasize the importance of observation. Teleological movement or final causes are causes that are typically difficult to observe, at least *directly*, while the efficient and material causes "could be assigned an empirical correlate" (Bunge, ibid.). A general and major shift in what was seen as the cause of being and change came about, and no longer were things (substances) seen as governed by "an inner principle of change and rest". Proponents of the novel alternative view understood this causal relationship quite differently. The "new" stone fell to the ground because of an outer force (or properties ascribed to lower levels "susceptible" to laws), not because of an inner striving or purpose. Modern science has in this sense been constituted by the idea of *efficient causes* being regarded as the starting point for any explanation as a whole (see Bunge 1963; Schmaltz 2014). Disputes over this causal principle (i.e. efficient causation) have been a focal point in philosophy ever since. The disagreements mainly concern how to define efficient causation and its status properly, rather than involving any disputation of its prevailing status.

If behaviour is always seen as *caused* by something external to that which is behaving, an 'external agent' as Aristotle called it, we will most likely end up with a view that Brian Ellis calls passivism. He uses the term passivism to designate those ontologies that consider entities in themselves to be "passive". By the term passive he refers to objects and phenomena of nature that are not "genuine causal agents capable of acting and interacting" – that, on the contrary, are "participants in processes that are externally driven and governed" (Ellis 2002, 3). Ellis identifies passivism with Humeanism. I identify passivism with a broader spectrum of ontologies. In my view, one can "obtain" this passiveness in at least two basic ways, either directly from Humeanism, or from an essentialist/reductionist view.[7] The main point of this chapter is therefore to uncover how this postulated passivism unfolds in different ways, especially within science, and how passivism connects to the question of naturalness. To venture forward we must find a starting point that allows us to investigate the complexity of the problem.

The focal point is not a theory of what science really is (philosophy of science), but what science takes to be the real being of nature – the ontology that science follows, explicitly and implicitly.

It is hardly the case that one can pin down the prevailing ontology of nature that science employs in terms of either essentialism or Humeanism or some similar philosophical theory. So, even though I claim that naturalness is not a concept that is well received within science because of the dominant ontology currently framing modern scientific activity, I do not suggest that it is an easy task to understand what this ontology consists of. There are, of course, many sources that could potentially lead us into the "right" understanding of the ontology of science. More fundamentally, however, we first need to agree with Thomas Kuhn when he asserts that what the scientist is actually doing is always guided by some basic commitment about 'what the world looks like' (Kuhn 1996, 5). The mere fact that an ontology is had, however, does not say much about its content, or how we should obtain a qualified understanding of it. The search for such an understanding may involve many aspects. I have listed five:

#1 What are scientists doing when they do science?
#2 What does the scientist believe that s/he does?
#3 What is the scientist reporting to others about what s/he does?
#4 What do others say that the scientists are doing? What task is the scientist expected to fulfil?
#5 What do the ideas from the history of ideas say that s/he is doing?.[8]

What this list of five questions first and foremost indicates is that the ontology of science is not accessible in a straightforward way. It is perfectly possible to have explicit assumptions about what you are doing (#2) that do not comply with what you are actually doing (#1). The scientist might believe that s/he is uncovering the *essential* properties of something, while his or her methods and ways of behaving are actually only means of uncovering the dispositions of things. It is also possible for a scientist to report or somehow convey to others that s/he is doing F when s/he is actually doing Z (#3). The conveying itself, and the things conveyed, may also vary according to the different expectations to which the scientist is subjected (#4). These expectations exist both because science is the 'truth source' of modern society, and because it is the driver of economic growth as the primary source of social 'progress' (through the application of technology), which arguably puts certain pressures on #2 and #3 (see section 2.8).

Historically (when our model of science was shaped by thinkers such as Bacon, Locke, Descartes, Boyle, etc.), until today, there has been much dispute about what science is and should be (#5). But this history does not inform us of the ontology of science itself. It might give us the sanctioned story, but that is not necessarily the best one, since it is often "hampered by consistency" (i.e. by understanding science through the history of ideas, we will be inclined to seek a picture that is consistent). By saying this I do not mean to say that science has 'many stories to tell' and that it is impossible to give a coherent description. Quite the opposite: I think that it is possible to give one reasonably coherent description of the ontology of science, but I also think that such a description must take into consideration that science displays itself in several ways, such that nothing should be taken at face value.

In this chapter, I intend to review the 'essentialist-necessity theory' of Locke and the 'contingency theory' of Hume. The plan is to show how these views fit into (what I understand to be a "correct" interpretation of) the ontologies underlying today's scientific praxis, and not the other way around.

The type of literature that has grown rapidly over the last decades are books that are intended to give a general overview of the specific scientific findings in a terminology that is more broadly accessible than that which would be found in the specialized sciences. Works of popular science present general claims based on scientific "findings". They are meant to be accessible interpretations of scientific findings and how they should be understood (e.g. Robert Laughlin (2005); Stephen Hawking (1988); Fritjof Capra (1975); John D. Barrow (2007); Richard Dawkins (1976); Lenny Moss (2004); Rupert Sheldrake (1981); Richard Lewontin (2000); Douglas Hofstadter (2007), etc.). However, the authors of such publications typically do not discuss how the substantive views cohere with *ontological* theories. (A typical example is John Barrow (2007) talking about the laws of the universe, without making clear what is meant by "a law of nature".) They don't normally touch upon questions like "What is a property?", "What is causality?" or "What is necessity?", but rather take a particular view on such issues for granted.[9] From a critical point of view, one may say that despite the success and much-needed presence of this literature, work of this kind contains problematic aspects that should be noted.

One problem is that the authors of such works purport to ask 'basic questions', but they seldom, if ever, transcend or challenge the ontological assumptions of the science that they portray. Thus they obscure the horizon from the vantage point of which one *could* see that ontological debate is needed. There might be ontological problems underlying what seem to be theoretical problems within a certain scientific field. For instance, the problems related to medical research based on RCT-methodology might be ontological rather than scientific (Kerry et al. 2012 and Eriksen et al. 2013).

A second problem is that of authors who try to expand or override scientific paradigms such as reductionism by pointing to examples. (Examples could be: Laughlin, Sheldrake and Lewontin.) These authors are typically making inferences from science to ontology, without appreciating that a philosophically sound ontology demands something more than generalizations from examples. There is nothing wrong with this approach so long as it does not cover up the need to complete this picture ontologically. It is evident that one will never get into a proper debate about the ontology upon which a given scientific description rests if one's ontology is derived from cherry-picked examples. An ontological discussion needs participants who are committed to coherence, not only to scientific findings. There are many opinions and ideas that may attain support from the deliverances of science, but when there is a major disagreement over what science says, it should be obvious that we will benefit from taking a look at the fundamental philosophical ideas that guide science into its "findings" in the first place.

As I have said, I believe that *passivism* in general guides the current praxis of science. In the chapters ahead, I therefore try to reveal some of the main sources of passivism.

2.4 Essentialism: John Locke

John Locke differentiates between *real* and *nominal* essences. An individual falls under the general category of nominal essence. Humans are apes (*genera*) that differ from other apes, for example by being able to reason in a special way. This is the well-known way to classify things that Aristotle developed in detail. Locke calls these categories (*species*) *sorts*, which rudimentarily resemble what we today would call *kinds*. Nominal essences, which reflect the categories that appear in language, are thought to be grounded in "a deeper" reality, namely, in *real essences*.

Locke is famously an empiricist. But not quite, since *individuals*, which are what we face empirically, can hardly be ascribed an essence. What is essential is essential to sorts, not to particulars (1690/1995, Book III, part IV, chapter 4). Without a 'sort' to place the individual within, we would not be able to *sort out* what could be *essential* to it and thereby its individuality. We therefore have to rely on this (unreliable) nominal essence (based on complex ideas) to get started on any queries about *real essence*.

The nominal essence of gold, Locke suggests, is a particular weight and colour and a certain degree of malleability and fusibility, etc. The *real essence* of gold, by contrast, is the "particular constitution which every thing has within itself, *without any relation to any thing without it*" (ibid., my emphasis). It is the "constitution of the parts of matter on which these qualities in their union depend" (ibid.). What constitutes a thing is an inner constitution of parts that is *independent* of any other thing, and from which the properties (qualities and powers) that we *experience empirically*, flow. Our nominal definitions, therefore, do not really refer to what we experience but to a reality "outside language". They relate to an inner constitution that is *intrinsic* to the thing itself.

Nominal properties and sorts supervene on real essences unconditionally (ibid., 356). In effect this means that in our everyday life we encounter things whose being we do not really know.

> For our senses failing us in the discovery of the bulk, texture and the figure of the minute parts of bodies, on which their real constitution and their differences depend, we are fain to make use of their secondary qualities.
>
> (ibid., 212)

We are familiarized with things through a nominalizing process that originates from the primary qualities and powers of things; we *think and believe* that our nominal categories resemble the real ones, while we *in reality* know nothing about the real essences of things (ibid., 373).[10] In thinking that our nominal essences refer directly to reality as it is, we are "happy" prisoners of the illusions of the cave (cf. Plato). Locke puts this in a most unforgettable way: "Though the familiar use of things about us take off our wonder, yet it cures not our ignorance" (ibid., 360). We tread on stones and handle iron but we

> know not their make, and can give no reason of the different qualities we find in them. It is evident the internal constitution, whereon their properties depend, is unknown to us. For ... what is the texture of parts, that real essence that makes lead and antimony fusible; wood and stones not?
>
> (ibid.)

It seems that Locke is in doubt as to whether this 'internal constitution' could ever be known, but by the *examples* he gives we could certainly assert that we know more about these postulated constitutions today.[11] A typical example that Locke gives is that we may be able to use a watch without knowing the internal constitution of its gears and nuts and bolts (ibid., e.g. 375). Leibniz (through his "spokesperson" *Philaletes*) in fact defines Locke's whole distinction between nominal and real essence with reference to the clock: "[O]ne may know the Strasbourg clock either in the manner of the clockmaker who built it or in the manner of a spectator who sees what it does" (Leibniz 1996, 304).

These *"minute parts"*[12] are what we today would typically call the *micro properties* of lead and antimony, wood and stones, known to us by the reductionist research programme that Locke's ontology indirectly initiated. The analogy of the watch reminds us of the various research programmes whose proponents try to reduce the workings of the mind to the workings of the neural network of the brain. This is obviously also what J.L. Mackie takes to be a reasonable interpretation:

> Since we can equate Locke's real essences with what we should now call the molecular and atomic structure of things, we may say that many real essences that were unknown in Locke's day are now pretty well thoroughly known by chemists and physicists.
>
> (1991, 78)[13]

According to Locke we should therefore not leave the production of knowledge to "illiterate people who sorted and denominated things by those sensible qualities they found in them", but rather to "philosophers and logicians, or such who have troubled themselves about forms and essences" (1995, 367). *That this pretty much defines the task and role of science should be obvious.* That, whenever accepted, it has led the most prestigious research programmes of our time such as 'the theory for everything', The Human Genome Project, The Human Brain Project to look for 'the minute parts' such as strings, DNA and brain cells should therefore not come as a surprise.

Locke infers from his idea of real essences that an improved understanding of the world will result in (nominal) concepts and categories that allow us to distinguish the being of things *sharply* (and not *vaguely*) (ibid., 368). He adds to this assertion that this must be the case since "God created the universe, and that he did so in an orderly way" (ibid., 362). A fuzzy nominal categorization of things therefore indicates that our knowledge is of a low quality. Locke is an essentialist.

It seems to me that Locke's ontology can be fairly well illustrated by what has happened within the 'taxonomy of life' since the discovery of the DNA molecule. The Linnaeus-based taxonomy system was typically generated from knowledge gained by observation of secondary qualities. The *tree of life* model generated more recently has had access to the "real essence" using molecular sequencing. This insight into the "real essences" of the system has changed some parts of it, but mostly it has just adjusted and corrected it. Although this is not always the case, it is what we would expect. The nominal essence (i.e. Linnaeus) is not something that is totally arbitrarily produced like mixed modes, but it is not completely precise either. It may therefore seem that the missing yardstick that hindered us from gaining full and precise knowledge was the knowledge of genes (i.e. 'minute parts'). Scientists who adopt a Lockean metaphysics will therefore feel great satisfaction in the discovery that the (postulated) "real' essences can correct our somewhat arbitrary system of nominal essences.[14]

The problem is that the story does not end here, because, to put it simply, the *tree of life* model has been challenged by another model, namely the *web of life*. Genetically, one can show that the flow of genes has not only streamed down the phylogenetic lines; genes have also been flowing across the branches, especially by way of horizontal gene transfer. This makes it more difficult to give a consistent description of the different kingdoms, taxa, species, etc., based on genetics alone.[15] What we see in this case, therefore, is that the fuzzy nominal knowledge does not receive the expected help from a better understanding of the "real essence".

Locke would perhaps take this as an indication that we have not reached the right level of real essences, and that we should in this case go further down to chemistry and physics to find the right reference for our nominal categories. However, although the hopes of finding sharper distinctions at deeper levels has been pursued, at the level of quantum physics one has famously found behaviour that one thinks can only be predicted in probabilistic ways. This discovery was and still is a surprise to science, but we need to remember that it is surprising *given* a research programme predicated on the metaphysics of Locke.

Locke's essentialism is distinct from Aristotelian essentialism, which specifically picks out the essence of something by characterizing the *behaviour* of the thing. It is not the inner physical constitution, but the behaviour of the whole substance that constitutes the form. (See Aristotle's argument against the materialists in section 2.1.) Such properties are indeed not hidden or harboured in the matter (*hylē*). But of course, this is also Locke's point: that what the Greeks and the scholastics called the ("real") essence are *only* nominal ones (see J.L. Mackie 1991, 86). According to Locke, nominal essence refers to something that these individuals have in common, namely a universal material constitution that every thing has within itself, independently of everything else. Mackie calls this 'corpuscularian science', as opposed to the scholastic way of doing science. (Robert Boyle and his way of doing science is the model in this case (ibid.).)

Locke advanced a concept of *form* as real essence (the source), understood as a kind of material base. (See section 3.2.) By rejecting the Aristotelian account of form (which was intended to counter the "materialist" position), he established one of the main reference points for modern science. Aristotelian form turned into *appearance*, and became associated with nominal essence. I don't fault Locke for this move, since it also seems to be a reasonable continuation of Aristotelian essentialism.[16] Moreover, the relationship between nominal and real essence is not only formal or conceptual; it is also a relationship where some kind of (causal) *production* and activity is involved. In the same way as Aristotle thought that the form was causally productive, Locke thinks that the real essence plays a productive role. *The real essences determine the being of what we encounter empirically.* (For further substantiation see Locke 1995, 334, 211, xxiii7, xxiii8, xxiii9 and xxiii10; Chappell 2007, 134; Mackie 1991, 9–10; Leibniz 1996, 294.)

Locke's move has had a tremendous impact on the history of science and philosophy. The idea of a corpuscularian science was truly a whole new idea about how we should understand the world, and in some ways one may say that this idea created science as we know it today. It seems to me that the pivotal move – away from "behavioural properties" and towards some kind of inner/intrinsic constituting essence – is something that all modern ontologies have in common, including the one underlying contemporary science. What Locke really proposes can be seen as a kind of *reality principle*. Things and phenomena cannot be considered to be known before we have pinned down their intrinsic constitution.

The following is one of *many* examples that would illustrate what I mean by this. A small article in *New Scientist* tells us that: "The world looks different if you are depressed". The reason and explanation given for why this is a fact is that "Depressed people have a shortage of neurotransmitter called GABA ... Depression is often thought of as just a mood disorder ... *now we know* it can even affect the way a person sees the world" (*New Scientist*, 29 Nov. 2009 my emphasis). I would say that it comes as no surprise that depressed people see the world differently, but we apparently need to *justify* any such claim with a reference to the activity of the intrinsic constitution for it to be a *true claim*.

Reductionism is not just one of many possible ontologies; it is the ontology constituting most modern approaches to reality. Stephen Mumford refers to Robert Boyle, to underline the same point when he says:

> All the mysterious powers in philosophy, passed down from Aristotle, can be explained in terms of shapes and structures ... gunpowder itself owes its aptness to be fired and exploded to the mechanical contexture of more simple portions of matter – nitre, charcoal, sulphur.
>
> (Mumford 1998, 12–13)

The point Mumford is making is that we, in general, and in science in particular, currently *tend towards* explaining manifest behaviour in terms of some kind of "inner constitution of the minute parts". C.B. Martin puts it even more clearly: "If we want to understand the fragility of glass, *standard scientific practice* suggests that we look at its internal structure – that is the parts of which it is composed and the way these parts are organized" (2007, 49, my emphasis). We may do this as Locke does, i.e. in terms of essentialism, or we may formulate it in terms of more clean-cut empiricist accounts (as in Hume's *minima sensibilia*); a categorical base (as in Armstrong); pointlike perfectly natural properties (as in Lewis); as distinctly contributing dispositions; etc.; but in all cases we seem inclined to imply that the behaviour of things is to be understood in terms of some type of *intrinsic constitution*, and that this constitution is of utmost importance since it is seen as the active and real aspect of what we see and experience around us.

What we want to explain in this book is the given behaviour of the being to which we are attending. If one reduces such phenomena to the levels below, one will also have to insist that the phenomena are caused by something that is other than themselves. If you are an essentialist you will have to say that things are *determined* by the essential behaviour of their parts. And so the story goes all the way down, to quarks and what have you. In this sense, any *reductionist account is also a passivist account.*

Aristotle was able to account for what I have called in this book "*qua*-wholes" due to his teleology. When he asked for what the horse "really is" he did not give an answer in terms of what constitutes the horse, but in terms of its ethological behaviour. It runs fast; it neighs in a special way; it breeds in a special way, because it is its nature to strive towards the realization of these properties that constitute its form. This is a horse *qua* horse. In Aristotle's case the production of this behaviour is explained by the *striving* towards realization. The parts constituting the horse are a necessary condition for this behaviour, but they neither produce nor determine the dispositional behaviour of the horse *qua* horse. An Aristotelian is not asking about what a horse is *qua* its necessitating constituents, but *qua* horse. This point holds at other levels of organization as well. When we ask "What is a molecule?" we will not, according to the Aristotelian, have answered the question by simply pointing to the way it is physically constituted. My view is that the activity of the *qua*-whole should be explained neither by the striving, nor by the "minute parts". There is a third alternative that will be fully discussed in Chapter 4.

2.4.1 Naturalness and the legacy of Locke

I have identified four ontological opponents to a concept of naturalness. These are: ontologies of pure necessitation, ontologies of contingency, ontologies of reductionism and "nominal ontologies" such as constructivism. Clear traces of all four of these sometimes opposing positions can be found in Locke's *Essay*.

In *An Essay Concerning Human Understanding*, Locke puts much emphasis on how he thinks our concepts are generated, and shows how words are defined by words, and why words can be arbitrarily related to the things they define (1995, III, IV, 6).

In so doing, he also sets the framework for what the arguments in the contemporary realism debate look like. If one affirms that there are real essences that nominal essences can be measured against, one has referents outside of language. Those who hold this view are *scientific realists*. Those who doubt the possibility of 'boundaries and categories set by nature' (ibid., 368) are postmodernists, or constructivists.[17] Locke also sets the standard in a way that makes these two positions dependent upon each other. Any reference to reality *will have to* refer to a reality that has a *fixed set of properties with clear distinctive features for each and every substance.*

The so-called linguistic turn is nowhere more indebted than it is to the presumptions that are made by John Locke in this case! People who don't believe in *distinct borders* between categories in nature would automatically turn out to be non-realists.[18] (For example, the existence of hermaphrodites is taken to indicate that realism must be wrong; very few queer theorists are scientific realists!) The failure to see how our knowledge could possibly live up to this "complete list" yardstick then leads us to either: (1) leave our realist aspirations behind; or (2) stay with the essentialist account but prescribe the means and methods for science in a way that is in accordance with the Lockean view.

For the realist, there will be a problem related to the way that we encounter things in daily life. Our normal understanding of things will be hampered by our nominal categories, so that we will need a special language to uncover the real essences of things. (And social constructivists will have great fun by showing that literally all words have a metaphorical etymology.) The behaviour and the properties that we encounter under normal conditions in our everyday lives will also have a dubious status. Layman-like descriptions will be compared to those given by "illiterate people" "who sort[ed] and denominate[d] things by those sensible qualities they found in them", rather than to those given by scientists "who have troubled themselves about forms and essences" (1995, 367). Our everyday description of the 'essential behaviour' of things is more in line with Aristotelian essences – and therefore, on my reading, with Lockean nominal essences – and it follows from this that, as realists, we should not take the description to refer to anything real. A social constructivist on the other hand does not say that nominal essences represent the truth. Constructivism is seen as constructivism for the reason that constructivists don't believe in essences at all. They think that the nominal essences are fundamentally constructed in the first place for the reason, of course, that their correlate (real essences) does not exist. Social constructivism depends upon Locke's essentialism. Constructivism is Lockean essentialism inverted.

If we are forced to choose between these two positions, no reintroduction of the concept of naturalness will stand a chance. The point of showing that constructivism is predicated upon Lockean essentialism, therefore, is to drive home the point that we need an ontological reorientation if we are to have any hope of reintroducing the concept of naturalness.

The third opponent of naturalness, empiricism, is also embedded in Lockean metaphysics. A full-blown empiricist (like Hume) does not accept the problem of *substances* (which brings Locke into the anti-empiricist task of dealing with essences (see Locke 1995, 341)). Hume only accepts simple impressions as possible candidates for something that could have a reference to "reality" – resting on the passive powers of the mind.[19] This view is famously called phenomenalism.

Hume takes this to its extreme by saying that we have no knowledge of things other than what we find in our impressions, and that we can only *assume* that the simple ones refer to some kind of reality. How these impressions are connected "in reality" we would have no way to know, because we do not and could not have any direct impression of how our impressions map onto any such postulated reality. Substances are nothing but a *bundle of simple impressions*, and we have no simple impressions of the relatedness making up each and every bundle. Therefore, whether there is something that can be called a kind or a kind's real essence, we will never be able to determine. Famously, we also cannot have any impression of the necessity relations that are postulated in a cause-and-effect sequence. Hume's position has contributed to a situation wherein we are given a choice between two modalities: either you think that connections are necessary (determinism) or you think that they are contingent or accidental. This is the modal dualism of Hume, wherein *propensities* have no place (see chapters 3 and 4). Locke does not hold this contingency view himself, but his philosophy contains the potential to develop into such a position, if we grant that Hume is a follower of Locke in the sense of purifying his empiricist impulses.

The last point that I want to make will be spelled out in a somewhat superficial way. My aim here is just to point to a connection that may become more important in the years to come (see Wapner 2003, and section 1.1). Although Humeanism and constructivism have a common ground in nominalism, they are positions that are not associated with each other. This is apparent in the development of those positions, as evidenced by the fact that logical positivists and constructivists/ nominalists such as Heidegger or Derrida do not communicate very well with each other.[20] For example, the logical positivists were some of the main critics of Heidegger.

However, the "counterfactual thinking" that is based in Humeanism (i.e. the supposition that the things that there are could have been different, and that it's just accidental that they are how they are) could be said to be an important feature of social constructivism (Hacking 1999, 6; see also Kukla 2000). If we see David Lewis as a neo-Humean who is the "headmaster of counterfactual thinking", and Berger and Luckmann (who wrote the book *The Social Construction of Reality* in 1966) as successors of Heidegger and the "headmasters of social constructivism", we may want to say that there are two quite different traditions that have *de facto* come together at this particular point, i.e. where counterfactual reasoning based on a Humean ontology turns out to be a possible candidate for the implicit ontology of social constructivism (as Hacking claims). Whatever arguments there are to be elevated against such a "unification", it seems to hold in practice. Social constructivists typically criticize environmentalists as being too naïve for not acknowledging that their defence of nature rests on a socially constructed concept of nature, such that the "nature" that they defend could as well have been different. This type of criticism comes from "leftists", deconstructivists and "debunkers" who like to intervene in any debate by saying that "even though our ways of understanding and organizing reality appear natural and 'real', they are just human-made products with which we try to cope with a *contingent and coincidental reality*" (see Wapner 2003 and Castree 2014).

2.5 Humeanism

Let us examine Humeanism from the perspective of granting that properties have to do with *behaviour*. "Being red now" is behaviour.[21] When we want to know what an electron *is* we want to know how it behaves. To know what it means to be negatively charged is to know negative charge as behaviour. Whenever we want to know about the structure, the weight, the relative position or the extension of the electron, we uncover these properties because we think that they matter when it comes to the behaviour of the electron. When we know *how* it behaves we would like to explain *why* it behaves like that. We may then appeal to, e.g. its *telos*, instantiated in every substance as an essence; or some transcendent form such as the "inner constitution"; or its *essence* (combined with laws); or laws (instituted by God); or "*relations*" (as I will do later); or we may simply say that what we see are something that we should call regularities, and that we cannot *say much more about them*. This last preference is a kind of starting point for the Humean position.

A crucial assumption that Hume makes is that *what is more than constant conjunction* needs to be necessity (Hume 1739–1740, 161–162 and 77). When behaviour is not necessary, we will, in Hume's account, have to say that the behaviour was contingent (ibid., 171). Since we cannot *observe* any necessary connection (or power, or efficacy), but (at the most) only constant conjunction, we would have no reason to assume that properties are connected *at all* (ibid., book I, section XIV). This is a very important point, because it restricts the possible spectrum of *modal* connectedness to only two: *necessity* and *contingency*. Hume is a modal dualist. If things are not necessarily connected, they are not connected at all.[22] That is, he could have considered 'propensity' as a possible candidate, or said that since we cannot observe necessity it follows that things are only "propensively" connected. To say as much would have been untenable for Hume, however, since propensities would have to be justified in terms of some kind of *de re* potentiality, which would, in a similar way as with necessity, not square with his commitment to sensualism (strict empiricism).

The idea of necessity (which again in Hume's mind is *the* idea of connectedness) does not originate from impressions, but from an "internal impression, or impression of reflection" (ibid., 165). "Necessity is something that exists in the mind, not in the objects" (ibid.). "Objects" are therefore connected contingently.[23]

A different way of putting this, which is quite common today, is to say that there are "laws", but that these laws are contingent. They are just statements of regularities that exist (Beebee 2006). In a different possible world, the laws could have been different, and so, therefore, could the behaviour. This seems to be the way a "Humean would answer" to the fact that science *de facto* operates with laws, and that many would claim that a science without laws is not a science.

In the history of philosophy, Hume's view is portrayed as an account that threatens the whole scientific undertaking. The Humean "view of nature" is taken to be one in which the beings are just floating around, bumping into each other accidentally (see e.g. Jones 1969, 319). There is no inner *telos* or inner constitution that makes things do what they do. The world is "loose and separate" (Hume, ibid., 54). Everything is determined by the contingent spatiotemporal relations into which things enter.

This is not without reason. We have already seen how Hume dismisses any necessary connections. He also broadens his critique by saying about (Lockean) powers,

> The efficacy or energy of causes is neither plac'd in the causes themselves, nor in the deity, nor in the concurrence of these two principles, but belongs entirely to the soul... . 'Tis here that the real power of causes is plac'd, along with their connexion and necessity.
>
> (ibid., 166)

The use of especially this phrase: "Anything may produce anything" (ibid., 173) underlines the total contingency of the connection between properties and the world, according to Hume. On the other hand, it is easy to see how Hume's account underpins the scientific endeavour in the sense that it places a relevant limit on what sort of questions scientists can and should address. Scientists (at least empiricist ones) can say something about facts, and can report data about tested regularities, but empirically they have no means to infer from these sorts of claims to metaphysical claims about how and why such facts have come about and how and why they are connected (in contrast to essentialists, who assume *a priori* that the essential properties of things guarantee that things belonging to the same natural kind will behave in accordance with this essence). Humean scientists can retain an agnostic attitude towards such questions (Mumford 2004, 33).[24] On the other hand, however, I agree with those who say that this is an inverted metaphysical claim, especially because a Humean has to assert that things are *discrete* and unconnected in the first place in order to say that we should remain agnostic about the way properties are connected. (See Mumford 2004, 27; and discussion below.)

In either case, the situation does not bode well for my purpose in this book, since I wish to argue that there are limits to how things should be constructed, manipulated and put together. A nanotech enthusiast would like the world to be like Hume's world – with loose and *separate* "units" that are contingently connected (especially if there were nevertheless some suitable kind of regularity as well), and I would say that a "Humean world" would be incompatible with maintaining the use of the word natural. 'Natural' would have to come with quotation marks – as it often does today. If there is an order in the world, it would, according to Hume, *at the most* be only an order *for* someone, e.g. for humans. One postulated order might be better than another would be for a particular sort of agent (e.g. humans). Even the act of theorizing naturalness could be seen as a hidden power game. Claiming that to anticipate any order at all would be to impose *my* order on others. (See also (sub) sections 1.3.1, 2.3 and 6.1.1.)

Humeanism is typically a nominalist position. The nominalist can claim, together with the Humean, that the world has no real order, and that any such claim will be a claim that really has to do with needs that are specifically human and social, such as the "need" for power, recognition, security and "external" guidance. (Friedrich Nietzsche is, of course, a nominalist in this sense.)

However, a Humean can maybe remain "agnostic on the question of how things are connected" (Mumford 2004, 27), but the price is that he or she needs a specific metaphysical theory about the *discreteness of properties* in the first place. This is a crucial point, and must be established in more detail.

In the *Treatise*, Hume argues against infinite divisibility. The motivation for doing so is that he distinguishes between simple and complex impressions, and says that simple impressions (and ideas) as such "admit of no distinction or separation" (1978, 2). If something is simple, then it has no parts into which it can meaningfully be divided. If simple impressions were thought to track the world as it is "in itself", but the real world had no simple units, Hume would be without referents for his *minima sensibilia* (the smallest sensible impressions), which referents he needs for his empiricist account to work. The idea of a simple impression is not just a regulative idea, but points to the existence of simple properties in the external world, without claiming (of course) that such properties exist. This, again, is why he argues against infinite divisibility. So, if the *relations* in the world are contingent there must be some units that are *distinct* and self-identical. There must be some distinct units between which the contingent relations are relations (ibid., 87).

Hume often carelessly uses the word 'object' for these units, but when he is more careful he uses the phrase 'distinct impressions' or 'distinct existences' (ibid., 635). (Hume should not talk about objects at all; David Lewis uses the phrase "pointlike properties".)

Georg Molnar calls this the *distinctness-thesis* (2003, 181) (see also the discussion in Mumford 2004, 53ff.). Such units must be independent of each other in order to be contingently connected. If they didn't have any intrinsicality, they would depend upon the existences of other properties, and would therefore not be such as to be contingently related in the first place. It is difficult to say what this Humean intrinsicality amounts to, but lately there has been some debate on the topic (especially in *Philosophy and Phenomenological Research*, June and Sept. 2001). I will say more about this issue in section 4.1 and subsection 5.5.3.

The important thing for now is to assess what follows philosophically from the distinctness-thesis. The major point, apart from the contingency thesis, is that the distinctness-thesis indirectly calls for a reductionist *ontology*, one wherein some units with some intrinsic characters are the fundamental constituents of the world. Hume expresses one of the pre-conditions for such a view in the following way: "Whatever is distinct is distinguishable; and whatever is distinguishable, is separable by the thought or imagination. All perceptions are distinct. They are, therefore, distinguishable, and separable, and may be conceived as separately existent and may exist separately" (1739–1740, 634, see also 86–87). Everything that can be separated by the mind exists separately. The world is built of separate intrinsically constituted units, which arbitrarily conjoin into clusters of properties ("objects"); the order of and between these units is contingent. The only "relation" between the discrete properties that Hume accepts is, as we have seen, constant conjunctions/

regularities. Constant conjunctions only tell us that two *"discreta"* appear together regularly. We may find that smoking and lung cancer appear together in a constant conjunction, but we cannot say anything about whether smoking causes lung cancer. (For something to be a cause, Hume requires that X comes before Y and *necessarily* makes Y come about.) It is therefore said about Hume's regularity view that its proponents are not able to distinguish between correlation and causal regularity (Chalmers 2008, 214). If we add this aspect of Hume's thinking to his general idea about simple and complex impressions, and bear in mind that complex impressions are constituted by simple ones, we have something close to what, for the moment, I have rudimentarily called reductionism.[25]

Potentiality is a modality that is problematic for Humean empiricism. "Potentiality" cannot be observed. And even though we enact elaborate security systems for an atomic plant or we carry avalanche gear while skiing in the mountains, the potential hazards anticipated cannot be observed directly in advance. We take these precautions in relation to something that does not (yet) exist in an empirical sense. Can they nevertheless be said to exist, or do they only exist in our minds?

Empiricists cannot accept potentiality as something that can be ascribed to reality. A potential being or a potential behaviour is obviously not something that can exist as an impression gained from the spatiotemporal world in a way that is consistent with how Hume thinks about observation, and it is therefore something that, from an empiricist perspective, cannot exist as such. Potentiality *as such* is on this account reduced to *logical possibility*. Or, as Nicholas Rescher formulates it: "Only actual things or states of affairs can unqualifiedly be said to exist, not those that are possible but unrealized. By definition, only the actual will ever exist in the world, never the unactualized possible" (1973, 215). Potentiality becomes, in Rescher's and the empiricist's view, the *merely possible* – which is another term for non-being. Potentialities are things that only exist in our minds, and not *de re*. Reality consists of *positive* facts present here and now. Potentiality as something *more* than the logically possible (non-being) is thus eliminated (see also Hume 1739–1740, 32).

The main way of dealing with this question, however, is to reduce the phenomenon in question and then see if there are any *actual* properties on the levels below that can account for the potentiality in question.

If we assume that an empiricist must admit that e.g. precautionary security systems on an atomic plant are a vital part of the atomic plant itself, and that we elsewhere take sensible precautions even though we take those precautions in relation to phenomena that "do not exist yet", we should also assume that the Humean empiricist can account for what seem to be *de re* potencies such as these. And to some extent it appears as though he or she can. Even though we cannot see directly, for example, how and to what degree a certain mountainous region is disposed to undergo avalanches, an empiricist will insist that we can observe this by, for instance, looking directly at the microstructure of the snow (which is empirically accessible) combined, perhaps, with the observable incline of the slope. By comparing actual (retaining in the memory) avalanches with different empirically accessible microstructures of the snow (structures that we may after a while get enough empirical data about to be able to make "predictions"), we would be able to observe constant conjunctions/regularities.

This is an odd position, however, because on the one hand it is founded on the idea that the microstructure somehow "causes" the avalanche, or at least that the question of avalanches should be answered by referring to "the intrinsic properties of the snow" (which in the end would be the simple impressions or the smallest distinct units; what Helen Beebee (2006) calls the "wholesome base of distinct existences"). On the other hand, a Humean cannot make any *inferences* or put forward explanations about the relationship between avalanches and microstructure, although he or she might observe a constant conjunction (cf. the problem of induction). The reason for this is that there is nothing about these parts that makes them do anything in particular (i.e. no necessitating essences or *de re* potencies etc.). What they do is what they do, and they can suddenly (for no reason) do different things. Their behaviour is in principle contingent, even if what we see often happens to be regular behaviour.

So why is it that the microstructure of the elements participating in the event "causes" the avalanche to come about? A Humean cannot answer this question, because it is a contingent result of the way the parts are arranged and aggregated. (The Humean therefore says that the joint effect (the avalanche) supervenes on the (contingent) behaviour of the parts.) Humeans don't say this because they think that the causal chains in question are too complex, or anything akin to that, but rather because they are committed to saying that knowledge gained at t1 cannot be trusted at t2, and the reason for this is, again, that "necessity cannot be observed". Here is a simple illustration which might be helpful in explaining the differences and similarities between Humeanism and (Lockean) essentialism.

In (Lockean) essentialism there is something about the part (its inner constitution) intrinsically that gives it the ability to contribute to an outcome via the same behaviour (property) in each and every instance. There is "something" that makes this contribution necessary. There is a "vertical" necessitation between parts and the whole. In Humeanism, the arrow is not an arrow of (vertical) necessity but at best a line of constant conjunction or regularity. But in *both* cases the "horizontal" relation *between the parts* is contingent. The parts and their lines are separated from each other (cf. the distinctness-thesis). So there are no arrows

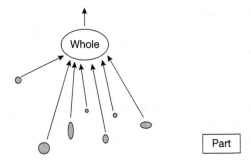

Figure 2.1 Singular contributors. Simple model representing the difference between essentialism and Humeanism with respect to parts, properties and the relation between properties. (See text.)

going horizontally between the parts in this illustration. The parts and their properties are not relationally constituted, and the whole is therefore just a sum total of the contingent or necessary behaviours of the distinct parts. This inevitably leads to some kind of reductionism, although there may be several ways to formulate this reductionism. The common and prominent feature that figures in the reductionism in both cases seems to be the *distinctness-thesis*. As I see it, there is no way to avoid reductionism if a distinctness-thesis is involved in or implied by one's account. (See chapters 3 and 4.)

The arrow pointing from the whole itself, on a (Lockean) essentialist account, would be an arrow of necessitation. The behaviour of the whole is necessary, being necessitated by its parts. (This whole may participate in a new part–whole relation.) On a Humean account, by contrast, what the whole does is contingent. Or, following a neo-Humean account, we would say that it would depend upon the contingent laws that happen to govern at the moment.

2.6 The experiment

The experimental method was used paradigmatically by Galileo Galilei, to verify his alternative cosmological views (Losee 1980, 55); Nancy Cartwright's claim, i.e. that the Galilean idealization "is at the heart of all modern physics" (1989, 188), is not controversial. The experimental method (as opposed to scholastic deduction from first principles) was acknowledged as a viable path to knowledge in the seventeenth century (Hacking 1983). The Copernican turn facilitated the suspicion that what we see is not what there is (Funkenstein 2005, 51f.). That is, unaided observation (and deduction) can deceive us! Our senses cannot be trusted (Descartes) and new methods are needed for the improvement of our "seeing".

We need to see behind the "accidental causes" and we therefore need experiments to reveal the real independent being of things. If accidental causes are not a part of the being of things, they will only disturb our efforts to understand the being of the things that we put under scrutiny. It is then feasible to do as Galileo did, and try to take away the external accidental causes (*causae accidentariae*), such as friction and other sources of "resistance". Refining the experiment will be thought "to produce a more stable, less noisy version of the phenomenon" (Hacking 1983, 231; Chalmers 2008, 216), i.e. the phenomenon will be seen to have some essential or intrinsic features that can be isolated and identified under ideal conditions.

I do not mean to suggest that this method was put forward in the seventeenth century as a defence for essentialist metaphysics. Experiments were designed first and foremost with the aim of carving out the *specific* causalities of things. In Descartes's *Discours de la Mèthode* the second rule is famously "to divide all the difficulties under examination into as many parts as possible, and as many as were required to solve them in the best way" (2006, 17). When teleological causes are abandoned, we lose direct access to the causal picture, because the parts are no longer parts that can be understood and explained in light of the teleological cause. (See Kant 1987, section 65.) We are left with a complex and chaotic causal web that immediately stands in need of clarification. What causes what, and in what way? In the absence of a teleological cause, the experimental method rescues us from everything that "stands out as so messy and imperfect" (Hacking 1983, 33). It is no longer thought that every part must make their contribution to the whole (that teleologically organize the parts). Parts and their properties are discrete and independent "actors" bringing about the whole.

One may also look upon the experimental method as simply a way to discover which properties *belong* to which object. By varying the conditions, Galileo found that the property of falling, for example, does not really belong to the falling object itself, but rather to a force that works on objects with mass. Separating something into parts, as Descartes advises, makes it possible to *locate* the *alleged* agents and patients in the complex phenomenon that we want to understand. To map the properties of things in order to see how these properties relate gives us neither (Lockean) essentialism nor reductionism as such. The fact that you think that properties can be isolated in an experiment does not *necessarily* imply that you think that those properties can or should be explained by properties on a lower level, but thinking so will *strongly suggest* reductionism and essentialism – that is: *passivism*.

Reductionism, as I have said, is the idea that a phenomenon can be understood and fully accounted for in terms of its constituent parts. The laboratory will be of great help in isolating (defining) each and every contributing part of the phenomenon (fully), making it possible to see how and in what way(s) the contributing properties of the parts constitute those higher-order properties. One who holds that this isolation is sufficient to account for the part–whole relation (as one would if one thought that the world is built of and has its agency in virtue of such 'independent parts') will need (Lockean) essentialism or humanism + "laws" and reductionism to underscore his or her research.

Humeanism cannot in itself authorize an inference from parts to a whole, since there is nothing in or about the parts that necessitates that they do what they do. Humeans therefore say that the whole somehow *supervenes* on the parts. But again, such a move does not get Humeans anywhere close to being able to predict the behaviour of things. From a Humean point of view, for instance, a researcher cannot say that a technology based on laboratory knowledge is perfectly safe. This possibility is available to the Lockean essentialist, however.

Experiments are traditionally constructed to uncover and understand some phenomenon. However, some (such as alleged constructivists) would say that experiments themselves help *construct* the phenomenon. For them, certain "real" phenomena do not exist before some conditions are put in place by humans (and there is no place in nature that is free from conditions). For example, it has been claimed that super-conduction did not exist before it was created in the laboratory (Hacking 1983, 229). Hacking argues that reality *is* "untidy", and that therefore experiments do not uncover reality, but rather replace it with an alternative reality (because to take away the untidiness is to take away the real phenomenon and *create* a new phenomenon). If we think that the "messiness" co-constitutes the phenomena, we will say that what we gain in the laboratory is constructed, and should be understood as constructed (when applied directly *in-vivo*). The *idea* of experimentation that Hacking opposes is a view that is dependent upon an essentialist account. Brian Ellis characterizes this view of experiments as follows: "The essentialist theory of laws ... enables ... to abstract from any external forces [accidental fuzziness] that may be acting upon it to say how it would be or behave in the absence of such forces" (Ellis 2002, 101). (I elaborate this issue further in section 5.4.)

Nancy Cartwright seems to have a quite ambiguous position on this question. On the one hand she says that any experiment must reflect the fact that the results come from the particular situation that has been created, but nevertheless uncover 'some reality'. ("The situation may be counterfactual, still it is realistic in some sense", 1989, 191). On the other hand, she says that the model created from the laboratory is unrealistic. "It is after all a representation, and not the real thing, so necessarily much will be left out" (ibid., 192). But what about extrapolation, then? Cartwright's opinion is that the "law that describes the happenings in the model" are *ceteris paribus* laws, but that the abstract law that is taken to hold in the background of the experimental model, and which is designated to range over more than the concrete happenings in the model, must drop the *ceteris paribus* clause, or else the abstract law would not work according to its "purpose" (ibid.). "In the abstract law the ceteris paribus conditions are dropped; and for a good reason, since this law is meant to bear on what happens in the more frequent cases where conditions are not ideal" (ibid.). To grant such an inference we would have to grant that the properties are somehow essential (the behaviour will be similar under different conditions in the Lockean sense) and not relational.

At first, Cartwright implicitly refuses the whole misconceived idea that we would need an essentialist account to go from *ceteris paribus* law to abstract law, because what an abstract law is, is just a description of a *capacity* (disposition). An abstract law describes what tends to happen and not what must necessarily happen. Thus it is not describing an essential property of some thing or some relation, but rather a capacity, according to Cartwright. However, what I find dubious is that she still says that such tendencies would be stable and invariant relative to new conditions (ibid., 191). Is she not then implying a Lockean essentialist twist after all, in the sense that what must make these tendencies stable must be some intrinsic essential properties of some sort, and that the 'messiness of the world' doesn't play a role after all?[26]

I strongly agree with Cartwright that what the scientist is *really doing* is investigating capacities and not some properties defined under some essentialist criteria, but in light of the five questions that I raised earlier in this chapter we have to ask: is this what the scientist thinks s/he is doing (#1), or is this what s/he conveys when s/he in some way or other puts their results into the *in-vivo* world (#3)?

2.7 Science: from *in-vitro* to *in-vivo*

The daily work of a scientist is characterized by meticulous cooperative work within a "well-defined" area of interest. Scientists are almost by definition studying 'the parts', which means that scientific work must in most cases take place under idealized conditions. An ecologist studies the interaction between two populations (which often also requires the use of "idealized" mathematical models); a molecular biologist studies one enzyme and its function; a chemist studies a special isotope of uranium, etc. Evidence-based medicine is considered to be "evidenced" if the study conforms to the standard of RCT (randomized controlled trials), which by designation refers to studies that have been conducted under different degrees of idealized conditions. Research that transcends these empirical differences in order to articulate how these (studies of the) parts work *together* are often considered to be speculative and therefore less valuable for those who want to have a career as a scientist. An exception to this is research that leads or may lead to technological products or some kind of profitable economic activity. A scientist or a scientific team that has found "a neurotransmitter", a "genetic sequence", a "new way to structure carbon", etc. is allowed to reflect on how their causal findings may 'change everything'. That is to say: how their single causal findings interact and may interact with everything else.[27] What kind of ontology is operating under the surface that makes scientists accept or silently overlook this clearly ungrounded discrimination?

To get a fuller picture of the ontology that is guiding the scientific activity we see today, it is far from enough to just discuss the ontology of science on the basis of the views of various philosophical theories. We also need to look at the role, the actual performance and the current understanding of what we like to call 'science'.

In so doing we should first and foremost not start by fooling ourselves into thinking that science is still pursuing knowledge 'from a disinterested position', where 'collecting facts about the world', 'solving the mysteries of the world', 'exploring the wonders of life' is the aim, as this would tie our conception of science to a 'nineteenth-century mode'[28] of inquiry. The motivation that lies behind today's scientific endeavours is far more schizophrenic, and there is good reason to claim that the quantity of research that is motivated by how the resulting knowledge can be used and applied and taken to the marketplace is increasing rapidly. It is more than unfortunate if science benefits from the position of autonomy afforded it in virtue of being portrayed in a 'nineteenth-century mode', if the enterprise of science is motivated by ends that transcend the values that guard its autonomy in the first place (Nelkin 1996). If applicability is the *leitmotif* of science, we will probably see that the core praxis of doing science (in terms of #1) is not what we think it is (in terms of #3, and #4) if we imagine that it is still in a nineteenth-century mode (the very mode that we associate with Maxwell, Einstein, Heisenberg and Bohr).

These scientists were not asked to estimate the probability of whether their research would lead to any patents, as is the norm for scientific employees at universities in the United States today. Neither were they confronted with the focus on application, technology and development in scientific journals. If we take a look at *Nature*'s sub-journals we will see that approximately two-thirds of these sub-journals gain their relevance from the possibility of application and product-making in some sense: *Nature Biotechnology, Nature Cancer Update, Nature Neuroscience, Nature Review Cancer, Nature Review Drug Discovery, Nature Report Stem Cells, Nature Materials,* etc.

This observation is not meant to underpin a speculative claim about the situation and role of contemporary science, but rather to illustrate an agreement that has occurred over the last thirty years about how science should be understood. The literature that has come out of this new understanding shows science to have changed its focus and emerged into a kind of second phase (see e.g. Ziman 1996; Latour 1998; Funtowicz and Ravetz 1993; Gibbons et al. 1994; Sztompka 2007). The current and emerging sciences are often called things like post-normal science, mode-2 science, post-academic science, etc. A recent concept that has also emerged is techno-science, designating the type of *science* that is solely dedicated to technical applications (nanotechnology, biotechnology etc., i.e. "I am *studying* bio*technology*"). 'Engineering sciences' is an older concept that nevertheless refers to the same intersection of activity between science and technology. In more general terms, we also see that academic life at the universities is increasingly taking place within the framework of what is called a "knowledge-based economy", wherein the *production* of scientific knowledge is seen as a precondition of the existence of a modern-day economy.[29] A reminder of a different relationship, one in which science and technology were more independent of one another, is the story of how aeroplanes were invented and further improved by engineers long before anyone really understood scientifically the principles according to which they work. Today, by contrast, we see that most inventions come directly from scientific knowledge. At least, this is the underlying thesis behind the knowledge-based economy doctrine that rules today's politics.

What is the importance of this shift in focus when it comes to the relationship between the ontology of science and the idea of naturalness? The first thing we should take into consideration is that a post-academic science will change how we should understand the *in-vitro/in-vivo* transition. In the previous chapter we discussed the role of the experiment and the ontological predisposition to passivism that is related to the experimental sciences as such. As science gains an even more prominent role in the knowledge-based economy (and given that experiments can be seen as the "mother" of this this type of technology), we can expect that post-academic sciences will add force to this philosophical tendency and not the other way around. I will try to justify this claim in a more substantial way below (see also section 4.4).

Gene technology is a technology wherein one or several DNA-sequences (a "gene") are moved from one organism to another, or within the genome of the same organism. The sequence that one wants to move is assumed to have specific properties that one would like the target organism to have and express as well. The sequence "expressing the trait" has previously been isolated, and the conditions under which it expresses the desired higher-level property have allegedly been mapped (e.g. it often needs extra promoters and enhancers – taken from yet other organisms – to "express the desired trait" within the new organism.)

Up to this point it is clear that the scientist to some degree must or should understand that this sequence belongs to a whole, and that the specific causal findings only hold under these laboratory conditions (*ceteris paribus*). If this is fully understood this would call for a careful mapping of the conditions that might change the working of the causal connection that has been found in the laboratory. The problem occurs if *this general* understanding of the limits of the knowledge gained in the laboratory gets relinquished the moment that this sequence is inserted into the new organism to become a *commercial application*. The commercial application demands something *new* from the causal connection gained in the laboratory – namely full predictability. For a specific technology to work as a technology, it needs strict necessity. The conditional "if p, then q" needs to be instantiated in the real world without exception. It needs this both to be regarded as safe, and to work at all. Technologies that *sometimes* work are not technologies (also because they would bring us into a conspicuous and obtrusive relationship with the technology, which according to Heidegger is a "non-working" technology by definition, 1927/1992, 102–103).

What seems to be the case is that this *need* reaches beyond the general understanding of the role that the gene played in the first place (#4 unduly influences #2 although the scientist is really doing something else (#1)). That is, to defend the idea that a gene can have a property of always delivering the same q under *any condition, one must invoke an essentialist ontology.*[30] What one has in the laboratory in the first place is a *general* knowledge that any function of the sequence is highly dependent on the conditions (the *ceteris paribus* clause). The *in-vivo* realization of this knowledge however throws the *ceteris paribus* clause out the window. Going from *in-vitro* to *in-vivo* is therefore also (in this case at least) vacillating between different ontological descriptions. Only under the regime of a Lockean essentialist ontology can the organism as a whole be portrayed as an assembly of such necessitating and recombinatorial units, which does not have a "nature" that is more than what is mereologically producible.[31] The new agent that is hosting the inserted sequence must be portrayed as a passive result of its inner constitution, and what it is able to do must be predicated on the background of its parts because what it is able to do, and the necessity by which it does what it does, is just a "passive" result of its necessitating parts, and not the result of conditions or relational partners that the organism faces as a whole (see sections 4.3 and 4.6)! The organismic whole and its qua-organismic relation to the environment *must* be discarded, or else the ontology (in terms of #2 and #3) backing the technology would not coincide with what is elsewhere assumed.

An example that is representative of this widespread type of reasoning is the *New Scientist* (18 Feb. 2006) cover story, titled "Get Up and Go": "A new wave of drugs will make it a breeze to go days without sleep, and give you a good night's shut eye in two hours. Are you ready for 24-hour living?" The author(s) of the article predict that in the future, but also in the present, we will be able to chemically manipulate the neurotransmitters in our brain in more specific ways, enabling us to control our sleep and enhance our mental abilities in general – and all this without any side effects.[32] What is taken for granted in this article is that sleep has solely to do with how the parts making up the brain work. This focus shuts out any alternative or supplementary understanding of what sleep and waking might be about for the organism as a whole. This is just one example out of *many* articles of the same type, in which the research referred to is itself highly dependent on not only a Lockean but also a reductionist ontology. It does not simply "collect" facts about the *correlation* (constant conjunction) between the internal workings of the physical brain and, in this case, different states of mind; it is also highly motivated by and crucially dependent upon how these "facts" *explain* higher-level functions, and therefore can be employed to *control* these functions!

The third and crucial point that I want to make in regard to the *in-vitro/in-vivo* issue is that a certain degree of "necessity" that is found on one level can be disentangled and "liberated" if we "go one level down". 'Liberty is down the stairs'. It is, for instance, quite laborious and more or less impossible to change my genome (at least my chromosomes) on a *biological level*, because there are so many "horizontal" relations that keep the genome the way it is,[33] but if we attend to the genome "directly" (three levels down) we will find that the genes can be *depicted* as being contingently related *relative* to the level above, especially if we assume that their parts and the properties of the parts are non-relational and discrete – relative to the level above. So going down one level not only helps to explain the level above (more efficiently or ontologically), but it also allows one to "dig out" *contingency-treasures*, providing possibilities that in effect widen our liberties. In this way, reductionism, Humeanism and our striving for freedom and emancipation have a strong connection that is neither scientifically nor ontologically validated. (Cf. endnote 4 in Chapter 1.)

An example that illustrates this point is a quite famous debate between Eric Drexler and Rick Smalley – two proponents of nanotechnology. Drexler's view is that it will be possible "to guide the chemical synthesis of complex structures by mechanically positioning reactive molecules". Drexler thinks that it is possible to build nano-factories that

> [C]ontain no enzymes, no living cells, no swarms of roaming, replicating nano-robots. Instead, they use computers for digitally precise control, conveyors for parts transport, and positioning devices of assorted sizes to assemble small parts into larger parts, building macroscopic products. The smallest devices position molecular parts to assemble structures through mechanosynthesis "machine-phase" chemistry.

To this, Rick Smalley replies:

> [L]et alone a self-replicating assembler – cannot be done simply by mushing two molecular objects together. You need more control. There are too many atoms involved to handle in such a clumsy way. To control these atoms you need some sort of molecular chaperone that can also serve as a catalyst. You need a fairly large group of other atoms arranged in a complex, articulated, three-dimensional way to activate the substrate and bring in the reactant, and massage the two until they react in just the desired way. You need something very much like an enzyme ... That is why I led you in my reply into a room to talk about real chemistry with real enzymes, trying to get you to realize the limitations of this approach.... . Any such system will need a liquid medium.

For the enzymes we know about, that liquid will have to be water, and the types of things that can be synthesized with water around cannot be much broader than the meat and bone of biology. But, no, you don't get it. You are still in a pretend world where atoms go where you want because your computer program directs them to go there. You assume there is a way a robotic manipulator arm can do that in a vacuum, and somehow we will work out a way to have this whole thing actually be able to make another copy of itself.

And further:

Much like you can't make a boy and a girl fall in love with each other simply by pushing them together, you cannot make precise chemistry occur as desired between two molecular objects with simple mechanical motion along a few degrees of freedom in the assembler-fixed frame of reference. Chemistry, like love, is more subtle than that. You need to guide the reactants down a particular reaction coordinate, and this coordinate treads through a many-dimensional hyperspace.

(in Baum 2003, 41)

Their quarrel concerns precisely the point above. Smalley says that there are (horizontal) necessary connections to be taken into consideration, while Drexler maintains that we can overcome those restrictions by *really* going one level down, where (he believes) such restrictions do not exist, and where the connections seem to be more or less *contingent*. On the chemical level, we see that the chemist thinks that everything is connected by things doing what they necessarily have to do (essentialism), while this behaviour appears to be contingent if we can change its "internal constitution" *at the level below*. This type of discussion is the same as the discussions between the proponents and opponents of GMOs. The opponents often put their emphasis on restrictions at the biological level (although they are of course not considered to be as necessary and impossible to bypass as the nano-tech example indicates), while the proponents try to show the contingency of these restrictions by pointing to the level below. Proponents would say that a genome is somehow just a contingent aggregation of singular genes that can actually be disentangled and reassembled however we like. Often, the opponents are called pessimists (and sometimes luddites), while the proponents are called optimists.

An important background factor that partly explains why these situations occur is that the techno-economic development "naturally" strives towards the widest combinatorial space possible. Technology – in combination with the economy – pulls the attention of scientists, engineers and consumers towards "new possibilities". In concert with these interests we have seen that in the last couple of decades it has become a social norm to be creative and open-minded, i.e. open to The New.[34] When we put things together in a new way, we can make products that can generate money. The wet dream of our western technological societies *is nano-technological*, with the prospect that we can entirely 'rebuild the world as we know it'.[35] As we see from what Drexler envisions, we would appear to be facing a future in which we can rearrange the world by way of manipulating matter on an atomic scale, making more or less anything we want (cf. Roco 1999, 1).[36]

In general, to envisage the possibility of this whole enterprise one "needs" (Lockean) essentialism. Essentialism grants that the whole that we see can be explained in terms of its parts, and that each and every part is independent of the other parts, and on top of this makes its particular and singular contribution by *necessity*. Combining the relative "horizontal" contingency on the level below with an upward "vertical" necessitation, one can postulate, create and dream about units that are contingently assembled (Hume) and causally determinate (Locke) at the same time. Although Humeanism is not compatible with essentialism and therefore represents a kind of alternative, it is by no means a helpful one, since it represents the same view, in the sense that it renders the whole a contingent result of the contingent aggregation of the parts. Humeanism adds to the assumption that everything can be assembled and reassembled in any way that suits our purposes.[37]

2.8 Reservations

At this juncture, we should balance the exposition that we have given thus far with at least two reservations.

The first reservation is of course that technology based in a reductionist science actually works. Pharmaceutical pills, GMOs and the techno-scientific regime work, and have no doubt had what is often called a tremendous success – although one might say that the success is conditional upon our acceptance of more or less problematic side-effects. An explanation of why this is the case would require elaboration and cannot be worked out in this chapter. In Chapter 5, however, we will encounter this issue again. (See esp. *Miracle-Argument* in subsection 5.4.1.)

The second reservation is this: even if we were convinced that the scientist believes and assures others (#2 and #3) that it is sufficient to "laboratize" in order to get hold of and describe the essential being of the part-takers in order to reach a full description of the whole – even so, the description might still be haunted by the fact that what s/he is *really* doing (#1) is going back and forth between the levels heuristically, *without really noticing it*. So, while the neuroscientist might think that the neurons and synapses etc. determine something like consciousness, sleep or whatever s/he would stand no chance if there were only neurons and synapses and no consciousness or sleep to be studied (see Poldrack 2006). To *see* the brain activity of 'sorrow' the scientist needs to define sorrow. It is not the case that one could just look at the biochemical properties of a certain area of the brain and state: "Yes, this is sorrow". The conclusion: yes this is sorrow, can only be reached *ex post facto*. If a reductionist and a Lockean essentialist explanation were able to really be convincing it should have been able to predict higher-order properties that we did not even know existed. But this is never the case (see sections 4.6 and 5.2). While the social scientist or the psychologist see great obstacles in *defining* and understanding properties like 'dominant behaviour', feelings like 'sorrow' and 'empathy' the natural sciences such as neuroscience seem to think that this is just a minor problem. This is indicative of the fact that e.g. a feeling like sorrow is seen to be a feeling produced by the brain and not by the circumstance where such a feeling is (or is not) a relevant feeling to have. Without this anticipation it would be impossible to assume that we 'now see sorrow or empathy expressed in this area of the brain'. Without a precise definition, the cognitive scientist and her exact scientific methods would be totally helpless in finding the corresponding biochemical activity labelled 'sorrow'. And even though this is a fact, we see that cognitive science receives massive attention and funding. The reason for this can only be that one is able to defend the view that 'sorrow' is causally traceable to certain brain states. Which, in effect, *is* a dismissal of the alternative claim that 'sorrow' is in reality "caused by" an intentional state that the agent is directed towards (for example the loss of a good friend).[38]

A different example showing the importance of *ex post facto* reasoning is the rationale behind the human genome project (HUGO). HUGO finished in 2001, but the results were just a very small part of the job inasmuch as they had mapped the "letters" of the genome, but not what those letters "mean". An account of how these genes were correlated with the behaviour of the organism as a whole was omitted completely. This was not something that was anticipated from the start. The fact that they virtually discovered that they could not read the "phenotype" from the "genotype" caused the project to crash (although this was covered up, Skaftnesmo 2005). It therefore came as a *surprise* that humans have far fewer genes than Basmati rice, and that the genetic difference between two closely related species of nematodes (*C. Elegans* and *C. Briggsae*) is four times greater than the genetic difference between humans and (laboratory) mice. This should also tell us something about the tacit reductionist assumptions that scientists go by in general, since there were so few scientists (although there were some) who predicted this outcome.

The following is a different example from another part of science concerning the same issue.

> These things are clearly true, yet they cannot be deduced by direct calculation from the Theory of Everything, for exact results cannot be predicted by approximate calculations. This point is still not understood by many professional physicists, who find it easier to believe that a deductive link exists and has only to be discovered than to face the truth that there is no link. But it is true nonetheless. Experiments of this kind work because there are *higher organizing principles in nature that make them work*. The Josephson quantum is exact because of the principle of continuous symmetry breaking. The quantum Hall effect is exact because of localization. Neither of these things can be *deduced* from microscopics, and both are transcendent, in that they would continue to be true and to lead to exact results even if the Theory of Everything were changed. Thus the existence of these effects is profoundly important, for it shows us that for at least some fundamental things in nature the Theory of Everything is irrelevant. P.W. Anderson's apt and famous description of this state is "more is different."
>
> (Laughlin and Pines 2000, 28, my emphasis)

The point is that the reductionist trades upon higher organizing principles, which in fact *cannot be deduced* from the minute parts, but this fact is not acknowledged, since he or she is so stuck in the reductionist paradigm, as the writers say. (That is actually the main point for the authors in this article. Their audience is *the whole community of physicists*, and according to Laughlin they are not easy to move away from their reductionist positions. The claim that scientists in general are reductionists is not an extreme position, therefore. In reality it takes a great effort to overcome reductionism in general. See chapters 4 and 5.)

A possible reason why they "find it easier" to believe in a reductionist scheme is that the majority of scientists do not notice that their line of argument is made *ex post facto*. By this *unnoticed ex post facto* reasoning, the scientist can convince herself that the whole is fully understandable and produced by the parts. The quantum Hall effect is only "explained" after the fact by the parts and it takes a lot of effort to see that this is actually not the case. When you do not *notice* that your argument or your findings completely depend on the heuristic movement between the parts and the whole you will end up with a reductionist account if that is what blindfolded you in the first place (cf. quote from Laughlin and Pines above).

So we do have the "same" data, but we have two different metaphysical descriptions of those data (#5), and therefore of what is really going on (#1). This means that scientists with these different descriptions *would* describe their own activity to both themselves (#2) and to others (#3) differently and, thus, incoherently. This disagreement can prevail as long as unnoticed *ex post facto* reasoning prevails.

My description of reductionism as the real guiding principle for the methodology of science therefore does not really reveal what is occurring, and my description of science is therefore wrong relative to (#1). But that's beside the point here, because at this juncture I am not primarily searching for what the scientist is really doing (#1), but rather what she thinks she is doing, and what she conveys to others that she is doing, because it is on the background of #2 and #3 that the scientist rejects naturalness. I think that what the scientist is really doing (#1) and cannot help but be doing, is researching the dispositions of things and coping with the complex relational nature of these dispositions. But this is neither understood nor conveyed by the scientist or by other stakeholders, and this makes it even more difficult to acknowledge the place and role that naturalness can play within science today.

What I have gathered in the last two chapters are at least three complex reasons, in addition to the philosophical ones, coming out of the elaborations on Locke, Hume in Chapter 1, as to why science displays a passivist ontology. The first reason is related to technological application, the second to contingency-treasures at lower levels, and the last to *ex post facto* reasoning. All of the factors I have chosen to emphasize here come down to a certain *attitude*, an attitude towards what can be done and what cannot be done with the passive beings that we encounter. An attitude towards what can be expected and interpreted when knowledge gained *in-vitro* translates into *in-vivo* situations.

When the nature of a whole is studied by way of studying its parts (because one thinks *a priori* that the whole is just a *passive* result of the behaviour of the parts), then the nature in question disappears. When a whole is thought to be a contingent result of the behaviour of its parts – and the *behaviour of this whole* is determined by its inner constitution (i.e. its parts) – the researcher is permitted to expect that if the whole is "equipped" with the right parts, producing the right properties, then it will make no (substantial) difference when or how knowledge gained *in-vitro* translates into *in-vivo* situations. If you don't acknowledge the relative independence of the existence of the whole, it is not easy to see how the whole could make a difference to the parts. Conversely, if (for example) the neuroscientist really understood that sorrow is a feeling that is related to the Human Condition, she would have to admit that it is "the loss of a good friend" that created the sorrow, and not the correlating brain state. She would then be able to appreciate the damage that stands to be done to *the state of being human* (the whole) if she and others choose to be a part of a belief system that systematically (either directly or through its technological offspring) allows its proponents to assume that (e.g.) 'sorrow' is caused by certain states in the brain. If she understood sorrow as a capacity related to the nature of being relationally connected to a world where such feelings can be an answer to situations that humans can and do encounter, and therefore were to "be" on this understanding (both inside and outside of the laboratory), then her research could be truly helpful, although *a lot less* important than it is taken to be today.

2.9 No naturalness, only nature

What I sought to understand better in this chapter is why naturalness has been abandoned by science, as claimed in Chapter 1. Why do things have certain behaviours, positions in time and space; colours, effects, etc., but no naturalness? I gave the general answer that both necessitarian ontologies and contingency-based ontologies are incoherent if we want to argue that the property of being natural can be ascribed to things. In this chapter I have tried to substantiate this claim more carefully by elaborating on the Humean and Lockean ways of formulating a philosophy "devoted" to these two modalities.

Doing so seemed to me to be insufficient on its own, however, because even though we might say that a scientist must go by a specific ontology, the mere existence of ontologies that preclude naturalness may not be the reason why *scientists* would repel naturalness. What I therefore tried to do was to show how these ontologies fit into a description of what I called the ontology of science. This is where reductionism was brought in as a separate factor, although I have also argued and showed how essentialism and Humeanism in various ways fit well as a metaphysical background for reductionism. But reductionism is also driven by other factors (e.g. economy, technology), which partly lie beyond its ontology and the ontology of Hume and Locke.

Why is reductionism so important? Reductionism is important because proponents of this view, in a strange and inconsistent way, do not accept the reality of wholes. Wholes *qua* wholes and the processes of generating these wholes, are the "things" that *could have been* ascribed naturalness. 'A horse is not a horse;

it is what it is because of its proteomic constitution'. Since the beings and processes that could be ascribed the status 'natural' are *a priori* explained away, we are not even able to begin a positive exploration of naturalness. It is perfectly "natural" that you will not be able to alter *the nature* of something if there is no nature THERE to be altered in the first place. And in this situation it does not really matter if such a being is governed by laws, by intrinsically productive essences or by contingent free-floating properties. Passivism fits all these sorts of ontologies. We may also say that these ontologies are accepted because they comply with a passivist understanding of Nature.

If we go back to Norman Levitt's interview and the editorial article I quoted from *Nature* (1.2.#5), we will see that the *whole* in question is exactly what is not present in their otherwise convincing argument. If they had recognized that the nature that they study or write about has wholes that have natures, and not just "contingent or necessitating parts", then they, too, would perhaps have seen that there was a nature there all along: a *something* in relation to which alteration and manipulation make a difference. They would have seen that when they ascribe gut feelings or particular cultural dogmas to people's reactions against "unnatural manipulations", their argument hinges upon their own particular *ontology* and that people's reactions are not necessarily a result of misplaced normative statements.

Before we end this chapter there is one last issue that is important to keep in mind. Throughout this book I argue that the concept of naturalness is not viable under a philosophical regime that allows only for the modalities of necessity and contingency. The reader may agree with this claim considered on its own, but disagree with the way in which I have portrayed the situation. For example, you may think that it is actually not correct that scientists go by those ontologies that support only these modalities. What about biology, medicine and so on? There is a long and a short answer to this, and I will simply pick the short one here: my claim still holds, because there are currently *no alternative ontologies* to which scientists working in those areas can refer to for their "alternative" claims. Although a biologist may claim that a biological trait only tends towards a certain outcome, he or she has *no ontological way* to support this view. The claim is ontologically vacuous and has no theoretical power to challenge views claiming that, for instance, the functioning of the brain is determined by the constituting parts of the brain. It may look like I am trading on a straw man, but I think this is wrong. If there is a straw man here, we would have seen a third modality involved in current scientific processes in addition to those of necessity and contingency. I would like to see this ontology that supposedly should have been at work "out there" all along. Where is it?

Notes

1 I refer for the most part to *Physics* and *The Metaphysics*. The versions are: *Physics*: Oxford 1996, trans. Waterfield and *The Metaphysics*, Penguin 1998, trans. Lawson-Tancred.
2 This means that things that exist by *technē* are not real substances. This is also the interpretation that Johnson argues for. However, Charlotte Witt thinks that this is not clearly settled by Aristotle (1989, 69, fn. 7 and p. 70).

3 In other words, this means that Aristotle is explicitly not a reductionist (or a 'materialist', as Aristotle calls it). It's very important to note that he was interested in the things *tode ti*: things here, right before us "as they are". A horse has properties *qua* horse! Properties such as the ability to be tamed, the ability to run in such and such a way, to mate in such and such a way, etc.: these are the properties of *the horse* – which count (among other properties) as essential properties of the horse (see Chapter 4).

4 See e.g. Diamond (1999).

5 A view like this also coincides with the "genomic era view" that emerged in the 1970s, which marked a radical shift in our ability to manipulate other living beings. According to Hub Zwart, there are two incoherent views that compete on this issue. One (propagated by scientists and biotechnology experts) is that biotechnology has "always been around", and that modern biotechnology is just a continuation of this historical record; the other is that the 1970s represented a discontinuation of this historical line. The arguments employed in the latter group frequently refer to the "monstrosity-argument" (Zwart 2009; see also Miller 2006).

6 See also Glacken 1976, part 8, ch. 2. What Glacken mainly talks about here is teleology in general. ('Is there a purposiveness in nature?') In this sense Newton, Galileo, Kepler, etc., could be said to hold a teleological world view, but that was mainly because they were Christians. Here I am referring to the specific teleological cause that Aristotle attributed to substances, and not "teleology" or purposiveness in general.

7 A more detailed exposition can be found in Lie and Wickson 2011.

8 This list is referred to throughout this book and I urge the reader to keep it in mind.

9 Sometimes, however, we find that the author of a book on physics asks metaphysical questions such as "What is really an object?" or "What is causality?" A typical example would be the claim that some philosophers today think of causality in terms of energy transfer. However, such questions are rarely asked from the perspective of an informed understanding of their philosophical magnitude. Instead they are built on a "folk-version" of what causality, objects or properties "really are".

10 Famously, Locke divides qualities into primary and secondary qualities. Powers describe the way these qualities behave under different circumstances on our perception and on each other. Secondary qualities are said to *be* powers, while primary qualities are seen to have something in addition, which we don't really know (see Chappell 2007, 134–135).

11 An alternative view to this would be to interpret the real essence as a *Ding an sich*, or an unknowable substratum holding the thing together, but with no features or properties in itself. The interpretation I give here is not uncontroversial, but it seems to me that it is taken to be one of the more plausible ones (see Mackie 1991, 76–83; see also discussion in Atherton 1998).

12 Locke uses different expressions depending on the situation. 'Real essences', 'internal constitution' and 'minute parts' basically refer to the same idea.

13 Although still unknown to us under a strict *empiricist* truth criterion. We might be able to observe some of the features on this level, but how they are combined is often postulated. For example, the atom and its exact constitution cannot be observed directly. It is famously said that the observation is based on models (cf. model-based reasoning).

14 See http://en.wikipedia.org/wiki/Cladistics (last accessed July 2015).

15 http://en.wikipedia.org/wiki/Tree_of_life_(science) (last accessed July 2015).

16 See esp. *Physics* 254 b39, where Aristotle says: "These are the cases where it might be difficult to see what it is that moves the thing". Aristotle points to some kind of *hidden factor* that makes e.g. air move upward. It is not unreasonable to suggest "minute parts" ("real essences") as a possible candidate for such hidden agents (as Aristotle calls them). He also says "[T]hey were changed … by whatever it was that produced them and made them light and heavy" (255 b36). This "whatever made them light and heavy" might be a clue for why Locke arrived at "real essences".

17 One way of defining the metaphysical thesis of constructivism is: "quarks are invented rather than discovered". (See Kukla 2000, 4.)

18 Locke's view of the distinctness of properties is not exactly an uncommon thought. The word 'determine' originates from the Latin word 'determinatio', which originally was connected to the properties of things or the definition of them and "their substance". "In this sense, that is determinate which has definite characteristics and can consequently be characterized unambiguously" (Bunge 1963, 7). In Locke's terms this comes down to: 'That which is determinate is that which is able to determine' – which also is quite a common thought in general.

19 Hume's view will be more carefully elaborated with references etc. in section 2.5.

20 Heidegger could be said to a "nominalist" in the sense that he would say that nature is some kind of contingent "mass" (*"vorhanden"*) into which we humans bring some order in terms of our practical relation (*"zuhanden"*) with what is *"vorhanden"*. There are many things to be said about this which would make this view less straightforward, but we might say that Heidegger has in any case been interpreted in this way, and that this interpretation has contributed to the intuitions and arguments that are available for the constructivist to use.

21 To see that properties have something to do with behaviour we may argue generally (as I do below) or we may state it even more strongly as a reality principle. The Eleatic reality test is such a principle, which I will come back to in section 3.0.

22 "As objects must be either conjoined or not ... *"tis impossible to admit to any medium betwixt chance and the absolute necessity"* (Hume 1739–1740, 171, my emphasis). When considering Hume's ideas about necessity and contingency we should also keep in mind that he argues against Descartes who says that everything that is rationally or conceptually connected is necessarily connected, and necessary in a way that is given by God.

23 This is of course a very tricky question. What is Humeanism and what is Hume's philosophy? Since Hume on one side makes no claims about reality, only about impressions and ideas, many will say that he avoids the metaphysical questions we ask here. On the other hand, he says that there is a difference between impressions and ideas, and that the reason for this is that impressions depict something in reality (liveliness) (ibid., 66). This is a theory of truth and he does in fact apply this to say something about "The World"! He says things like "Anything may produce anything else" and, as we have seen, "necessity is something that exists in the mind and not in objects". In fact, that is what it means to be an empiricist – *one who will first and foremost believe in the existence of those things that are empirically accessible.* Granting that we are cautious of making Hume into an ordinary metaphysician, I would say that we have good reason to anticipate that a Humean will say that the connection between things and the behaviour of things is *contingent*. I say this as carefully as I can because Hume often allows himself to oscillate between being an empiricist and being a sceptic: after saying loud and clear that there is no connection, he also says that he would not know whether we might "find the principles that unite our successive perceptions" (ibid., 636).

24 At the *outset*, therefore, a "contingency account" such as Hume's cannot be combined consistently with a "necessity account". That would be philosophically incoherent.

25 Although complex impressions do not amount to complex wholes in reality, Hume's way of thinking here is strongly indicative of the claim I make.

26 I generally agree with Cartwright here, although I would formulate the solution differently (see subsection 4.5.3).

27 It might be the case that this claim stems from reading too many popular science magazines over the years (esp. *New Scientist*), but that does not mean that I am wrong.

28 Robert Merton's CUDOS-rules ('Mertonian norms') can serve as a depiction of this "nineteenth-century science mode" (Merton 1942).

29 A typical example is the discussion document on the strategy for the University of Oslo 2010–2020. Under the heading "Global Trends important for the University of Oslo", we can read the following:

Competence, knowledge and technology will be the most important features in a competitive and sustainable knowledge economy. More and more is expected from the universities to take societal responsibility in this sense. The capacity to take part in the production of new knowledge and new technologies and to get this knowledge and technology to circulate swiftly between the sectors of our society has become crucial and decisive in the global market economy.... . Both in the EU and the OECD and in the new and emerging networks between universities there is a common understanding that this modernization will be radical. This will demand that the universities formulate their role in society more clearly [sic: i.e. not differently but more clearly!], develop more professional leadership and understand their role as an engine of growth in the local and global economy and further; create a stronger dynamic and integration between education research and innovation (my translation).

30 The reader may substitute "parts" being determined by essences with "parts" being determined by laws. But you will arrive at the same ontological problem. The kinds of laws that you have found that govern the behaviour of "parts" in the laboratory will not really be applicable to other situations than those conditions found in the laboratory unless you think that these laws necessitate the behaviour of the part under all other conditions too. As argued previously, this is one of the pathways where passivism is instantiated.

31 One typical way to explicate this underlying techno-scientific value can be found in Miller (2006). Miller argues that GMOs are better and safer organisms compared to those that have been developed through traditional (phenotypic) selection because the technology works in a much more exact way. His assumption is that the insertion only involves a very specific and locatable change of the genome, while traditional breeding involves far more complex changes. To characterize this as being more exact he *needs* to rest his argument on an essentialist ontology in the way that I have described here.

32 The general notion applied to this type of cognitive enhancement is that of 'Nootropics'.

33 It is possible to provoke mutation by ionizing radiation and through application of chemicals (Miller 2006, 57), but these methods can hardly be called biological.

34 See Bell (1976/1993).

35 See e.g. Roco 1999. I urge the reader to take a closer look at this.
   A more realistic model is called NBIC convergence (Nano, Bio, Info and Cogno), or simply 'converging technologies', wherein these disciplines are seen as sufficient to create an integrated whole that can reshape the world as we know it (Roco and Bainbridge 2002).

36 Eric Drexler, who is, no doubt, the father of this idea, was (admirably) inspired by the Roma-Club report "Limits to Growth", which came out in 1972, to find a way to overcome the limits postulated in that report (Regis 1995). The result was the idea that we could disassemble and reassemble the world as we like, at a very low cost. Nano-science was specifically developed as a field where science, technology and economy were pre-integrated from the start.

37 Alfred Nordmann argues, in a very interesting article (2009), that nano technology (and science) is the first kind of science wherein the researchers and the developers actually embrace unpredictability or what they call the emergence of surprising properties. Nordmann points to the total ontological indifference and ignorance that underlie this research programme. It is a combination of the romantic idea about self-emergence and the idea of engineering nature from the bottom-up. ('Let us stack some atoms together and see what happens; probably there will occur some interesting properties that we can use.') The problem is, of course, that when they abandon essentialism, they leave behind a platform from which they can claim that some given technology will be safe or even functional. And that is why they randomly oscillate between these two positions. An example of this is the following taken from the report on nanotechnology referred to above (Roco 1999, 6): "Simulations and modelling also help them evaluate the infinite number of nanostructures they could, in principle, try to

build. Simulations can help steer researchers toward fruitful directions and away from dead ends." Later (p. 7) the authors of the report talk about the prospects and wonders (and not the dangers) of self-assembly, as if the atoms necessitated the behaviour on higher levels, and the technology would have full predictability. This can again be seen as a strange mix between essentialism and Humeanism.

38 I need to add that this is just an example, and that all scientific fields typically have disagreements related to this issue. See e.g. http://www.theguardian.com/science/2014/jul/07/human-brain-project-researchers-threaten-boycott (last accessed July 2014).

References

Aristotle (1996) *Physics*, Oxford University Press. (Translation Waterfield)

—— (1998) *The Metaphysics* (trans. H. Lawson-Tancred), Penguin

Ashby, E. (1978) *Reconciling Man with the Environment*, Stanford University Press.

Atherton, M. (1998) "The Inessentiality of Locke's Essentialism", in Chappell (ed.) *Locke*, Oxford University Press.

Barrow, J. (2007) *New Theories of Everything*, Oxford University Press.

Baum, R. (2003) "Nanotechnology", *Chemical and Engineering News*, vol. 81.

Beebee, H. (2006) "Does Anything Hold the Universe Together?", *Synthese*, 149.

Bell, D. (1976/1993) *The Cultural Contradictions of Capitalism*, Basic Books.

Berger, P.L. and Luckmann, T. (1966/2011) *The Social Construction of Reality: A Treatise in the Sociology of Knowledge*, Open Road Media.

Bunge, M. (1959/1963) *Causality*, Meridian Books.

Capra, F. (1975) *The Tao of Physics*, Shambala Publications.

Cartwright, N. (1989) *Nature's Capacities and their Measurement*, Oxford University Press.

Castree, N. (2014) *Making Sense of Nature*, Routledge.

Chalmers, A. (2008) *What is this Thing Called Science?*, Open University Press.

Chappell, V. (2007) "Power in Locke's *Essay*", *The Cambridge Companion on Locke's Essay Concerning Human Understanding*, Cambridge University Press.

Dawkins, R. (1976) *The Selfish Gene*, Oxford University Press.

Deckers, J. (2005) "Are Scientists Right and Non-scientists Wrong? Reflections on Discussions of GM", *Journal of Agriculture and Environmental ethics*, vol. 18.

Descartes, R. (1637/2006) *Discourse on Method* (trans. D. Clarke), Penguin.

Diamond, J. (1999) *Guns, Germs and Steel*, Norton Press.

Ellis, B. (2001) *Scientific Essentialism*, Cambridge University Press.

—— (2002) *The Philosophy of Nature*, Acumen.

Fox, M.W. (1990) "Transgenic Animals: Ethical and Animal Welfare Concerns", in P. Wheale and R. McNally (eds.) *The Bio-Revolution: Cornucopia or Pandora's Box*, Pluto Press.

Funkenstein, A. (2005) "The Revival of Aristotle's Nature", in M.R. Jones and N. Cartwright (eds.) *Idealization XII: Correcting the Model*, Rodopi.

Funtowicz, S. and Ravetz, R. (1993) "Science for the Post-Normal Age", *Futures*, September.

Gibbons, M. et al. (1994), *The New Production of Knowledge: The Dynamics of Science and Research in Contemporary Societies*, Sage.

Glacken, C.J. (1967/1976) *Traces on the Rhodian Shore: Nature and Culture in Western Thought from Ancient Times to the End of the Eighteenth Century*, University of California Press.

Hacking, I. (1983) *Representing and Intervening*, Cambridge University Press.

—— (1999) *The Social Construction of What?*, Harvard University Press.

Hawking, S. (1988) *A Brief History of Time*, Bentham Dell publishing Group.

Heidegger, M. (1927/1992) *Being and Time*, Blackwell.

Hofstadter, D. (2007) *I am a Strange Loop*, Basic Books.

Hume, D. (1739–1740/1978) *Treatise on Human Nature* (trans. L. A. Selby-Bigge and P. H. Nidditch), Oxford University Press.

Johnson, M. (2005) *Aristotle on Teleology*, Oxford University Press.

Jones, W.T. (1969) *A History of Western Philosophy, from Hobbes to Hume*, Harcourt Brace Jovanovich publishers.

Kant, I. (1987/1790) *Critique of Judgement* (trans. W. Pluhar), Hackett Publishing Co.

Kuhn, T. (1962/1996) *The Structure of Scientific Revolutions*, Chicago Press.

Kukla, A. (2000) *Social Constructivism and the Philosophy of Science*, Routledge.

Latour, K. (1998) "From the World of Science to the World of Research?", *Science* 280.

Laughlin, R.B. (2005) *A Different Universe – Reinventing Physics from the Bottom Down*, Basic Books.

Laughlin, R.B. and Pines, D. (2000) "The Theory of Everything", *Proceedings of the National Academy of Sciences*, January.

Lee, K. (1999) *The Natural and The Artefactual*, Lexington Books.

Leibniz, G. (1764/1996) *New Essays on Human Understanding*, Cambridge University Press.

Lewontin, R. (2000) *The Triple Helix: Gene, Organism and Environment*, Harvard University Press.

Lie, S.A. and Wickson, F. (2011) "The Relational Ontology of Deep Ecology: A Dispositional Alternative to Intrinsic Value?", in A. Aaro and J. Servan (eds.) *Environment, Embodiment and History*, Hermes Texts.

Locke, J. (1690/1995) *An Essay Concerning Human Understanding*, Prometheus Books.

Losee, J. (1980) *A Historical Introduction to the Philosophy of Science*, Oxford University Press.

Mackie, J. (1976/1991) *Problems from Locke*, Oxford University Press.

Marris, C. (2001). "Public views on GMOs: Deconstructing the Myths", *EMBO Reports* 2(7).

Martin, C.B. (2007) *Mind in Nature*, Oxford University Press.

Merton, R. (1942) "The Normative Structure of Science", in R. Merton (ed.) *The Sociology of Science, Theoretical and Empirical Investigations*, Chicago University Press.

Meyer, G. and Sandøe, P. (2001) "Public Debate and Scientific Ignorance", *EurSafe 2001 Third Congress of the European Society for Agricultural and Food Ethics*, October 3–5.

Miller, H.I. (2006) "Biotechs Defining Moments", *Trends in Biotechnology*, vol. 25.

Molnar, G. (2003) *Powers* (ed. S. Mumford), Oxford University Press.

Moss, L. (2004) *What Genes Can't Do*, MIT Press.

Mumford, S. (1998) *Dispositions*, Oxford University Press.

—— (2004) *Laws in Nature*, Routledge.

Nelkin, D. (1996) "The Science Wars: What is at Stake?", *Chronicle of Higher Education*, July.

Nordmann, A. (2009) "Enhancing Material Nature", in F. Wickson and K. Kjøllberg (eds.) *Nano meets Macro*, Imperial Collage Press.

O'Neill, J. (2003) "The Varieties of Intrinsic Value", in A. Light and H. Rolston III. (eds.) *Environmental Ethics – An Anthology*, Blackwell.

Poldrack, R. (2006). "Can Cognitive Processes be Inferred from Neuroimaging Data?", *Trends in Cognitive Sciences*, 10 (2).

Regis, E. (1995) *Nano – The Emerging Science of Nanotechnology: Remaking the World – Molecule*, Little, Brown Co.

Reiss, M. and Straughan, R. (1996) *Improving Nature: The Science and Ethics of Genetic Engineering*, Cambridge University Press.

Rescher, N. (1973) "The Ontology of the Possible", in M.K. Munitz (ed.) *Logic and Ontology*, New York University Press.

Roco, M.C., chair (1999) *Nanotechnology: Shaping the World Atom by Atom*, National Science and Technology Council.

Roco, M. and Bainbridge, W. (2002) "Overview: Converging Technologies for Improving Human Performance", in M.C. Roco and W.S. Bainbridge (eds.) *Converging Technologies for Improving Human Performance*, Cluwer Academic Publishers.

Schmaltz, T.M. (2014) "Introduction to Efficient Causation", in T.M. Schmlatz (ed.) *Efficient Causation – a History*, Oxford University Press.

Sheldrake, R. (1981) *A New Science of Life*, Blond & Briggs.

Skaftnesmo, T. (2005) *Genparadigmets Fall*, Antropos.

Sztompka, P. (2007) "Trust in Science", *Journal of Classical Sociology*, vol. 7.

Verhoog, H. (2003) "Naturalness and the Genetic Modification of Animals", *Trends in biotechnology*, July.

Wapner, P. (2003) "Leftist Criticism of Nature", *Dissent Magazine* (winter).

Witt, C. (1989) *Substance and Essence in Aristotle*, Cornell University Press.

Ziman, J. (1996) "Is Science Losing its Objectivity", *Nature*, vol. 382, 29 Aug.

Zwart, H. (2009) "Biotechnology and Naturalness in the Genomics Era: Plotting a Timetable for the Biotechnology Debate", *Journal of Agricultural and Environmental Ethics*, June.

Part II

A positive concept of naturalness

A philosophical word that I like to use is 'compossible', not because it is a beautiful word, but because it harbours a lot of meaning. It is a word that brings me back to the essence of this book. It is a word that I have from David Armstrong. It is a fusion of the word 'possible' and 'combination'. What is possible to combine? This is really what naturalness is about. On each side of the physically possible stands a *dubious* realm. On the one side, the supernatural, which goes beyond and is "more than" that which is physically compossible; on the other side, that which is "less than" the physically compossible, but which some people for some reason think involves combinations that are not natural.[1] It is generally believed that the natural laws set the limits for what is possible to combine or not. Anything less than "physically possible to combine" is contingent and arbitrary on a modal dualist view. Claims about naturalness are therefore in principle mind-dependent.

It requires a whole ontology to establish *de re* potentiality (propensity) as a modal option (see section 3.3 in particular). It is not enough to say that we "see propensity" in the broad and massive use of statistics in science – not if we want to establish that something less than necessity can be *real*, at least. The use of statistics is not the same as a theory of the realness of those phenomena that are captured by statistics.

Some people and some cultural groups think of GMOs as being unnatural. It is definitely physically possible to make GMOs but some still think that this does not make a difference for the case that they are unnatural. Today we have an unfortunate situation where all those things that are "less than physically compossible" are regarded as depending upon cultural and ethical beliefs. Science is said to be neutral in this matter, but this is where science really can change societies and cultures.[2] When scientists say that they cannot really say how things *should* be combined, they are saying that everything that is less than necessary is freely compossible and that everyone who tries to "naturalize" this realm has made a categorical mistake. Is it true that everything falling short of necessity must be contingent? If so, then every statement that says otherwise must be a sheer product of our minds. This means that everyone who believes (including constructivists) that "physical compossibility" is the only manner in which things are *really* related also must believe in this story underlying the position and role that science plays in present-day societies.

In the previous part of this book I have tried to show why scientists in general reject a concept of naturalness, and what kind of consequences this has for environmental ethics, the making of technologies from scientific knowledge, and in general for how science contributes to the human alteration of nature in a way that is not neutral. The *alleged neutrality* is only conceivable if most of us accept passivism as the only possible and therefore neutral ontology. To challenge this situation we therefore need to consider a different ontology, not least because this will show that passivism is not the only candidate for a realist conception of scientific activity. Even though one may not like or support an ontology of dispositions one may nevertheless consider dispositionalism as a serious alternative to passivism. If this alternative is taken seriously one would also have to realize that the passivist ontologies are not uncontroversial ontologies to go by in the first place, something which would be an immensely important admission in itself.

What I will try to do in this second part is to propose a positive concept of naturalness. I have pointed to several problems in the first part; the second part might be regarded as simply an attempt to propose solutions to these problems.

Notes

1 In a more detailed and less dubious picture we can say that beyond the "physically possible" we find the mathematically and logically possible, and beyond that the supernaturally possible. On the side of "less than physically possible" we find the chemically possible, the biochemically possible, the genomically possible, the proteomically possible, etc. And even this picture could be more detailed of course.
2 See e.g. Dworkin (2000), who points to the cultural importance of the way that we perceive our lives in relation to what is *given* (by the Gods/destiny/blind chance/physically possible) and what is left for human choice (443f.).

Reference

Dworkin, R. (2000) *Sovereign Virtue*, Harvard University Press.

3 Dispositions

3.0 Introducing dispositions

Disposition ontology is quite a "new ontology".[1] This ontology has a record that goes back to (at least) the 1970s, and has been in continuous and expanding development since then. Philosophers like C. B. Martin, D. H. Mellor, Georg Molnar, Karl Popper, Rom Harré, Roy Baskhar, Nancy Cartwright, Sidney Shoemaker and more recently Stephen Mumford, Brian Ellis and Alexander Bird, have been central figures. We might say that Harré, Madden, Cartwright and Bhaskar were mainly focused on philosophy of science, while Molnar and Martin were focused on metaphysics. It is the Molnar/Martin branch that we will try to follow here ('the Australian school', we might call it).[2]

Moving further back in time, we could of course point to the role that the Greek word *dunamis* played in the philosophy of Plato and Aristotle. *Dunamis* is often translated as *capacity* (Plato, e.g. *Sophist* p. 247) and/or potentiality (Aristotle, *Metaphysics*, Θ 3), (while *energeia* is more like the manifestation of the *dunamis*; *dunamis* means energy/'power *at work*').

As we have seen, however, there is a teleological tendency present in both Aristotle's and Plato's ontology that is at odds with the way the notion dispositions are interpreted and understood today. The similarity but also the difference between the Greek way of understanding dispositions and the contemporary understanding is important, since many, at least at first sight, think that recourse to dispositions represents the revival of "Greek Metaphysics". To appreciate these similarities and differences we must first understand the current and contemporary concept of dispositions.

The word 'properties' refers back to the way that we characterize some sort of being or entity. Yellow, negative charge, 20kg, salty, capacity to reproduce, wavelike, carnivore, beautiful, biodiverse, rare, etc. are examples of properties. Properties are what we refer to when we are asked to define something. Dispositions are said to be particular types of *properties*. In some accounts we also see the term 'properties' swapped for the term 'dispositions', meaning that there are no other kinds of properties than dispositions. In the standard account, dispositions are properties that describe what some given entity is able to do and to forbear. In a more neutral language, we would say that a disposition ascription means that the object would give "some characteristic manifestation in response to a certain kind of stimulus" (Bird 2007, 3). When dispositions are manifested there is always something happening. This means that "*a* power has directionality, in the sense that it must be a power for, or to, some outcome" (Molnar 2003, 57). Dispositions relate directly to behaviour – linguistically the suffixes '–ile' or '–ble' are used to convey "dispositional meanings" – fragile, drinkable, adaptable, visible, etc. Dispositions are properties that are defined on the basis of our knowledge about what a given thing is *able to do*. Our knowledge of the world is often directed towards these properties and is always implied in what we call categorical statements. We can understand what "F is G" means because we are often able to see what "F is G" means in terms of behaviour. F is 20kg would mean very little to us if we did not know what kinds of behaviour came out of such "categorical information". A world in which dispositions are included is a world in which "[p]articular objects and substances are causally powerful and causally responsive. They are able to do things and have things done to them" (Mumford 2007a, 39). A *disposition is a certain* **readiness** *that an entity has to perform specific kinds of behaviour under specific kinds of conditions*. (F is G means that F is ready to r, given Y.) It is therefore standard to say that dispositions are what the conditional (p $\rightarrow$ q) really refers to.[3]

There are, of course – as always between philosophers – disagreements as to how we should incorporate dispositions into a given ontology. Some prefer to say that dispositions are all there is. This position is called *pan-dispositionalism* or *dispositional monism* (see Mellor 1974; Shoemaker 1980; Mumford 2004; Bird 2007). Others prefer to say that some of the properties of a being or an entity are *not* dispositional. Such properties are often called *categorical properties*.

Properties that are said to be categorical may be thought to live side by side with dispositional properties or they may be thought to be the only *real* ones. Those who think the latter may suggest that dispositional properties supervene on categorical properties, either via laws or just as a matter of fact, or that dispositions are just helpful *placeholders* for the real properties that are categorical.

Philosophers who hold this position are called *categorical monists* (e.g. Armstrong 2005, 315; Quine 1974, 10; Lewis 1997, 149[4]). Philosophers who think that they can live side by side hold a *mixed view*, which is the idea that both types of properties are equally needed. Those who commit themselves to this mixed view may be *dualists* (Place 1996; Molnar 2003; Ellis 2002)[5] or *monists* (Martin 2007; Heil 2003; Mumford 1998).

This roughly captures the range of positions held by those who take an interest in talking about dispositions.[6] What are categorical properties? There is no firm agreement on which way to define this concept, but for the moment it is enough to say that these are occurrent properties "properties of shape and structure, especially the microstructure of the object" (Mumford 2007b, 83). Some say that these are properties that are "necessarily manifesting" (Mumford 2006, 481; Bird 2007, 66). We might recognize categorical properties better if we by way of preliminary point in the direction of what Locke and Descartes called primary qualities (quantitative structural properties).

The Eleatic Stranger in Plato's *Sophist* claims:

> I am saying that a thing really is if it has any capacity at all, either by nature
> to do something to something else or to have even the smallest thing done to
> it by even the most trivial thing, even if it only happens once. I'll take it as a
> definition that *those which are* amount to nothing other than *capacity*.
>
> (p. 247e)

This statement is of crucial importance in this book and for the dispositionalist
approach in general. The reason for that is that it evokes the very *reality principle*[7]
that the disposition ontology accepts, conveys and goes by.

According to the Eleatic, there is unmistakably some kind of close link between
"causal" powers and *being*. What something *is* can and should be *identified* via what
it *does or has the capacity to do*. It is not as if something is what it *is* and then
subsequently has behaviour glued to its identity. Properties that have no capacity
to do anything have difficulty passing this reality test. They are not real. Therefore:
to understand what something *is*, is to understand what it *does and can do* – i.e. to
understand its behaviour or behavioural capabilities. To *understand* what is real is
therefore to understand the (*de re*) possibilities of beings. A being has capacities to
do different things – and the things it is able to do characterize its being. This is
what those engaged in science or in the production of any other knowledge system
should keep in mind, according to this reality principle.

Broadly, an empiricist would have a different reality principle, consisting of
whether something is *überhaupt* accessible to our *senses* or not. Something is
spherical if it appears spherical (given a geometrical definition: having a surface
where all points are equidistant to the centre). According to the dispositionalist,
however, something is spherical if it has the causal powers of a sphere, or if it
behaves as a sphere does in a given temporal state (Mumford 2009, 2 and 3).
Dispositions are properties that are causally potent in this way (Mumford and
Anjum 2011). This leaves "other properties", such as categorical properties, in an
awkward status: either they are (really) dispositional, or they are redundant – out
of work (Mumford 2007a, 83). They are properties that don't pass the Eleatic
reality test (see also Mellor 1974 and Bird 2006 for the same argument). This issue
will be discussed in a more detailed manner in the chapters to follow.

3.1 Real potentiality?

De re potentiality is about reclaiming what the mediaeval philosophers called
natura naturans. According to *Historisches Wörterbuch der Philosophie*, the
differentiation between *natura naturata* and *natura naturans* originates from Arabic
and Latin translations of Aristotle. This translation fit well with the "Judeo-
Christian doctrine, the distinction between Creator and the created" (Glacken
1967, 196). A central issue for the mediaeval philosophers was the question:
should we worship God through his "ongoing potent creativity" or his product
(ibid., 167ff)? Should this product (*natura naturata*) be taken as an exemplar of his

greatness and divinity,[8] and should we take this product to be a starting point for the better understanding of God ("interpretationism") (ibid., 206f, 232)? On this account, the *activity* and potentiality of things that Aristotle designated for the substances *themselves* would be something that could be traced back to the divine and the concealed powers of God (ibid., 229).[9] In other words, what we see is the product; what is concealed is the creation – the potent creativity underlying the product. The story seems to go like this: the active potent powers that Aristotle attributed to the things themselves (the *hylo-morphian* view) were attributed to God in mediaeval times. Later, when God's role was considered to be that of initiating the creation and of giving rules for the behaviour of things (laws), the *natura naturans* was reduced to such laws (e.g. Schneewind 2003, 81). (Even later in this story God is no longer seen as a necessary part of the picture – believing in the big bang theory or something similar seems nowadays more rational.) Thus, we are now left with the *natura naturata*, passive and inert entities that are *determined by laws* or what Hume preferred to call constant conjunctions. The reader will hopefully see throughout chapters 3 and 4 that the dispositional ontology is able to "internalize" *natura naturans* again – without invoking either Aristotelian telos or "God the Creator".

The status of potencies or propensities is thus a crucial question in this book. If the modal status of *de re* potentiality can be reduced to so-called 'logical possibility' or 'logical necessity', then we will have failed to show how this ontology can underpin an idea of real potentialities in nature, and by that also the fact that 'nature is active'.

How can something that is only potentially X or Y, nevertheless be real? Dispositions seem to be something like "not yet actual", or what is frequently called 'unactualized possibilia' ('dis-positions'). Dispositions apparently cannot be touched or smelled in a four-dimensional world. Dispositions therefore seem to have a kind of ghostly existence. And if they are reduced to or seen as conditional claims (propositions) – where "dispositions" are seen as propositions about a possible (or actual) behaviour of some entity – then most of us will hesitate to place them in the realm of the real. Instead we will be apt to agree with Nicholas Rescher's statement that "Only actual things or states of affairs can unqualifiedly be said to exist, not those that are possible but unrealized. By definition, only the actual will ever exist in the world, never the unactualized possible" (1973, 215). So what can make us divorce dispositional possibility from logical possibility or mere possibility? This is, of course, a huge question to which there are no easy answers. But the dispositionalist insists that dispositions are actual even though they are not manifested.

The distinction between a disposition and its manifestation is crucial to the dispositionalist. In fact, it is this distinction that secures the very actuality and reality of the disposition. The dispositionalist would normally say that it is the manifestation that has conditions, or is conditional, while the disposition itself is unconditional. That dispositions are unconditional, i.e. that they 'exist independently of everything else', is taken to be a crucial argument for saying that they are real (including when they are not manifested). "When I say that a particular sugar-cube is soluble ... I am saying that it is actually soluble now, not that it could be soluble if some other condition obtained" (Mumford 1998, 64). Let's say that I buy a camera, and a friend of mine smashes it on the floor. I would assume that it had the disposition to take pictures even though that disposition was lost after the smash. This assumption is why I would expect to get a new camera from the person who smashed it. Dispositions are in this sense *said to be* actual properties that support *de re* potentialities (ibid., 74).

The best examples of this crucial point can be taken from the area of risk and risk assessment. We take precautions against risk in a way that assumes that dispositions are something that continuously exists. We don't take precautions in a way that assumes that dispositions occur only at the moment they manifest. The *risk* does not come into existence when it is manifested – it is something we acknowledge, prepare for, and act on before it is manifest, or else we would not call it a risk but something else.

For example, we ski in a way that assumes that the disposition for avalanches is there (or is not there) all along. The security system of an atomic power plant assumes by its very existence that the disposition for an uncontrolled meltdown is there *now* (Mellor 1974). There is nothing ghostly about having the disposition for "adaptability" for example. If something lacks adaptability *now*, it will not be able to adapt now. A stone, for example, lacks the capacity to adapt and therefore has no adaptability *now*. It is *logically* possible that a stone could adapt, but it is not a *de re* possibility, i.e. a dispositional possibility. If this sheet of paper is not "readable" *now*, it will not be readable when I turn on the light either.

Dispositions are universals (or, alternatively, tropes) that are actual "even when they are not actualized". This means that manifestations should be *isomorphic* to their dispositions, which is to say that a given disposition can only manifest in one way (e.g. Molnar 2003, 60 and 195). Assuming this isomorphic relationship, we can assert that a certain bearer ("thing") has the dispositions that it is said to have when the dispositions are manifested. If an "electron" does not display negative charge under prescribed conditions, it does not have negative charge (which eventually would make most of us doubt that it really is an electron – but that is a different issue). If we were to say that a given disposition could have different manifestations, we would not be able to identify the disposition through its manifestation. If the *same* properties could do different things, they would need to operate with some kind of property essence or a so-called *quiddity* to keep their identities intact throughout their different doings, the presumption of which would be highly undesirable for a dispositional account.

When we test whether a certain entity has a certain disposition and we find that under the prescribed conditions it does not manifest in the expected way, we will be right in inferring that the object does not have that disposition. By accepting this implication we can assert that objects or bearers that do different things do not have the same properties.

This brings us directly to another argument in favour of the claim that dispositions are real. We can be wrong about disposition-ascriptions. We can scientifically investigate whether or not some entity has a postulated disposition, and we can be wrong in what we expect to find. Consider, for example, the disposition-ascription "heal-ability". Some say that a homeopathic pill has the ability to heal, while others would disagree. Some would say that it is possible to recover from certain types of illness with the aid of "healing hands", while others would dismiss this as a possibility. What makes the ascriptions of such dispositions true? The question is certainly not whether or not it is logically possible that there exist such dispositions; the question is whether these are real potentialities or not.

A certain entity may have a wide array of properties (dispositions) that are not manifested at a particular moment. In fact, any entity will at all times have an infinite "sum total" of (possibly un-manifested) dispositions (Martin 2007, 31–32). Thus even though a dispositionalist is a realist, s/he is not necessarily committed to the *finite description thesis*.[10] However, this point must be sharply distinguished from saying that entities can have just *any* disposition, and also from the idea that some dispositions are essential to the object in question. The fact that we cannot give a definite list of the properties for a given entity does not mean that, for instance, a stone can *fly*. When it comes to essentialism, there are several philosophers who would say that dispositionalism favours this older ontological position (e.g. Ellis 2001, 2002), while others might disagree. It is certain, however, that dispositionalism does not imply that we are committed to either essentialism or conversely some kind of nominalist ontology.

3.2 Categorical properties

In discussing the nature and status of categorical properties I am motivated by at least three reasons: (1) they are an important or rather indispensable part of the general debate about dispositions; (2) they play an important role in the position that I seek to develop here; and not least (3) they are an important part of the debate about reductionism that I intend to show can be most accurately highlighted and discussed in the context of the more specific debate about dispositions.

As we may have seen already, the parties to the disposition debate have dedicated a lot of time to the issue of whether or not dispositions are real. For the purpose of this book, we may sum up the arguments presented thus far in the following way. Dispositions are real. This means that dispositions are what they are and exist in the way that they do independently of the conditions surrounding the object that does or does not carry them. This means that dispositions are *intrinsic*. To say that something has a particular property, e.g. the floor is 'slippery', is to say something about what the floor is like right now independently of whether someone actually slides on the floor here and now or not. This dispositional property can be tested. Such testing is not, *in principle*, different from the test that we would have to perform to see whether the proposition 'there is a dog next door' is correct or not. The reality of the potentiality is secured by something that is actual, and the potentiality has an existence that is independent of its manifestation under particular conditions; dispositions are properties that exist unconditionally. What the dispositionalist is saying then is that dispositions are *intrinsic* (to the bearer), a notion that, as we will discover, is a central concept for the issues that are raised by this book.

This way of defining dispositions, i.e. the stressing of un-conditionality/ intrinsicness, does not differ from the way in which categorical properties are defined. Categorical *means* un-conditional (Mumford 1998, 64).[11] The categorical monist does not accept the statement that dispositions are intrinsic, because she thinks that it is the categorical properties that are responsible for this apparent intrinsicness. According to the categoricalist, the examples (e.g. nuclear power plant) that are typically used to underpin the intrinsicness of dispositions do not show that dispositions are real; they might as well show that dispositions are only *ways to describe* how categorical properties determine the behaviour of the things involved.

A categorical monist thinks that it is the categorical properties that determine the behaviour of the entity or the "dispositional properties", and which make the dispositions *seem* intrinsic (Armstrong 2005, 315). For the categorical monist, our world has only one type of property, and that type of property is categorical. To explain why things with such properties *behave* the way they do, we have laws at our theoretical disposal. Dispositions are thus seen as preliminary and nominal placeholders for something that eventually should be explained by scientific inquiry as "*arrangement and interaction of small bodies*" and the laws that govern them (Quine 1974, 10). Quine formulates this view as follows:

> The dispositional idiom … forms families of terms not on the basis of structural or causal affinities among the physical states or mechanisms that the terms refer to, but on the basis of a sameness of style *on our own* part in *earmarking* those states or mechanisms.
>
> (ibid., 11, my emphasis)

For instance, when the categorical state of "feeling sad now" is detected in the neural interactions of the brain, then the phrase 'feeling sad now' is needed as an *earmark* for detecting that categorical base. Further, the categorical monist will say that dispositions are what they are in virtue of their categorical base, where 'in virtue of' literally means 'be-cause of' (Quine 1974, 8).

Trained philosophers will see that this position is one way to formulate what we would normally call a materialist or physicalist ontology (although this does not mean that all physicalists are categorical monists: you *can* also be a dispositionalist and a physicalist). This specific debate between those who are categorical monists and those who think that dispositions are irreducible and real properties gives us an opportunity to see the older debates about physicalism, materialism, reductionism, etc. in a somewhat fresh and new light.

First we need to ask what categorical properties are. The purported real-ness of categorical properties has been poorly questioned in comparison to that of dispositions. What are they?

> Now consider the so-called categorical properties. It is quite difficult to find, anywhere in the literature, a specification of what exactly is intended by 'categorical property' and it is symptomatic of the vagueness of the distinction accepted thus far that a number of different things are usually put forward as

examples of the categorical. The list of ontological categories includes occurrences, episodes, shapes, structures, and molecular substructures. Most obviously, but least committally, a categorical property is any property which is not a dispositional property – a contrast which cries out for the addition of some positive content.

(Mumford 1998, 75)[12]

My view is that categorical properties are designated as properties that are somehow necessarily manifesting "their full potential" (Mumford 2007b, 77). This has to do with their main distinctiveness, which is their postulated independence, i.e. that they exist independently of everything else. In this case, this means that there is nothing "within" or about the properties that could contribute to any further change. They are unchangeable and have no further potential to be changed by external conditions. If they could, they would be dispositional. They are truly unconditional.

However, being unconditional in this way also means that they can "do nothing", and a theory that cannot account for what *happens* in the world is a bad theory. "Purely categorical properties like shape, arrangement and symmetry … will not determine that something should happen next, rather than nothing" (Franklin 1986, 63). Categorical properties are therefore often linked to laws. No categorical property, taken alone, affects anything else (Mumford 2004, 175); it would need laws for its actions or its animation (ibid.). "Categoricalism about properties goes hand in hand with the view that laws are contingent and "tell" the properties what to do (or describe the patterns of regularity they happen to be parts of)" (Bird 2007, 44). When something happens, it happens because some law "tells the property" to do X. If laws are changed, the same property will do something else. In a different world, with different laws, we could have laws such that electrons would do different things. This is highly favourable, says the categorical monist (at least Armstrong and Lewis), because it means that properties can be recombined in an almost endless arrangement, depending upon the laws that govern them. This also goes to show their "passivity". (In a dispositional-monist world, by contrast, the property does what it does and cannot do anything else.) For David Lewis this aspect of categoricalism combines very well with his idea (the Humean idea) that the world consists of distinct properties that have an endless potential for combination and recombination. Hence he does not think that laws exist in themselves.

If a categorical monist does not add laws, he or she is a so-called Megarian. This expression – 'Megarianism' – goes back to Aristotle, who criticizes a school of thought that in his mind applies especially to "philosophers from Megara". (A common label for this philosophy today is actualism.) Megarians think, according to Aristotle, that capacities or potentialities (*dunameis*) do not exist, or rather that something has its properties only when they are actualized or manifested. Aristotle makes fun of this school when he says that the carpenter gains his capacities (dispositions) whenever he engages in carpentering and uses his hammer, and then *loses* his capacities whenever he drops the hammer on the floor. More broadly, according to Aristotle, it means that

[A]nything not currently happening will lack the capacity to happen ... So our brilliant Megarian friends will now have done away with all generation and process ... [I]f something is currently sitting it is never going to arise.

(*Metaphysics* Θ 3, 1047a)

This also shows why a (true) Humean faces a problem when s/he rejects the notion of laws. Laws determine what the things could possibly do. The ontological category "laws" is the price you have to pay for a passivist description of the beings that exist. (It is, however, also possible to have a passivist ontology that is also dispositional, see Groff 2013.) To reformulate: in a categorical monist world we are faced with pure matter that is animated by the laws that govern this matter. This is what one gets if one follows the physicalist/materialist intention all the way through its implicative lines.

There are, of course, a number of problems connected to this position.

(a) The first problem deals with an important but theoretical issue, namely what the identities of such properties are. If they are something that laws work upon, then they must be something in themselves, independent of the laws. They must have some kind of "specific–unspecific" being. They must be quiddities, which is a highly unfavourable thing to be! (Black 2000). "The matter is straightforward for categorical monism, for on that view the identity of categorical properties is primitive and so is primitive determinate. This is just what is meant by saying that they are quiddities" (Bird 2007, 138).[13]

A general argument against categorical monism is to draw attention to the fact that dispositions and categorical bases can vary independently of each other. Dispositions can for instance have 'multiple-realizers' as Hilary Putnam says (1975, see also Mumford 1998, 102). This is meant to show that dispositions are not determined by their categorical base. If there are no determining relations between the categorical properties and behaviour (dispositional properties), and we cannot say that the categorical base (+ laws) accounts for the behaviour of the bearer, or that dispositions are placeholders, then we cannot say that the behaviour (manifesting dispositions) is determined by categorical properties.

(b) There are countless examples of situations in which we may have the same disposition but a different categorical base, or the other way around. One simple example is that we can have different materials filling the same dispositional (functional) role. Both wood and asbestos wallboards can work as protecting surfaces on a house, and both "skin wings" on bats and feather-wings on birds work as wings (i.e. have the same disposition to fly). The story about the so-called "eyeless-gene" may serve as a good example of: (1) how wide-ranging and common this categorical monist view is; and (2) how it fails to be able to account for the situations in which there is obviously no determining relation between the categorical properties and the dispositions. One of the earliest experiments that gave the researchers clear evidence that genes somehow "generate" phenotypic traits were experiments on *Drosophila* (banana fly) wherein the experimenters managed to inhibit the "eyeless-gene" from expressing, and saw that the *Drosophila* became blind. This was used as one of many examples of what is called the central dogma of molecular biology.[14] However, some years later Webster and Goodwin (1996) found that if you let these eyeless banana flies reproduce for some further generations, you see the banana flies regain their eyesight, even though the "eyeless-gene" is still absent. The organism can therefore be seen as having generated a new "categorical base" for the same dispositional property. (See also Punzo et al. 2001.) Situations in which we can see that there is no relationship of determination between a categorical base and a given disposition are widespread in nature. There is, for instance, no determining connection between DNA and the properties of genes. There is no determining relation between the amino acids making up the protein and the way the protein *folds*. And indeed – a determining relation is what is required for this position to work. Otherwise one has to explain why something occurs that exceeds the elements that are present in the base, and why one would want to insist upon a reductionist position that is not borne out in real life.

(c) The main reason why dispositional monists find categorical monism untenable is that its proponents fail to explain how inert categorical properties can give rise to something like dispositions – and if they could (in virtue of laws), they would need to assert the existence of property essences in order to do so (quiddities). The dispositional monist says that the categorical base can be eliminated because it is redundant – it is impossible to define it as an ontological category that is different from the dispositional aspect. If the disposition can be said to have actuality, then even the most "obvious" categorical properties (such as shape and structure) are, upon second thought, dispositional. "To say that something is hard, for example, is tacitly to point to its disposition to behave: it would resist penetration if its surface was pressured" (Mumford 2009, 97). Shapes, structures, etc., all have causal effects, which means that they are, by definition, dispositional! It is therefore impossible to even think of a property that is "fully realized". All properties, insofar as they are properties, are properties that *do* something, and on the Eleatic Stranger principle, that is also what makes them *real*. The most striking argument, therefore, is the argument that if categorical properties play a role that is somehow causal, then they must – for that very reason – be dispositional properties.

The purpose of a commitment to categorical properties is for one to be able to "say" that these properties in some sense and to some extent cause the dispositional properties to be what they are. The chemical bonding of H_2O is supposed to *explain* why water behaves as it does, and *explain* this in the sense that the bonding plays the causal role. But as we have said: the problem is that this role would make categorical properties dispositional in virtue of the definition of dispositional properties as properties that do something. The dispositional monist therefore says about categorical properties: 'We don't know what properties of this type are; if they are something, they would be quiddities. And we don't know what they do, because if they do something they would be dispositions.'

(d) A major advantage for the categorical monist, and a major reason why categorical monism seems intuitively appealing, is that the categorical base can be said to *ground* the dispositions. Without a categorical base, many would say, dispositions are nothing but free-floating potentialities that never get realized. "Why do people think that dispositions must have categorical grounds underlying them? Well the clock tells the time because there is such-and-such an arrangement of little bits inside it" (Blackburn 1990, 62). Without a categorical base or ground, the dispositional properties would be what Armstrong calls "always packing, never travelling" (Armstrong 2005, 314). However, there is a question whether or not this way of thinking is based on a false premise. The idea of a ground or base is also the idea that there is eventually a fundamental ground where everything else is grounded. Is this idea just a metaphysical assumption? Jonathan Schaffer asks this question in his article "Is There a Fundamental Level" (2003). Schaffer starts with an outline of how a so-called fundamentalist (categorical monist) will rely upon the following assumptions:

> The fundamentalist starts with (a) a hierarchical picture of nature as stratified into levels, adds (b) an assumption that there is a bottom level which is fundamental, and winds up, often enough, with (c) an ontological attitude according to which the entities of the fundamental level are primarily real, while any remaining contingent entities are at best derivative, if real at all.
>
> (498)

He attacks (b) by showing or claiming that there are neither logical nor empirical reasons that can make us take (b) as a given. He traces the argument that "there is a fundamental level" back to Newton, and then further back to the atomists, the latter depending analytically on this assumption (ibid., 504). He concludes that *empirically* there are no reasons why we should privilege 'fundamentality' over what he calls 'infinite descent' when we choose our metaphysical positions (ibid., 505–506 and 512).

> Should we not discover a complete microphysics (or should we at least continue to discover ever deeper novel structures) this would provide evidence for infinite descent. Should we discover a complete microphysics, this would then provide for supervenience-only fundamentality and allow for fundamentalism and Humeanism.
>
> (ibid., 512)

An important point for Schaffer in this paper seems to be to convince current metaphysicians – who, according to him, prefer some version of fundamentality (physicalism, Humean supervenience, epiphenomenalism, atomism) – that they should keep the option of infinite descent alive. As a part of this aim he ends his paper by describing what infinite descent would mean in more detail. "The most striking feature of an infinite descent is that *no level is special*" (ibid., 512). The micro-level is not privileged, because it does not explain anything more than the levels above. They are 'ontologically equal'. "Because there can be no privileged locus of the causal powers, and because they must be somewhere, they are everywhere" (ibid., 513). The point is that there are no entities that specifically govern while others are either supervenient or governed. All entities are both governing and governed.

> So, infinite descent yields an egalitarian metaphysic which dignifies the whole of nature ... I believe that I am both composed of and dependent on certain cells, which are in turn both composed of and dependent on certain molecules, which are in turn both composed of and dependent on certain atoms, which are in turn both composed of and dependent on certain subatomic particles, which are in turn both composed of and dependent on certain quarks and leptons. We just don't know whether this chain stops. But from this perspective it seems obvious that my realness does not in any sense turn on whether there are preons and so on below, or not. To see that there is no evidence for fundamentality is already to regain the macroworld ... [And] once regained, [it] is not easily lost, even should real evidence for fundamentality arrive.
>
> (ibid.)[15]

For the issue being discussed throughout this chapter, Schaffer's view makes a difference when it comes to the asserted necessity of finding a "base for everything else". What should be clear from this is that the metaphysical idea of categoricality depends further upon the metaphysics of (what Schaffer here calls) fundamentality.

(e) One could also ask whether so-called grounding properties really are or could be independent in the designated and relevant sense. Most scientists today agree that the properties that we ascribe to the minute parts of our reality are themselves structure-belonging properties. An electron that is negatively charged is precisely not a property that is un-conditional in the way that the categorical monist assumes that it is. Rather, it is conditional upon the other reciprocal parts on the subatomic level, in such a way that we cannot properly speak about the properties of electrons in isolation. (See e.g. Dorato 2007; Esfelt 2004; Schaffer 2003, 504.) It would not help much to *call* something a categorical property (i.e. "independent") if such properties are totally dependent upon their relations to other parts in the system. If nothing can be singled out as independent, discrete and monadic,[16] then we cannot have an "entity" that can do the job of unconditionally grounding the world as we know it anyway.

3.3 Problems for the dispositional monist

The dispositional monist tries to defend the idea that it is things themselves that are active, that the properties of things are not just a passive structural base that external forces work upon, but rather that the things themselves are active in a way that does not call for external determination and animation. This is what makes dispositionalism an alternative to the present-day passivist ontologies of nature, one that in many respects resembles what we have discussed in the previous chapter. And for purely philosophical reasons one might, for the moment, admit that dispositional monism seems stronger than categorical monism. However, dispositional monism has also problems of its own. Our effort to solve these problems will lead us to the position that I will favour and that is a modified type of so-called neutral monism (section 3.6).

There are three main problems for the dispositional monist: (1) how can dispositions be actual? (2) what gives dispositions their identities; and (3) what grounds dispositions?

(1) *How can dispositions be actual?*
The "categoricalist" asserts, as we have already seen, that the "actuality-aspect" is secured by the categorical property. To this Mumford replies:

> By a potency, a power-theorist means a real potentiality and thinks that Armstrong is wrong to say that these are not real. The dispositionalist takes them to be real in their own right, so they do not require to be actualised in their manifestation in order to themselves attain actuality. The Eleatic stranger is on the side of the dispositionalist here.
>
> (2009, 100; see also 2004, 174)

This argument, which we have also seen previously, seems to answer the question. On the other hand, is Armstrong completely wrong in requiring a kind of empiricist test for something to be actual and real? Wouldn't such a test also be strongly in keeping with our intuitions?[17] Is it not something about this pen that exists here and right now (in space and time) that is actual in the "empiricist sense" – an aspect that is *something*, and *then* eventually a readiness for something else – a something that endures independently of conditions? In short don't we need something that '*fills in space*', which is *there* already? (Blackburn 1990, 62.)

Mumford and other dispositional monists say that a disposition carries this actuality already. It is not so, they say, that we first have something actual (*natura naturata*), and then something potential (*natura naturans*) owing its being to this actuality. The point of using the notion of a disposition instead of that of 'mere *possibilia*' is that dispositions are something specific: that a stone on the ground (here on Earth) could start to fly is logically possible, but it is a mere possibility; that the stone can yield nutrients to the surrounding soil, by contrast, is something more than a mere possibility. Dispositions are also specific and real potentialities in the sense that they can be specifically falsified. A mere possibility would be the same mere possibility even if it was tested and the result returned negative, and the reason for that is that it has no actuality. If dispositions were not actual, they would not be specific and not falsifiable. The accusation that dispositions lack actuality seems to be a claim that is raised by those who never accepted that dispositions are something more than mere possibility in the first place.

What seems to be assumed but not clearly spelled out, however, is that a dispositional monist world also needs objects. A *circle* does not have any dispositions, but a ball with circular shape has dispositions (connected to the fact that it is circular). I think that we can all agree that if nothing were manifested in the world, we would not have dispositions either, and it is also generally agreed that dispositions need what the dispositionalist calls bearers (objects) (which is of course counter to Humeanism, whose proponents claim that "properties" are the only real entities of the world). Bearers are something that is manifested, here and now, but bearers are not properties. Although bearers are a part of any dispositional account, bearers and the role of bearers have not really been focused on in the disposition literature (something that could be attributed to the fact that analytical philosophy is dominated by Humeanism and therefore by scepticism towards 'objects' in general). Many of the questions that are implied and many of the intuitions that are not accounted for here can be addressed by paying more attention to the fact that the manifestation of a set of dispositions must result in some kind of object or process, and that this object or process is (of course) not the same as a disposition. We will return to this in greater detail later. (See sections 4.4–4.6.)

(2) *What identifies the disposition (if its manifestation is just a new disposition?)*
This is the problem of regress: if we assume that all properties are dispositions, we will have the following situation. If disposition A is a disposition to do B, but B is a disposition to do C and C is a disposition to do D, then we do not really know what disposition A is a disposition for, i.e. we do not know its identity because it is not fixed by anything. We said that a disposition is isomorphic to its manifestation, but if the manifestation is yet another disposition there will be no way to identify the disposition. It is therefore said that any search for the *identity* of a disposition will plunge us into a vicious regress (Swinburne 1983).

The reply that Mumford gives to this is to state again that this is a problem that "can be turned into an advantage" (2004; 2009, 100), given that we don't anticipate that the identity of the disposition is determined by its intrinsic features, but rather by its relational being. The *way* that Mumford formulates his answer is very much in line with the position that I take in this book, so it is important to give some various examples of how he does it.

> The nature and identity of a property cannot be determined alone ...
> Every property gets its essence in relation to other properties. And given

that there is a finite number of them, on a scientific realism about properties (Armstrong 1978), then that gives us circularity rather than an infinite regress.

(ibid., 101)

The regress is not vicious, says Mumford. He compares the situation to that of a dictionary wherein each word is defined by other words, and wherein this situation poses no problem as long as we can get into the dictionary (circle) (2004, 186). In a more general sense, it is easy to see that this is not only a solution to the identity problem, but also a positive world view. In *Laws in Nature* he formulates it thus:

> The world is analogous to a jigsaw puzzle. Each jigsaw piece can fit with the rest only in one way. It can connect to a number of (all) its neighboring pieces, but its shape and colouring allow only a single place for it in the complete picture … In this sense, the place in the whole picture is necessary to the piece.
>
> (2004, 184)

This is put up in contrast to Lewis's mosaic tiles where "Each mosaic tile is completely self-contained, has all its properties (shape, colour, etc.) intrinsically, has no connection (metaphysical, causal, necessary) with any other tile, and may fit alongside any other tile or tiles to make any picture" (ibid., 183).

Mumford says that his jigsaw metaphor catches the main point of accounting for identity, but he adds that it is inexact in some other ways (i.e. the metaphor does not catch the way in which each piece has its particular way of being "intrinsic" and the way in which relations can be less rigorous than the metaphor suggests).

Another response to the regress problem that adds an additional aspect to the relational view that we will explicitly argue for in the next part of this book, is the following:

> [T]his position has a relativistic nature. No property has an essence independent of the relation it bears to other properties. Hence, to be a property F is just to bear certain relations to all the other properties, G, H, I … in virtue of the causal powers of F (and reciprocally the powers of G, H, I …) A property/power F must be a property/power for a further property/power, partly because *this is what it is to be a property*. Without bearing such relations, F would not be a property… How, otherwise, would the property F have any nature? This nature is relative to other properties, and each of those has its nature relative to the others. This might lead one to think that no property has any nature. We have seen, however, how a notion of absolute spatiotemporal location has become replaced by a notion of relative spatiotemporal location. A relative

location is good enough and so too is a relative nature for properties. Given that the alternative is an absolute nature, a notion that seems hard to defend or even conceptualize, we should accept relative natures.

(Mumford 2007c, 148; my emphasis)[18]

What Mumford first and foremost maintains here is that the identity of something and the identity of the properties of things are not determined by some intrinsic inert essence (quiddity), but rather by the relational whole of which the entities are a part (on this aspect see also Bird 2007, 139).[19]

An obvious problem that Stephen Mumford does not address here is the problem of holism. If something is defined by its relation to other things, how can there even be some*thing* at all. A relational account demands that there is something that is related, but how do we guard against the *relata* disappearing into the *relation*? This is an issue that we will discuss at length in Chapter 4.

A more obvious solution to the problem stated here is, as we have seen, to say that the manifestation of a disposition is not a further *disposition*, but rather a (new) bearer (thing) or a process.

(3) *What grounds dispositions?*

A dispositional monist will of course say that any ground, on closer inspection, will be dispositional. "As has been frequently pointed out, if the microstructural properties are themselves dispositional, then this sort of analyses will not by itself achieve any ontological reduction of powers to non-powers" (Molnar 2003, 131). What makes the dispositions endure, and what makes them actual, are properties at lower levels that are *themselves* dispositional, says the dispositional monist. One problem about this argument is that it is developed only as an argument against categorical grounding. While the categoricalist would like to see inert properties that hide nothing and therefore are allegedly not reducible to anything else, and which for that reason seem basic and capable of grounding anything else, a philosopher like Stephen Mumford will ask why we should "accept a fundamental level of properties that is utterly inert and powerless, everything is passive and nothing is active" (ibid.), and further: "How could such a dead world support that which is built upon it? [Lewis calls this Humean supervenience.] How can it produce a world in which things happened?" (ibid.). The main argument is therefore that a dispositional ground is a better alternative than a categorical grounding. The question is: why should the disposition ontology be a part of this "grounding discussion" at all? Whether one thinks that dispositions can ground themselves or whether one thinks that they need categorical properties, it may be useful to ask if this is really a question that the dispositionalist must answer. Might it not be the case that the dispositional monist has been lured into a quarrel where the terms of the problem have been defined by the categorical monist, and where one seems to be forced to come up with some discrete monadic entity 'at the bottom' as an answer to their metaphysically loaded questions? (Cf. Schaffer (2003) opinion discussed above.)

3.4 Combined views

Combined or mixed views are, as we have said, views where categorical and dispositional properties equally belong to a description of the world as it is. These combined or mixed views can come in either the dualist or the monist variant.

3.4.1 Property dualism

Stephen Mumford identifies three aspects of such a position that must be taken into consideration when we want to identify a dualist view (1998, 95ff). *The first aspect* is the idea that there are two ontological types of properties in the world; e.g. there is a way that beings behave and there is a way that they are structured. *The second aspect* is the idea that the one type of property cannot be effectively or principally reduced to the other in such a way that talking about the one type of property would really just be a way to speak about the other. *The third aspect* is the idea that even though there is no completely shared *identity* between the two types of properties, the dualist must be able to provide an explanation for how they are connected (Mumford 1998, 98).

The last provision seems a bit strange, however. Wouldn't we rather say that the dualist holds the view that we cannot (typically) provide an explanation for how these properties are related? The relationship has to be contingent in some way. If they are connected by identity they would not be ontologically different. If they are causally connected in the way that one causes the other to come about, then one of the properties would be reducible to the other. And likewise, if they are connected 'by supervenience', then one of them would be reducible to the other again (i.e. something that explains another thing cannot be identical to that which it explains, but that which is explained can still be reduced in terms of causation or supervenience).[20] A true dualist must believe in the possibility that inert, fully actualized properties like categorical properties can ground dispositions. If you believe in external laws or supervenience you cannot be a dualist. If you believe in categorical properties and think that dispositions are more than this you are a (masked) dualist.

At this point we have touched upon an important, difficult and continuously overlooked tendency that shapes the debate on dispositions. The majority of dispositionalists who are labelled dualists, neutral monists and even dispositional monists are in some way or other categorical monists. The reason why I argue that this is the case is because, as we will see later, the only way to secure the realness and independence of dispositions is to argue that they are relational. But most dispositionalists think, without qualification, that they are intrinsic, and will therefore have to say that reductionism is the only way to secure the independence and realness of dispositions.

In the (dualist) literature it is often the case that dispositions are, in the first instance, assumed to be *de re* properties of the world – for example, via the argument that a categorical base can be multipe realized. But when the dualist is challenged to account for the relationship between categorical and dispositional properties, s/he is more or less forced to back out to develop different arguments that in the second instance *reduce* these properties to categorical bases. U.T. Place (1996) is, as far as I can see, notoriously ambivalent in this sense. On the one hand, he assures the reader that dispositions cannot be reduced to categorical properties (ibid., 60); on the other hand, he says that dispositions are (fully) "caused by" the categorical base (ibid., 115).

In most cases the alleged dualist position seems to end in categorical monism, therefore. This means that there are at least two types of categorical monist: one who openly admits to his or her position, and one who is in disguise. Their common denominator is reductionism.

The problem that I see with this debate is that it hinders us from further exploration of the issue that is at stake here. It seems that the dualist label scares off those who initially grant that dispositions are different from categorical bases. They either fall back on the position that dispositional properties can be reduced after all (causally or by supervenience), or they say that it is the categorical base that is the problem and that what is posed as categorical is really dispositional (identity). If, instead, we can show or convince ourselves that these two types of property are connected in *another* way (not by identity, not by causation, not by supervenience), that will invite further exploration of the question of how dispositions come about if they do not come about in virtue of their categorical base.

3.4.2 Neutral monism

Neutral monism is the position that Stephen Mumford holds in his book on dispositions (1998). 'Neutral' for not giving priority to one property over the other, and 'monism' for the arguable fact that the difference between the two types of properties is not a difference in "ontological category". This view is a modification of C.B. Martin's 'limit-view' (sometimes called the 'two-sided view', 1994, 184).

Martin's 'limit-view' seems to be a different way to handle the issues discussed in the monism/dualism debate. Although the following is not expressly argued for by Martin or by anyone else, one may interpret Martin as saying that dispositions and categorical properties are *formally* related concepts. What Martin in any case *says* is that dispositionality and quality ("categorical properties") are *aspects* of what we call properties. This actually resembles the way form and matter are *formally* related in Aristotle's *Hylomorphean* view (section 2.1). Martin says:

> To speak of a qualitative property is to take some real property at the limit of only its potency-free pure act of being, which of course it never is; To speak of a dispositional property is to take some real property at the limit of only its capacities and dispositions, which of course it never is ... The limit view should not suggest that there are degrees of dispositionality or quality of some real property ... It isn't that an intrinsic property or quality is purely qualitative but dispositionality is "supervenient" on it. Properties are indissolubly qualitative-cum-dispositional or dispositional-cum-qualitative. The dispositional is as basic and irreducible as is the qualitative and there is no direction for one's

being basic in a property and the other supervenient. To separate one from the other as the really basic property is philosophical artifice and error.

(1996, 132–133)

Translated into a modal vernacular (which might not capture the full complexity of the discussion), we might say that if we are talking about something that is actual (an actual structural state), we also always imply something about how this can and will dispose towards certain outcomes (the possible behaviour of …), and if we are talking about something being a disposition we also always already imply something being "actual". It seems that Martin suggests that the concepts that are discussed typically transcend the empirical investigation of their content. The fortunate thing about this is that he (indirectly) shows that it would be a mistake to think about connectedness as if that had to be done in terms of causal, supervenient or law-based connectedness. Therefore, questions regarding whether these properties are necessarily connected or contingently connected, or whether or not one of them is determining the other, etc., do not pose the issue correctly, since the dispositional and the categorical are always already connected in the first place. The one cannot ontologically go without the other. They are formally connected.

This is how I interpret Martin, although I have seen that others have interpreted his position to be that dispositions and qualities are identical (Armstrong 2005; Engelhard 2010). It would be strange if Martin's position were to come down to this, since it would immediately fall prey to the objection "How can the two features (properties) be specified as both being distinct and yet identical?" (Engelhard 2010).

So far so good, but how can we use this view as more than a suggestive guidance for thinking about these matters? Martin provides no cases to support his position other than examples such as "The dispositionality and quality of any intrinsic property is similar to the way shape and size are of extension", which are not very helpful for those who want to think that he is talking about one of the most important questions in metaphysics and science and is saying something beyond how we should *talk about* this relation. The view that he proposes in this debate therefore remains an indicative gesture. In other words, we are back to Aristotle and perhaps Kant,[21] but without any reference to either Aristotle or Kant, or the substantive discussion that they themselves felt obliged to provide in *their* versions of this 'limit-view'.

However, the neutral monist (Mumford 1998) is more than willing to fill out this formal principle with the substance that Martin lacks.

Mumford (1998) formulates his view in the following way:

Reductionism in either direction is both unnecessary and an incorrect way of looking at the relationship between the dispositional and the categorical. What we have are two different ways of denoting the same properties. One way is in terms of what possibilities those properties bestow on their possessors. The other incorporates a wider class of descriptions involving features such as shape, structure and molecular structure. [This is] … two modes of presenting the same instantiated properties.

(p. 190)

The substance that I claimed that Martin did not provide (but Mumford does) comes in the form of a merger between the limit-view *and* a theory of levels:

> [N]ature consists of hierarchically ordered levels where at each level there are entities and properties that can be characterized dispositionally or structurally and whether they are dispositional or structural characterizations depends on their explanatory relations to other entities or properties within the whole of which they are a part.
>
> (ibid., 214)

The incorporation of *levels* into the categorical/dispositional issue is to my mind crucial for this account to work. The incorporation amounts to something like this: *The categorical is not a property in its own right; it is just something that is categorical in* **relation** *to what is dispositional on "the level above".* Seen at "its own level", it is dispositional. Water has dispositions and the categorical base for these dispositions is to be found at the level below, the molecular level (H_2O). H_2O, on the other hand, has dispositions, and the categorical bases for these dispositions are found on the level below, i.e. the atomic properties making up the molecule H_2O, etc.

If someone asks: "but how are dispositions and categorical properties related?" we can answer, with Martin, that they were never unrelated. Since they are already connected, we are not committed to saying one thing or the other about contingency or physical necessity (Martin 1996, 135). They are formally (not contingently or necessarily) related such that if you talk about one aspect, you immediately also imply the other. Talking about how water really behaves (dispositions) does not exclude the fact that it *is* structured *one way or the other*. But saying that it is somehow structured and takes up a place in space does not tell us what this structure will necessarily do (dispositional aspect).

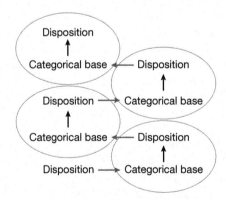

Figure 3.1 Dispositions can become categorical bases. Simple model representing the merging of level theory with neutral monism. What is a disposition on one level may become a categorical base for dispositions on the level above.

The difference this makes is that such a view does not *prevent* us from saying that, e.g. the categorical base determines the disposition or vice versa (in general or in some specific instance); it just *prevents* us from saying that they are fundamentally related *in virtue* of the one determining the other, or fundamentally unrelated *in terms* of the one being contingently dependent upon the other.

I support neutral monism in this book, and one of the reasons is that there is a way to say that *the categorical base does not determine the disposition without also implying that there is no relation, which would otherwise lead us into dualism.*

On this account we are not committed to answering the question of how the one can exist totally independently of the other, as we would be if we were to claim that the relationship is causally contingent (e.g. how could the mind behave in a way that is not determined by the neural structure of the brain?). Another example of a formal connection is the fact that to say that shape does not determine size does not imply that shape and size are not connected.

A problem for the debate has been exactly this issue: that the participants (and even Martin and Mumford themselves) have not appreciated that the limit-view is one that does not require its defenders to explain how the two aspects are related in terms of necessity, contingency causation and/or supervenience. This said, the lack of clarity is understandable since categorical properties have filled the "actuality-role" in this debate. It is understandable that Alexander Bird says that he "cannot agree with Martin or Heil" on their limit-view, and that "properties must be one or the other", *since* categorical properties are seen to be fully inert properties that need laws for their animation. If they are already posed as something separate and fully inert they would need laws, not dispositions. Bird's move into dispositional monism is therefore more than understandable. The standard interpretation tells him that categorical properties are part of a completely different account. This is a question that we will investigate in forthcoming chapters. But for the moment, we will have to put this special definition of the limit-view into semi-brackets, because it will be too messy to bring this into the discussion before the current debate is concluded.

3.5 The categorical and dispositional revised

In the course of this discussion, we have come close to the conclusion that the categorical/dispositional distinction is semantically confused. I think that this is correct in the sense that "traditional categoricality" belongs to a discourse that is different from the discourse that underscores the reality of dispositions, and that bringing these concepts together and treating them as if they did belong to the same theoretical whole leads to a confusion wherein semantics covers up deeper disagreements. I believe, as the discussion above has shown, that there is a real problem related to the *endurance* of the disposition, which I don't think that Mumford or any other dispositional monist has solved.

This is what I have chosen to call *the problem of intrinsicality*. What makes it possible for dispositions to endure "in-between their manifestations"? It seems that there indeed must be something that "fills in space" – something that is present here and now, which is not dispositional as such. But is this 'something' categorical properties? If it were, we would still need to deal with the problem of how inert, fully actualized properties can give rise to potencies like dispositions – and also, therefore, with a type of dualism and with the related problems of how these two ontological categories can eventually be connected. (This is a problem that categorical monists have created for themselves, and which they are currently trying to mend with a series of nomothetical theories or other technicalities.)

We saw in section 3.2 that the categorical monist was committed to the following three points:

1   Discrete non-related properties.
2   Unrestricted compossibility.
3   Behaviour accounted for by contingent laws.

All of these commitments show that categorical properties are at odds with a world of dispositions, and they explain why the dispositional monist has abandoned categorical properties altogether, but they also explain why the dispositional monists unfortunately face the problems that they do.

The *dispositional* monists seem to think that opening the door for the main *intuition* that underlies the *categorical* monist view ('filled in space') will lead to a resurrection of categorical properties (as defined by the categorical monists). They are therefore suspicious of the "filled-in-space speculation" in general. There is a reason why the dispositional monist still "worries about" categorical properties and uses every opportunity to pose their own view in contradistinction to it, although it is acknowledged (see Bird 2007) that this account is far from being a relevant part of a dispositional account *in the first place*. I believe that the reason for it is that the dispositional monist has not yet found a way to account for the intrinsicness problem. As we have said, it does not help to *say* that dispositions endure, or to postulate that they are actual or that it would be absurd to think that they are not intrinsic (Molnar 2003, 108). It must be shown concretely how dispositions can endure between their manifestations.

Thus, in presenting the main problems facing the dispositional monist view, I have framed the case in such a way that the following three points come out as plausible:

#1   The "categoricalists" have a legitimate complaint with respect to their 'filling in space' concern, which dispositional monists have not yet managed to answer in a satisfying manner.
#2   The arguments for categorical properties and dispositions come from different ontological regimes, regimes that cannot be combined. Categorical properties as defined in this debate can/should not be used for the 'filling in space' role.
#3   The arguments that the dispositional monist has against the categoricalists' claims are somewhat weak in the sense that they rest *too much* on apagogical arguments, which is not a promising way to proceed if we accept #1 and #2.

We have now finally arrived at the point at which the introduction of *enduring manifestations* seems opportune. Enduring manifestations have some traits that are similar to categorical properties, in that they are something that can be said to be "actual" in the intuited sense, and that can be said to be categorical in the *level-specific neutral monism* sense specified above (see section 3.6). They are not, however, categorical in the Lewis/Armstrong sense because they are "relationally created" and are of course much more concrete than Lewis/Armstrong categorical properties in that they are *manifestations of dispositions*.

There are a few places in the current literature where notions like enduring manifesting dispositions are mentioned (e.g. Mumford 2006, 481), but we have yet to see any systematic way in which the question of manifestations as such has been worked out fully (i.e. providing something like a "philosophy of manifestations"). Enduring manifestations may be thought to give us a rather dull and demystified answer to this huge "highflying" metaphysical question, but I think that if it is simple and it works, then it has an advantage over the alternatives. We do not have to add anything more; rather we have only to explicate the role of the metaphysical concepts that this ontology *already* operates with (cf. Occam's razor). This fact also adds a further dimension to what we have said about the connection between "categorical properties" and dispositions. The emphasis of a revised neutral monism view is that this relation is formal. It is formal in the same sense in which the relationship between dispositions and manifestations is formal. (We do not, e.g. ask: "Does the disposition cause the manifestation", since of course 'manifestation' already presupposes 'disposition'.) There cannot be one without the other, yet they are connected by neither causality nor identity.

What seems to be wrong with categorical properties is not that they are categorical. Rather, they are said to be some kind of mystical ground that, for *internal* theoretical reasons, is needed for the role it plays (inert, fully actualized, independent, etc.). If, instead, it could be shown that there are properties that are manifest, and that this manifestation plays a role in *itself*, and that the properties are also relationally constituted – such properties would, to my mind, service the dispositional account in a very suitable manner.

3.6 Modified neutral monism

This might seem to be a dull local debate within one of the many corners of philosophy. I would suggest, however, that what we have discussed are highly potent general questions, which pertain to other parts of philosophy as well as to how we view the world in general. For instance, if we don't have a concept of dispositions, then we will be inclined (as many are) to think that the only alternative to physicalism (and reductionism) is vitalism, spiritualism or something similar. And if we don't have a viable concept of how relationalism could actually work in practice, then we will be sceptical about any kind of holistic idea, seeing it as amounting to some kind of mumbo-jumbo solution. Many scientists stick to some kind of (blurred) physicalist ontology because they cannot see an alternative. Similarly, many explain their religiousness by saying that reductionism cannot explain what they see. If one accepts dispositions as real, which is actually common practice within science today (in terms of #1), it should be of interest that doing so is fully theoretically defensible, and is not just something that one (subtly) encounters through the force of the phenomena. Boring "self-sufficient" philosophical discussions such as the one that we have gone through here are therefore highly needed in, and indirectly called for by, today's situation. A conclusion to the discussion is also required, before we develop our particular view on dispositions further.

Thus far it seems as though we have to be either categorical monists or dispositional monists, because categorical and dispositional properties belong to different theoretical wholes altogether. This is partly right, but also completely wrong, mainly because categorical properties do not have to be categorical in the Armstrong/Lewis sense, but also because given the way in which *we* interpreted the neutral monist view, it is really not in conflict with the *dispositional* monist view.

The neutral monist account has dispositions 'all the way down'. But dispositions can play the role of categorical properties (in the sense of 'filling in space') in virtue of their manifestations. Manifestations "work categorically" in a level-specific sense when that which is manifest is manifest *continually* (but also when manifest for a very short period of time; see section 4.6). The manifestation of the dispositions of H and O is H_2O. This manifestation is the "categorical base" for *water, as long as the manifestation endures. In other words, manifesting dispositions are the very "basis" that has been interpreted as the internal constitution determining the essential properties of the level above.* This is the crucial point that will be worked out in greater detail in section 4.6.

What is still insufficiently accounted for, however, is what kind of "property" the manifestation is. The simple answer to this is to say that "the categorical property" is not a property at all, and that it is not a base that *has* properties either. If it were a property it would be dispositional (here we fully agree with the dispositional monist). If it is a base that *has* properties, it would soon become clear that it would be something that can be defined as such (and then it would be a quiddity). But it cannot. This is exactly the point regarding the *monistic* relation between dispositions and manifestations. Dispositions and manifestations should be reciprocally defined in the most intimate way.

Since there is a kind of "categorical base" involved in this account, the intrinsicness issue will not appear to be as acute as for the dispositional monist. However, this question is very complex. In the next chapter we will try to work out the relational account of dispositions further, and a key question there (in the second half) will be 'If dispositions are individuated by their manifestations, and if all manifestations are a result of relational dispositions coming together, how can they be individuated by something at all?' Therefore, a possible suggestion to a solution of the identity problem will not be fully stated before section 4.6.

By way of these preparations I hope to have established a ground that can allow us to embark on the most important issue to discuss, namely: does the "categorical base" (enduring manifestation) determine the disposition? Even though dispositions and enduring manifestations are not first and foremost related in *virtue of* causation (but rather formally and reciprocally), we must still assume that the enduring manifestation X, compared with manifestation Y, makes *some* difference when it comes to dispositions.

The idea in this chapter was to show how and why the debate over dispositions, their realness and role should lead us in the direction of a modified neutral monist view. In posing the modified neutral monist view I have had at least six "objectives".

1   To display the arguments that show, if only in a preliminary way, that dispositions are real and cannot be reduced to categorical bases or conditionals.
2   To show more carefully why "dispositionalists" say that the identity of a thing is related to what the thing does and is able to do.
3   To show, in a preliminary way, that dispositions can be viewed as relationally constituted.
4   To show, in a preliminary way, that the dispositional monist view is inescapably in need of some "variety" of a categorical base, but not the one that is normally discussed, and that if such an amendment is made, the problems that the dispositional monist faces can be (easily) solved.
5   To show, in a preliminary way, that even if the categorical base does not determine dispositions and their manifestations, we will not end up with a dualist ontology. The reader must decide for him or herself whether or not s/he thinks that this solves many of the classical philosophical questions, which to my mind it does (although that is not the main objective here).
6   To prepare the ground for a relational view that is not 'fully relational'. Emphasizing the role of manifestations is a part of this preparation.

At some point in the following chapters of this book, you will see that I use the expression 'categorical properties' or 'categorical base' where I see that it is needed to bridge the gap between this account and the way categorical properties are normally talked about. Where this bridging is not important, however, I will just use the shorthand expression 'enduring manifestation', or just 'manifestation-aspect'.

Notes

1 Dispositions are also frequently called powers or capacities. Some see it fit to also distinguish between these expressions in terms of content, but I will only engage in that discussion where necessary and will primarily use the term 'disposition'.
2 This is the rough version of a kind of historical review that I learned from Stephen Mumford in a personal communication.
3 There is a comprehensive debate related to this issue of whether dispositions can be reduced to conditionals. (See e.g. Martin 1994; Mumford 1998; Lie 2010.)
4 One could not really say that David Lewis participates directly in this debate and we cannot therefore really say that he can be characterized as a categorical monist. But we might assert that he would have been, given his neo-Humean view on the relation between dispositions and conditionals, his view on laws, and the fact that he thinks that everything (including dispositions) supervenes on point-like properties.
5 Some of these thinkers do not themselves subscribe to dualism, but rather have the position ascribed to them by others; e.g. Mumford (1998) argues that Place and Prior et al., are dualists and e.g. Bird (2007) states that Ellis and Molnar are dualists, or have a

mixed view and cannot possibly be anything "less" than dualists since they state that such properties are totally "unmixable" (see ibid., 44).

6 For an overview of the possible positions held within the field of dispositional ontology, see Bird *Nature's Metaphysics* (2007, 4). Stephen Mumford's book *Dispositions* also contains a much broader and more elaborated and detailed outline of the arguments associated with these positions. Mumford's book is weaker on the pan-dispositional view, but this is certainly due to the fact that this view was not as developed and elaborated when the book was written as it is today (Mellor and Shoemaker being the key exceptions). Mumford himself made a shift in position from a mixed view (called neutral monism: see section 3.4.2) to dispositional monism (2004 chapter 10; and see esp. Mumford 2007c).

7 Eleatic reality test for short – a phrase taken from Armstrong (1997, 41) who has taken it from Graham Oddie.

8 Exemplarism: ibid., 201 and Hegge (1978, 58).

9 And consequently, the road is open to what Keekok Lee calls extrinsic teleology which, according to Lee, is the first step towards a teleology provided by humans – since humans eventually are also regarded (by humans) as the only being which is an end in itself (1999, 47).

10 A finite description thesis is a thesis that there is a finite set of properties (and objects) in the world and that we can reach a point where we have (or can come very close to) a full description of all these properties. The Laplacian demon trades on this thesis. David Lewis takes this thesis for granted when he says that:

> [W]e may reasonably think that present-day physics already goes a long way toward a complete inventory. Remember that the physical nature of ordinary matter under mild conditions is very well understood. And we may reasonably hope that future physics can *finish* the job in the same distinctive style.
>
> (1999, 292, my emphasis)

11 However, etymologically it means *according to the stream of voices at the square* – "*kata-agou-rein*".

12 However, in this book (*Dispositions*) he ultimately concludes that categorical properties have a role to play.

13 Two philosophers who hold the same view of categorical properties are David Armstrong and David Lewis. There is, however, a disagreement between them when it comes to laws. They both agree that laws are contingent. For Lewis, the contingency of laws is what laws are about. Since laws are contingent and the things that they say something about are causally inert, laws must be *external* to the things themselves. But Lewis does not think that laws *govern* the inert things, although he thinks that every possible world somehow has its fixed laws. This means that, for Lewis, the same thing (or rather its counterpart) in world 1 can have a different law (a different behaviour) in world 2. Armstrong thinks that laws can *govern* the relations between distinct entities (relate the universals of state of affairs), but he also thinks that those laws are external to the beings themselves, because he too thinks that they are contingent. The things themselves and how they behave are distinct. They *are* something, but what they are is not specified, before we see the actual laws operating. Their identity is specified by the laws that reign contingently. Properties such as this must have an essence that *is* something, but is so without being specifiable. A *quiddity*. In Lewis's language these are called 'point-like properties'.

14 It was Francis Crick who came up with this phrase expressing the idea that information goes from DNA to RNA to proteins. It is called a dogma because it assumes that there is absolutely no "causality" going the other way around, e.g. proteins cannot cause genes to be the way they are, etc.

15 When reading the article it is not completely clear whether Schaffer's point is simply to show this option or to argue that this is the best option. However, I think that the last

sentence in the quoted statement should convince us that Schaffer is interested in more than just 'showing the option'.

16 See Bird 2007, 139.
17 Engelhard (2010) calls this 'the dualist intuition'.
18 Mumford has developed his relational account in the direction of a vector model, together with Rani Anjum. (See Mumford and Anjum 2011 and section 4.4 and subsection 4.4.1.)
19 Although, as we said previously, the answer Mumford gives here does not seem to be consistent with the answer he gives when he talks about the intrinsicness of dispositions, where grounding dispositions looks more monadic, in the sense that they are self-grounding. We will come back to this in section 5.4.
20 Reductions in terms of laws or supervenience seem to be the best options. If dispositions are reduced by causation, then categorical properties look more like dispositions.
21 I am here thinking of the way "form (twelve categories + time and space) *and matter (Ding an sich)*" *are inevitably/formally* connected, not of the content that is specific for Kant's philosophy.

References

Aristotle (1998) *The Metaphysics* (Trans. Lawson-Tancred), Penguin.
Armstrong, D. (1978) *Universals and Scientific Realism*, Cambridge University Press.
—— (1997) *A World of State of Affairs*, Cambridge University Press.
—— (2005) "Four Disputes about Properties", *Synthese*, vol. 144.
Bird, A. (2006) "Potency and Modality", *Synthese*, vol. 149.
—— (2007) *Nature's Metaphysics*, Oxford University Press.
Black, R. (2000) "Against Quidditism", *Australasian Journal of Philosophy*, March.
Blackburn, S. (1990) "Filling in space", *Analysis*, March.
Dorato, M. (2007) "Dispositions, Relational Properties and the Quantum World", in M. Kistler and B. Gnassounou (eds.) *Dispositions and Causal Powers*. Ashgate.
Ellis, B. (2001) *Scientific Essentialism*, Cambridge University Press.
—— (2002) *The Philosophy of Nature*, Acumen.
Engelhard, K. (2010) "Categories and the Ontology of Powers: A Vindication of the Identity of Properties", in A. Marmodoro (ed.) *The Metaphysics of Powers: Their Grounding and their Manifestations*, Routledge.
Esfelt, M. (2004) "Quantum Entanglement and a Metaphysics of Relations", *Studies in the History and Philosophy of Modern Physics*, December.
Franklin, J. (1986) "Are Dispositions Reducable to Categorical Properties?", *Philosophical Quarterly*, vol. 36.
Glacken, C.J. (1967/1976) *Traces on the Rhodian Shore: Nature and Culture in Western Thought from Ancient Times to the End of the Eighteenth Century*, University of California Press.
Groff, R. (2013) "Whose Powers, Which Agencies", in R. Groff and J. Greco (eds.) *Powers and Capacities in Philosophy: The New Aristotelianism*, Routledge.
Hegge, H. (1978) *Menneske og naturen*, Antropos forlag.
Heil, J. (2003) "Levels of Reality", *Ratio*, September.
Lee, K. (1999) *The Natural and the Artefactual*, Lexington Books.
Lewis, D. (1983) *Collected Papers*, vol. I, Oxford University Press.
—— (1997) "Finkish Dispositions", *The Philosophical Quarterly*, vol. 47.
—— (1999) *Papers in Metaphysics and Epistemology*, Cambridge University Press.
Lie, S. (2010) "Naturalness Reconsidered: Dispositions, Ethics and Ontology, PHD Dissertation, University of Tromsø.

Martin, C. (1994) "Dispositions and Conditionals", *Philosophical Quarterly*, vol. 44.

—— (1996) *Dispositions: A Debate* (with D. Armstrong and U.T. Place), Routledge.

—— (2007) *Mind in Nature*, Oxford University Press.

Mellor, H. (1974) "In defence of Dispositions", *Philosophical Review*, vol. 83.

Molnar, G. (2003) *Powers* (ed. S. Mumford), Oxford University Press.

Mumford, S. (1998) *Dispositions*, Oxford University Press.

—— (2004) *Laws in Nature*, Routledge.

—— (2006) "The Ungrounded Argument", *Synthese*, vol. 149.

—— (2007a) *David Armstrong*, Acumen.

—— (2007b) "Filled in Space", in M. Kistler and B. Gnassounou (eds.) *Dispositions and Causal Powers*, Ashgate.

—— (2007c) "Power, Dispositions, Properties: A Causal Realist Manifesto", in R. Groff (ed.) *Revitalizing Causality: Realism about Causality in Philosophy and Social Science*, Routledge.

—— (2009) "Passing Powers Around", *The Monist*, vol. 92.

Mumford, S. and Anjum, R.L. (2011) *Getting Causes from Powers*, Oxford University Press.

Place, U.T. (1996) *Dispositions: A Debate* (with D. Armstrong and C. Martin), Routledge.

Plato (1997) *Sophist*, in J. Cooper (ed.) *Plato Complete Works*, Hackett Publishing Company.

Prior, E. (1982) "The Dispositional/Categorical Distinction", *Analysis*, March.

Punzo, C. et al. (2001) "The Eyeless Homeodomain is Dispensable for Eye Development in Drosophila", *Genes and Development*, vol. 15.

Putnam, H. (1975) *Mind, Language and Reality, Philosophical Papers*, vol. 2. Cambridge University Press.

Quine, R. (1974) *Roots of Reference*, La Salle Ill., Open Court.

Rescher, N. (1973) "The Ontology of the Possible", in M. Munitz (ed.) *Logic and Ontology*, New York University Press.

Schaffer, J. (2003) "Is there a Fundamental Level", *Nous*, vol. 37:3.

Schneewind, J.B. (2003) *Moral Philosophy from Montaigne to Kant*, Cambridge University Press.

Shoemaker, S. (1980) "Causality and Properties", in P. van Inwagen (ed.) *Time and Cause*, Reidel.

Swinburne, R. (1983) "Reply to Shoemaker", in L.J. Cohen and M. Hesse (eds.) *Aspects of Inductive Logic*, Oxford University Press.

Webster, G. and Goodwin, B. (1996) *Form and Transformation*, Cambridge University Press.

4 Dispositions and relational realism

4.0 Introduction: relational realism

Relational realism is an ontology. I favour relational theories in general, and the current theory in particular, for at least four reasons.

1   First, I favour this theory because I think that relational realism is the best account of how the world looks and really is. What I like about this theory is that it contains more detail and "technical" solutions in terms of how the world is related and how we can and may understand this relatedness than do any competing theories. I have found that the dispositional ontology has elements that make it possible to give a more detailed and "falsifiable" ontological description of the relevant subject matter. Not being able to do so has often been a problem for proponents of relational ontologies, who often are more or less relying on a benevolent reader when claiming that 'everything is connected'.[1]

2   As previously explained, theories of naturalness are often associated with essentialism. To give an account of the nature of something looks very much like describing the essence of that thing. I think that it is simply wrong to make this association. In general terms, the nature of something is connected to the natures of other things, and this is exactly what makes naturalness a contemporary and relevant philosophical subject. The nature of the hen is not to be found inside the hen itself, but in how and why it relates to other organisms and elements in the world. The nature of the hen can only be attended to by attending to those relations that constitute its nature. But it is not enough simply to state that this is the case. We also need to give a detailed and convincing account of why and *how* this is the case. Only an account of this type can convince sceptics and contribute to necessary changes within science, technology and how we relate to nature through management and other types of dealings in general. As we have seen, one of the major reasons why we don't accept naturalness within certain domains today is because it looks ontologically unfeasible. It is therefore unavoidable that rethinking naturalness will require that we consider and develop an alternative ontology that is able to give 'naturalness' a new foothold.

3   I have argued that reductionism is incompatible with a satisfactory concept of naturalness. The 'something' in "treating *something* in accordance with what we call nature" must be something that cannot be reduced, since that would of course make it impossible to "treat it in accordance with its nature". The parts are, on a reductionist account, just discrete "contributor units" that are contingently assembled in order to create the hen. If they are more than that, then the hen would be more than its parts as well, i.e. the parts would not be sufficient to tell me something about how I could *fail and succeed in my efforts to treat something in accordance with what we call its nature".*

Reductionism is a particularly stubborn opponent. Reductionism seems intuitive; it is difficult to spot (in all its facets); and it has a firm and acknowledged ontological basis. What I have found is that only a relational ontology can seriously explain and at the same time challenge reductionism. It is important to challenge reductionism by trying to explain how it works *in the light of an alternative*. In the absence of a viable alternative, one may accept reductionism just because it seems to be the only option or may think that the reductionist account is neutral or non-reductionist when that is not the case. To adhere to a non-reductionist account requires an active and perceptive effort, as reductionist accounts seem to be the default position. My aim is to show how a viable and strong theory like the dispositional theory can truly be an alternative to the many reductionist ontologies that dominate today's science and world views.

4   The last reason why I think that we should accept a relational realist account of the world is that it solves difficult problems within the dispositional theory itself. A potential difficulty that non-technical readers may encounter in this chapter is that I try to give a *general account* of a relational theory of the world through internal debates going on *inside* the domain of dispositional theory. I urge such readers to focus on how these specific discussions and solutions apply to the more general issues of reductionism and naturalness.

4.1 Reductionism and intrinsicality

We can put *empirical* "evidence" on the table to support the idea that given properties cannot be reduced to micro-properties (multiple realization), and we can refer to special phenomena like fractal organization, strange attractors and the quantum hall effect, etc., to argue against a reductionist account (e.g. R.B. Laughlin), but this should not be confused with what would be an ontological argument for the same claims. To my mind, the disposition theory is an ontology that gives its proponents the capacity to defend a non-reductionist position *theoretically*, in contradistinction to the many attempts to do the same by pointing to empirical examples. One of the major advantages that the approach affords is that it helps us to understand *why* wholes and their properties cannot be reduced to their constituents. A universal argument such as this also shows that the irreducibility holds at all levels of nature and that it applies to more than the most typical discussed cases such as whether the mind can be reduced to the brain, social phenomena can be reduced to biological phenomena or whether life can be understood in terms of molecular sciences.

In my view, reductionism is not such a complex question. I believe that the quarrel over different types of reductionism stems from a situation in which there is no viable or compelling alternative to reductionism, and wherein we subsequently cannot find a way to deal universally with empirical findings of phenomena, as for instance found in cases of multiple realization. If we can justify ontologically how and why 'higher-level beings' are and must be as real as 'lower-level beings,' then we will not be forced to permit our theoretical discussion to be guided by *empirical* evidence (underlining only that reductionism is the correct default position, but that "there are unexplainable exceptions").

If we are to assess and really understand how and why, for instance, methodological reductionism, ontological reductionism and theory reductionism work and do not work, we need to have a more general account of what reductionism is. A general theory will also make it easier to see *how and why* constituents on the level below *do* belong as a viable part of any explanation of the phenomena we are talking about, after all (see section 4.6). In my view, the disposition ontology can provide us with such a theory.

We may start the line of argument by claiming that dispositions have a relational nature, and that it is this very relationality that constitutes the irreducibility of the phenomena. I call this position relational realism. The most difficult and profound challenge to this account comes from the concept of intrinsicality. The issue is complicated, and we cannot arrive at a position that would require us to throw away intrinsicness as such. What we need to assess is whether we have understood intrinsicness in the correct way.

As we have previously seen, intrinsicality allegedly refers to properties that something has *independently* of anything else (see e.g. Molnar 2003, 39 and below). It is assumed that this is what it means for something to have properties that belong to the thing itself: *independence*. Intrinsicality therefore presupposes the distinctness-thesis, that things and/or properties can and do exist independently of other things and/or properties, thus making a relational ontology impossible in the first place. Given this premise, it comes as no surprise that the discussion about instrinsicality is not about whether or not properties are or could be independent, but rather about which properties are intrinsic and which are extrinsic. A further premise in this debate is that it is only intrinsic properties that are real. This premise is, as we have seen, vindicated by John Locke, and it has not been seriously challenged since. I have called this the 'Lockean reality test': 'properties that do not depend on their relations to other properties are real'. The distinction between primary and secondary qualities, which is still recognized by many philosophers today, is itself dependent upon or explained by the intuitiveness that comes with intrinsicness. Thus Duncan Pritchard typically explains the difference between primary and secondary qualities in the following way:

> The point is rather that the colour of an object is not intrinsic to the object in the way that its shape is, but instead depends upon there being perceivers who respond to the object with the appropriate visual impressions.

(2006, 80)

When intrinsicality is implicitly used as a synonym for 'real', as is frequently done, one who makes such an equation is thereby committed to an account that has already ruled out relational properties as being real in the first place. On such an account, relational properties are a special type of property that is called an extrinsic property (see below). The easiest way to get a realist ontology out of the dispositional ontology would be to appeal to categorical properties, which are supposed to be independent as such. We have seen that this is what the categorical monist does by pointing to fully actualized properties or minute parts at lower levels.

As we have seen, however, proponents of the dispositional monist ontology also argue that it is a "realist ontology" simply by claiming that dispositions themselves are intrinsic, i.e. independent. This is the reason why I have said that I would prefer to call the realism problem of dispositions "*the problem of intrinsicality*". The fact that dispositionalism seems to depend upon intrinsicality for its realism claims can be seen in George Molnar's *Powers* (2003), wherein he allocates more than one chapter to this issue. Mumford and Alexander Bird also emphasize in several places that 'intrinsicness is essential to dispositions'. (See also *Stanford Encyclopaedia of Philosophy*, 'Dispositions'.)

There is, however, a great deal of confusion surrounding this dispute. On one hand, there seems to be widespread agreement that (most) dispositions are so-called intrinsic; on the other hand, there also seems to be widespread agreement that dispositions are relational.[2] But how can relational properties be said to be intrinsic? This seems to be a contradiction in terms.

Brian Ellis defines intrinsicality in the following way: "it is a property that something has independently of any other thing", adding that a much more precise definition is not easy to obtain (2002, 51). The intrinsic being that something has is the being that we "see" when it is not, according to Ellis, subjected to external stress. When a rubber band is stretched, or whenever some given material is subjected to "what the engineers call stress" it deviates from its natural shape. He adds that actual shapes are often "made up of two *distinct* parts: an underlying intrinsic shape, and a superimposed distortion" (ibid, 52, my emphasis).

Langton and Lewis[3] have a definition that may be regarded by some as more precise than Ellis's. Molnar gives us something that can be considered an improvement to this definition, at least for a dispositional account (2003, 1.4.5).

The common feature that runs through all of these definitions is that they assume that properties or dispositions must be *either* intrinsic or extrinsic. For instance, Langton and Lewis start out with the thesis that an intrinsic property is something that something has independently of the situation, or independently of the thing being "*lonely or accompanied*", as they say. An example for the sake of the argument is: if I am angry only when I am accompanied, the property of being angry can be said to be extrinsic, but if I am angry *also* when I am lonely, then it will be said to be intrinsic. All of the qualifications that they make throughout their paper do not really change this basic assumption, viz., that properties are *either* intrinsic or extrinsic. From the perspective of a relational view, however, properties are neither intrinsic nor extrinsic in this sense. Properties, all properties, are relational and therefore dependent already. Their relatedness is not something that comes in addition to properties postulated as intrinsic. One cannot talk about properties independently of their relatedness.

This said, I don't think that it is enough simply to brush away Molnar's (and other dispositionalists') thesis that 'realism about powers carries a commitment to intrinsicality'. It is clearly the case that we would like to differentiate between dispositions and manifestations. If not, the dispositionalist would be a "Megarian". We would like to say that manifestations depend upon the situation, while the dispositions do not, i.e. we would not like to hold a position where we would have to say that the dispositions of the bearer change in accordance with the situation. The fact that dispositions remain invariant vis-à-vis the situation is what makes us say that dispositions are real and actual, and this is what differentiates mere *possibilia* from dispositions. This is what lies behind Molnar's strong emphasis on this question. If I have the property of being "angry" independently of the situation, we would say that this is a disposition – a property that I have intrinsically.

The problem is that we cannot solve this difficulty by just *insisting* that dispositions are intrinsic, and by pointing to examples where "we can see" dispositions endure across different situations, since this is really not a theoretical answer. Solving this problem means that we will have to be able to answer to further questions:

1   *Can we retain the "intrinsicality" of dispositions without committing ourselves to the distinctness-thesis or to a reductionist account?*
2   *If we go for a relational account, is it then possible to avoid pure relativism where the relata disappear into the relation* (which would of course be devastating for any relational account since there could be no relations in a world without relata)?[4]

We may start to provide an answer to these questions by suggesting that 'intrinsically' does not necessarily mean that *properties themselves* are independent as such. It is rather the other way around. Properties are intrinsic in the sense that they belong to an *object* in a particular way. It is *the object or the bearer* that has properties intrinsically. Properties are not intrinsic in themselves.

We will soon see how this makes a difference. Preliminarily, we can say that this makes it possible to say that intrinsicality is not really about *independence* but rather about *adherence* or location. If we can find a way to say that a property *adheres* to a certain bearer we will, as far as I can see, solve both the intrinsicality issue and the problem of 'relata disappearing into the relation'. This claim will not get its full exposition before subsection 4.5.3. However, before we can go further into the question we need to give an account of what it means to say that dispositional properties are relational.

4.2 Relational realism

Brian Ellis's notion of intrinsicality tells a broader story about the world wherein what we see must be understood and explained via *distinct* and intrinsic natural kinds, involving *distinct* and intrinsic dispositions, which come together and create the world as it is. To unwrap the realness of this world, we must detect and trace how all these dispositions behave in isolation, in order to see their intrinsic behaviour, and then *subsequently* see how they combine with other dispositions. This means of course that reality will only come to light under *in-vitro*/idealized conditions.

The preferred view in this book is that properties *are* relational. Properties are relational before they are "intrinsic" or "extrinsic". I have called this position *relational realism*.

What is meant by relational realism? In section 3.3 I pointed to the fact that Mumford sees himself as a relationalist. For Mumford, being a relationalist about identity means that:

> [T]his position has a relativistic nature. No property has an essence independent of the relation it bears to other properties. Hence, to be a property F is just to bear certain relations to all the other properties, G, H, I … in virtue of the causal powers of F (and reciprocally the powers of G, H, I …).
>
> (2007b, 148)

Alexander Bird says something similar in "The Regress of Pure Powers" (2007): "For the dispositional monist, the essences and hence the identities of entities are to be determined relationally, rather than purely intrinsically" (ibid., 15, see also pp. 11ff.). In C.B. Martin's case, I think that we can say that he develops his relationalism through the question of causality. "[A]ny particular dispositional state is itself *only* one among many other dispositional states that together form reciprocal dispositions partners for their particular mutual manifestations" (ibid., 3). Properties are in his view by definition already relational.

Because I support the Eleatic principle, I think that identity and causality are closely linked.

I therefore think that a definition should contain both of these elements. We may define relational realism thus:

> The being of some being is determined by its doing. The doing of a being has a dispositional character and this character is determined by the existence of other bearers and their dispositions. The disposition P has its specific identity P in virtue of its relations to dispositions Q, R, S, etc. Having a **specific** disposition to do something is only possible and specified by the dispositions of other beings. An object with only one "property", completely alone in the universe, would accordingly not have any properties.

It is important to keep in mind that it is not the properties themselves that "are related"; it is the bearers. Dispositions and their manifestations occur in the relational field in-between such bearers.

Dispositions are notably thought to be impotent in the following sense: A man may ask you, "Why does one get sleepy from (smoking) opium?" And you may answer, "Because opium has a *dormitive virtue*." The other man may reply, "Your appeal to the disposition of the opium explains nothing. To have a *dormitive* virtue is simply to have a property that puts people to sleep. You are going in circles."[5] Thus, even though we may say that dispositions "are important", we could just as well say that they explain nothing because it is unclear how they themselves come about. It is claimed, therefore, that to appeal to dispositions is to appeal to 'just-so explanations'.

To explain why opium really has this *dormitive* virtue, we arguably need to find what is often referred to as the relevant *active ingredient*. Reference to it would allegedly give us the ultimate explanation. But does it follow analytically or by causal necessity that morphine would lead to a *dormitive* effect? Does it follow analytically or in any other way necessarily that the complex molecules that make up morphine would lead to a *dormitive* effect? The explanation of the active ingredient ("categorical base") is only rational if we *solipsistically assume that properties are not relational in the first place*. As soon as we consider the possibility that the *dormitive* effect might be a relational property, we will have to acknowledge that the appeal to a lower "categorical" level will be as trivial as we saw in the dispositional explanation above. If going one level down is supposed to automatically give us an *explanation*, it will be because that which exists 'one level down' *necessitates* the disposition. But the fact that morphine gives a *dormitive* effect is *not* necessary. What explains the dormitive effect in a non-trivial way is a relation, not "intrinsic" dispositions or the active ingredient on the level below.

Consider the following case. Let us imagine the unbelievable, and visualize cyanobacteria that were able to talk, three billion years ago when oxygen was directly poisonous for any kind of living being. What would these creatures have said about the following proposition: "Oxygen is poisonous for living creatures because it has a poisonous virtue?" Maybe, while laughing gently, they would have said what we are saying about similar cases today: "Yes but that's trivial. Where is the active ingredient?" But is it trivial? Today we see clearly that it is not. Oxygen does not have a poisonous virtue; it is rather a necessary ingredient for being alive for most organisms.

It is only relationally that oxygen is poisonous, not "intrinsically". Just as it is only relationally the case that opium has a *dormitive* virtue, not "intrinsically". It is only from a relational point of view that we can understand why the complex molecules of morphine stimulate certain receptors of the brain in the way that they *de facto* do. It does not *follow* from the "active ingredient" in opium, or from the particular set-up in the brain, that the reaction will give 'a *dormitive effect*'. If it did follow, it would have to follow necessarily, and who would be ready to defend such a claim? In short, to transcend the damaging problems that the triviality claim poses for the dispositional ontology, one *must* go beyond non-relational accounts of dispositions.

The general claim put forward by reductionists can be posed as the claim that dispositions can be reduced to their postulated "categorical base",[6] or to dispositional properties present on the level below. To argue for relationalism is therefore also a way to argue against reductionism. It is relationalism that explains why dispositions cannot be reduced! This claim is still weak and I have only indicated my main arguments for it here.

4.3 Reciprocal dispositional partners

It has been a long-established criticism of any reductionist account that phenomena seem to be more than the sum of their mereological parts (see e.g. Bunge 1963, Chapter 6). The dispositions of hydrogen and oxygen would make us think that, if conjoined, they would work as a powerful explosive. Instead, the result of this fusion is water, something capable of extinguishing fire. In biology, this principle is even more in evidence (e.g. Moss 2004, 76).

We have previously referred to Martin's relationalism by calling attention to how he suggests that dispositions always "form reciprocal disposition partners for their particular mutual manifestations" (2007, 3).

Martin opposes what he calls the "two-event model" of causality (or what is normally called *efficient causality*). This model is the classical Humean (or more accurately Cartesian) model where there is a cause and an effect in a time sequence, with one active and one passive part of the equation.[7] Martin's alternative suggests that dispositions work conjointly. This he calls 'reciprocal disposition partnering'.[8] David Armstrong interprets Martin's view as an action–reaction model (2005, 312), or generally as *interaction*. I think that Armstrong has misconstrued Martin's view, since Armstrong's interpretations smuggles the two-event model in through the back door, without our noticing. There is no action (first) and then reaction, according to Martin. On the contrary, reciprocal means contemporary and equally constitutional. I believe that the following quotation supports this way of understanding Martin's point about, and view of, dispositional partnering:

> You should not think of disposition partners jointly *causing* the manifestation. Instead, the coming together of the disposition partners *is* the mutual manifestation; the partnering and the manifestation is identical. This partnering–manifestation identity is seen most clearly with cases such as the following. You have two triangle-shaped slips of paper that, when placed together properly, form a square. It is not that the partnering of the triangles causes the manifestation of the square, but rather the partnering *is* the manifestation.
>
> (2007, 51)

The reciprocity is something that is essential to the disposition; it is not something that accompanies its being. "What makes the sugar cube dissolve?" Martin asks. Is it the dissolver or the solvent? Neither: it is the partnering of the two. Without the one, you would not have the other. "Any partner is co-equal with the others for their mutual manifestations. *Nature comes in package deals*", Martin says (2007, 3, my emphasis)

A match will not light when there is no oxygen in the room. If we do not have the "partnering-view" that Martin has, we will in most cases construe "oxygen in the room" as a *background condition*. By calling oxygen a background condition, as is done commonly in the course of conditional analysis and generally by proponents of the hypothetico-deductive method, we preserve the idea of the two-event model of causation and more generally the idea of a *distinct* non-relational property that causes a particular event to come about (i.e. "What causes the iron-piece to expand? Answer: Heat"). It is only because oxygen is abundant that we regard it as a background condition. Had it been scarce, we may have regarded it as the causal factor or maybe even the triggering factor. But oxygen (or rather air containing 21 per cent oxygen) is not just a background condition or triggering factor; it is an entity with certain dispositions – dispositional properties that must be in place in a certain quantity in order for the match to light.

In a conditional analysis, a world of A's and B's are presumed, and (painstakingly) one also has to make room for background conditions. The relational view of dispositions is a world in which dispositions are reciprocally dependent upon each other and wherein the manifestation of these dependencies is mutually brought about.[9]

4.4 The combinatorial puzzle

This subject, the combinatorial puzzle, can be taken as a specialized and limited philosophical debate; alternatively, one may view it as a debate that has a larger and wider implication for science in general and for similar philosophical debates in other traditions. In any case, it should be obvious for any informed reader who is interested in debates about 'parts and wholes' in science or elsewhere that the combinatorial puzzle carries a special importance when it comes to accentuating crucial questions within this area.

Non-relationalists claim that wholes are results of what John Stuart Mill calls 'the composition of causes'.[10] The problem is that *empirically* we know that some/many/all wholes are not computable from the knowledge of each and every participating cause, and that they ontologically cannot be the net result of the composition of causes. From the knowledge of how the parts behave, we cannot infer how the whole will behave, or what the dispositions/properties of the whole will be.

This is, as I said in the previous chapter, a well-known debate between reductionists and so-called holists. Some wholes have *emergent properties*, as we say (see e.g. Laughlin and Pines 2000; Morrison 2006). Mill says that there are so-called heteropathic laws operating in such cases, which he typically calls special cases.[11]

Georg Molnar, whom I would *not* characterize as a relationalist, formulates the problem raised by the combinatorial puzzle for the dispositional account in the following way: "The important question, for us, is what happens when a number of distinct powers [dispositions] combine to yield a single effect?" (2003, 196). The reason why this question poses a problem is *isomorphism*. The reader might recall that isomorphism is about the identity between the disposition and its manifestation, and that we cannot have "same disposition different manifestation". A certain manifestation must point to a certain disposition. This is allegedly the way we can even identify something as disposition X.

Previously, in *Powers*, Molnar also emphasized the intrinsicality of dispositions (Molnar 2003, ch. 1.4.5 and part 6). This means that he took as a starting point that dispositions are distinct in the sense that they bring the same singular contribution in any (different) situation. Molnar gives us an account wherein distinct and independent dispositions come together and create a polygenic result.[12]

Stephen Mumford, who supports a relational view on dispositions, somewhat awkwardly confesses to a similar understanding. In *Passing Powers Around* he says:

> Powers sometimes work with each other, and sometimes against each other, to produce jointly the events we find in the world around us … Each power makes exactly the same contribution to the production of an event, irrespective of the other accompanying powers … If we want to know exactly what contribution a particular power can make, the best way would be to *screen off* all the other factors that could interfere.
>
> (2009, 103–104; my emphasis; see also Mumford 1998, 211 and 229; 2004, 172; 2007b)[13]

The problem is: if manifestations are *always* mutual manifestations, we would never be able to 'screen off all the other factors'. What we seem to have in reality is a situation wherein we have presumably the same powers, but they manifest differently because their contribution *allegedly* is the same while the manifestations are different. The question is how this can be the case if the manifestation is *isomorphic* to the disposition. The key problem for Molnar and Mumford is that we never see the manifestation of a singular power.

Molnar's solution is to discriminate between *effect* and *manifestation*. He argues that it is possible to compare the *manifestation* with the *telos* of some given (human) action and the polygenic *effect* with the unintended effects of human actions (2003, 197–198). Emergent and/or polygenic effects: the joint manifestation is just a *contingent* side-effect of the action of each and every power.

To my mind, this is a desperate move to accommodate what seems to me to be a fact: the nature of manifestations is that they are always mutual and never singular. Unless we can figure out a way to "screen off all the other factors that could interfere", we will always be faced with mutual manifestations. One way to get out of this problem is to criticize an even more hopeless position, which is what Molnar does when he criticizes Mill for applying a 'vector addition story' to the polygenic phenomena. But how would Molnar's own solution work when applied to the same example that he takes from Mill?

In this example, we encounter two horses pulling a barge from each side of a canal with the result (manifestation) that the barge moves straight ahead. Here we have two dispositions creating a polygenic result. According to Molnar, Mill has to say that the barge is pulled straight ahead because the two horses (powers) pull in each direction *in sequence*. Molnar calls this view "naïve realism". He suggests that the two powers ("horses pulling") are "manifesting" themselves as a single power, but that what we get is only the *effect* (similar to unintended consequences), not a genuine (and non-contingent) manifestation of the two powers taken in isolation (ibid., 198). Molnar clearly thinks that there are no other types of partners involved when only one horse is pulling. But of course this is not the case. Usually we say that to test one factor we need to bring in the *ceteris paribus* clause, meaning that we keep "all other things being equal". This means that the dispositions of the ground that the horse walks on, the harness between the horse and the barge, the currents in the canal etc. are similar to the situation where both horses are pulling. However, keeping these dispositions equal does not mean that they have been screened off. They are still there as manifestation partners (and accordingly the manifestation must in reality be a manifestation of two or more partners, which is a joint manifestation of these manifesting partners).

So, if there really are two discrete powers at work here, pulling separately but resulting in a secondary by-product, what's the difference from Mill? Molnar would still have to explain how these two discrete powers work in tandem, *even if* we were to agree to his differentiation between (true) manifestation and the side-effect. It's how they work in tandem that is of interest, not whether or not the result is the result of the 'telos' or the side-effect of the 'telos'. This shows that Molnar's solution is only a technical solution to the combinatorial puzzle.

A relational account would start with the claim that you could not describe the dispositional contribution of the one horse without also describing the disposition of the other. How one of the horses pulls immediately affects how the other pulls. Theoretically speaking *Ceteris paribus* does not take away the dispositional partners; it only keeps them equal. The barge/horse story is very similar to the situation that we have when we want to understand how the centrifugal force (or inertia) and the gravitational force work together to create the orbit of different celestial bodies. This was the problem that Johannes Kepler was faced with when he wanted to understand and represent this situation mathematically: how to measure and estimate the influence of one of the powers when this power's contribution is *immediately* influenced by the contribution of the other (Kepler 1992, 547–572).[14]

C.B. Martin has quite a different solution to the combinatorial puzzle. Martin does not believe in levels or any sort of stratification in nature. He thinks that every whole can be traced back to "the causal operativeness of its *constituents*".[15] Parts are "interactive" and not rigid. A certain part (e.g. quark) has many dispositions. When these fundamental parts enter into partnerings with certain other partners they manifest disposition f, l, k while other dispositions r, s, t when partnering with other parts. When hydrogen enters into a partnering with oxygen then we see other dispositional properties (of its constituting quarks, leptons, etc.) manifested, compared to the properties manifested when it enters into a partnership with peroxide. This simply explains the whole and the behaviour of the whole for Martin.

It seems to me that Martin thinks that this solution is final and sufficient because he thinks that the initial problem is that the parts have been deemed as rigid, and that it is only when you consider the parts to be rigid that you will find it mysterious that constituted wholes have "novel" and emergent properties.

There are two reasons why I think that Martin's reductionist solution is not a good one. The first reason is that Martin may be able to explain the sheer and joint manifestation of the partners (protons, neutrons, etc.), but he cannot explain the *behaviour* of the manifestation. And explaining the behaviour is what it takes for the casual operativeness of quarks and leptons to explain the creation of a horse (or a unicorn: ibid., 2). Quarks have the disposition to combine and form hadrons; they do not have the disposition to code. And further, the gene has the disposition to code, but not to metabolize food or grow (see subsection 4.5.1). Although made from quarks, the behaviour of the horse, its dispositions, cannot be explained by the quarks – *no matter how dynamically they combine.*

The second reason is that Martin identifies the dispositions of the constituents with the dispositions of the whole, which is something that one would do if the manifestation of the whole were the manifestation of the constituents. This means that we have a vicious circle. Or rather: if Martin ends up saying that the quark (in togetherness with a huge array of dispositional partners) has the disposition to manifest a golden-horned unicorn, he will face the problem of the assumed *relata* disappearing into the relation. The relational whole (the combined manifestation) will *entirely define* the specific disposition of the entity (quark) that we are discussing, and he will therefore be left with no way to identify the specificity of the *relatum* (the quark) – a result that would *really* violate what the idea of isomorphism demands in order for a dispositional theory to work.

In *Getting Causes from Powers*, Stephen Mumford and Rani Lill Anjum (2011) propose that we understand causal interaction in terms of a vector model (in contrast to David Lewis's neuron diagrams). This model enables us to visualize how different dispositions/powers work together: how they facilitate, inhibit or make no difference for each other, etc. The main goal of this model is to show that necessity between cause and effect never takes place because a causal power (disposition) can always be interfered with and countervailed by other powers. Causation is *always* taking place in 'vectorial spaces'; therefore, no necessity. Although Mumford and Anjum agree with the mutual manifestation model of Martin, they cannot help representing dispositions/powers as having singular and independent identities and agency, which then only *eventually* work together, inhibiting, facilitating, intensifying each other, etc. A relational realist such as I am would say that this account encounters the same problems as Molnar's and Mill's do, and that their argument against necessitation is therefore also wrong-footed from the start.[16]

4.4.1 A possible solution to the combinatorial puzzle

The internal discussion that we have seen between different positions within the disposition camp shows that there is no easy solution to the combinatorial puzzle in general. The heart of the problem lies in the fact that we need to explain how something can be "distinct" and "relational" at the same time. Ontologies that are committed to the distinctness-thesis (e.g. Humeanism and certain dispositional accounts, etc.) or to "strong" relationalism (e.g. structural realism and, in effect, Martin's no-level view), start out with problems that will only create more problems and technical trickery. I think, however, that the dispositionalist ontology can solve this problem provided that we are careful in using and distinguishing between *objects* (bearers), *dispositions* and *manifestations*.

Everything starts with the Eleatic stranger, also in the case of relational realism. The relationalist argues that nothing is able to have a disposition or do what it does independently of anything else. What something does is part of a joint action – the "something" is always conjoined with other entities to form "a unit" with novel dispositions. This is simply how relational realism works, and it allows us to explain the combinatorial puzzle *a priori*. This gives us quite a different picture of what dispositions are; they are not singular discretely free-floating properties that *sit* on the bearer. It is the bearer that is the primary "agent". It is the bearer that is *in* the situation, not the properties/dispositions as such. If we want to "screen off other factors" in order to see how a disposition really manifests, we will just get a 'new package deal'. If we think that the object will manifest the same disposition independently of the situation, i.e. bring the same contribution (as Molnar and Mumford say), then we are essentialists.

The alternative view is simply to say that whenever the contributors get into new configurations they might or might not contribute with different dispositions (as Martin says). It depends, and what it depends upon are the contributions from the *other* partakers. For example, to even see and appreciate the fact that the surface structure has a disposition to reflect light you would need to know the contribution of the sun/light bulb emitting light. You know about this disposition because you know about the dispositions of the other partakers. It is not as if the disposition that a surface structure has to reflect light (seen as colour) is a free-floating disposition that that structure has in and by itself. It is a disposition that it has because there *are* the eye- and light-partners in the world in which surface structures exist.

Does this mean that the contribution of one partaker necessarily changes whenever there is a new situation? This may be the case, but it also may be the case that one or several partners have the same contribution in the new situation. In *situation 1*, in which the manifestation is, let us say, green (a green-coloured ball), we might assert that e.g. the sun gives the contribution x, the eye gives the contribution y, while the surface structure of the ball gives the contribution z. In *situation 2*, in which the manifestation is a red colour, we might assert that the sun/light bulb/etc., gives the contribution x, the eye gives the contribution y, while the structure of the ball gives the contribution *w*. But the nature of the dispositions involved is of course still relational. The new contribution (provided by the new structural surface of the ball) is not given independently of the other partakers and the manifestation(s) that they bring about. *It is these other partakers and the joint manifestation that literally defines the specific contribution of the "single" partakers.* With other partakers, the *contribution* of the structure of the ball might be different. Contributions cannot therefore be screened off and singled out in and by themselves. They are only what they are in relation to other partakers. What Molnar calls effect (the joint manifestation) is not contingently related to the contribution of the partakers; it is rather "picking out" what their specific contribution is. Without the "joint" manifestation, we would not be able to pick out *the singular* contributors. Mumford and Anjum's argument against necessity is, to simplify, that 'a necessary connection can principally and always be prevented from being manifested', but this argument against necessity comes as an answer to the following question: "That *a* caused *b*, suggests that *a* made *b* happen

(Woodward 2003), but why should that automatically mean that *a* necessitated *b*? Could there not be an account of causal production without necessitation?" (2011, 47). If you start out by accepting that causality takes place between singular, discrete a's and b's (single-track causation), then (I think) *their* argument against necessitation is the best that you can achieve. On this account, however, there is no discrete independent contributor to start with, and therefore no necessitation other than *ceteris paribus* necessitation either. There is no necessitation *in* nature. To bring about an effect you need more than one partner and the effect never comes from the partners alone, but is also created by what the manifestation *eventually* "meets" when manifested. This effect is not a necessary result of the causes in any case, much less an effect originating from a single contributor.

To understand this thoroughly it is necessary to examine the relation between parts and wholes more carefully, especially in relation to manifestations. The two horses and the barge (+ many other dispositional partners) form a *new* unit (not very durable) that has new dispositions. Hydrogen atoms and oxygen atoms conjoin and make up a (durable) unit of molecules with novel dispositions that can manifest – for example the novel disposition of being able to be drunk by certain organisms. When those dispositions are at work (*energeia*) they manifest something, and this something is a *new unit*, which *eventually* has further dispositions. It is therefore a misunderstanding to think, e.g. that the partaking dispositions have novel dispositions themselves (i.e. *that* would amount to a view where properties have properties, which have new properties, which have new properties, etc. (see Kim 1999, 25)). It is the *manifestation*, the result of the partnering of dispositions that has "novel" dispositions. "Emergent dispositions" arise from "non-emergent" dispositions because they "non-emergently" mutually manifest some thing that *eventually* has "emergent" dispositions.

What a mutual manifestation creates is a *product* – a new whole that exists more or less durably in space and time and which therefore, by definition is *singular*. It is this *product* that has novel dispositions, not dispositions directly.[17] Dispositions are relationally constituted, but they create singular beings. It is the fact that the manifestation is singular that makes it possible for us to even think and (wrongly) anticipate that there *are* discrete "singular" *dispositions* in the first place. The contributors to a manifestation are singular because they themselves are manifestations of contributors from the level below.

Some might concede that certain *dispositions* have further dispositions/powers (e.g. Mumford 2007, 142); for example, we might think that the disposition of being red ("red-able") involves "a multiplicity of powers" (ibid.), but I think this is inaccurate. It is only when red is *manifested* that the disposition of being red can have a (further) multiplicity of powers. As *unmanifested*, being red can only be manifested as red (when the right manifesting partners are "in place"). We might, however, say that the disposition red has *iterative* dispositions, such as attracting men (e.g. red lips and fingernails), signalling danger to herbivores (red mushroom) or indicating that a star is "dying" (red light), but the iterativity presupposes that the original disposition has been manifested as something that exists in space and time first.

I have said that to know the particular contribution of one bearer you would have to know the contribution of the other bearers, because the contribution of one part *de facto* depends ontologically on the contribution of the other. It is the contributions of the light and the eye that make it possible for the surface to have its dispositional contribution. So, when we *say* that 'sweet water' is the manifested state of affairs that shows us that the sugar cube has the disposition of being dissolvable, this is not strictly correct, because what we also *see* is the *dissolving* disposition of water. In other words: we cannot observe directly whether it is the water that is dissolving something or the sugar cube that is being dissolved. What we observe is the manifestation 'sweet tasting water', and we infer *eventually* that this is a manifestation of dissolvability (or whatever disposition we may have in mind). We may think that we can "see" the singular contributor in advance, but this is not possible according to this relational theory. This is not possible because it is not possible for one disposition to have one manifestation. Manifestations are in principle the manifestation of two or more dispositions. That the manifestation is always a joint manifestation does not mean that there are not "singular" contributors, however. As argued above: the manifestation *is* singular (it needs to be since it is manifested in space and time), and it is manifestations that constitute single contributors. (The manifestation can be durable or just last for a very short time: see section 4.6, §4.) Since we never see a "single manifestation" directly, we can only infer that bearer x gives the contribution D when partnering with y, w, z, etc. To single out the different contributors you therefore need to know the contribution from the other contributors, and to know the contribution from the other contributors you need to see their joint manifestation. It is when you see the joint manifestation of what happens when you put a solid stone in water that you allow yourself to *infer* that *sugar is* dissolvable (as opposed to the stone: granting that you assume that water has not lost its dissolving disposition when partnering with the stone). It is in light of the *inference* we tend to make *in advance* that we may *eventually* say that we can "see" the dissolved sugar cube as a manifestation of the dissolvability of the sugar cube. (This is why keeping all things equal works, though only because we also have the ability to *infer* from observation.) It seems that it is whenever we overlook this *order* of reasoning that we are misled to think that "sweet water" is a directly observable manifestation of dissolvability. It is often because we as humans have certain interests, I guess, that we interpret the joint manifestation as a manifestation of a singular disposition, a singular cause-and-effect relationship.

And this is what lies at the heart of the combinatorial puzzle: we are comparing postulated singular manifestations with conjoined ones, as if there really were single ones. "What is it for manifestations to combine", Georg Molnar asks, and by this question he states that it is the joint manifestation that has to be explained, not the "singular" one – which, according to the relational account argued for here, is to turn the issue on its head, since there are no singular ones in the first place. What we see, therefore, is that Molnar's construction of the combinatorial problem is misconceived in the first place. This is not strange, since he has already said that isomorphism requires singular manifestations. I think that the intuition that lies behind isomorphism is correct – namely, that there are single contributors and therefore "single" dispositions – but that it is wrong to think that this means that such dispositions could "show themselves" as single manifestations.

I will end this chapter by emphasizing how the relational account laid out here threatens reductionism. What is the ultimate reason why novel dispositions cannot be computed from the knowledge that we have about the dispositional behaviour of parts? The ultimate reason is that there is a manifestation between the dispositions of the parts and the dispositions of the whole. There are not two elements involved in a reduction; there are three.

1   The contribution-aspect.
2   The manifestation aspect.
3   The behaviour-of-the-manifested-object-aspect.

There is a special way in which relational realism taps into these three aspects. The first way is by dint of the fact that the contributing parts don't make their contribution independently of the other parts. To know the particular contribution of one part you would have to know the contribution of the other parts. To know the properties/dispositions of the manifested object (3) you would therefore also have to know the *relational partners* that this new manifestation might meet and "join" up with! H and O manifests (together with other partners: such as temperature, pressure, etc.) H_2O. H_2O in turn has its dispositions partly due to the relational partners that water meets. When we talk about the properties of H_2O we are no longer talking about the manifestation of the coming together of H and O. We are therefore no longer talking about H_2O (2), but water (3). Water is the combination of the manifestation aspect and the further dispositions that this aspect "gains" by meeting "its" partners. I call the interface that occurs between the manifestation and the new partners that meet this manifestation *qua-face*, and I have called this whole view a modified neutral monism view (section 3.6).

The study of oxygen and hydrogen will not tell me about the partners that their joint manifestation will meet "qua-facely". It is only because we know *in advance* that water vapours at a certain degree that we can go back to "explain" this by pointing to the molecular structure; forgetting that temperature, air pressure, etc. is what "really causes" water to evaporate. We are asking, "Why does water evaporate *at a certain temperature?*" and immediately forget that it is the temperature – together with other partners *at the qua-face level*, not the molecular structure – that primarily "causes" the water to evaporate, cf. the dormitive virtue case. (See also section 4.6.)

4.5 "Relational problems"

We have already mentioned some of the problems that relational realism will face. Some of those problems were touched upon in section 3.3, when we looked into the problems that dispositional monism has to deal with. We saw that dispositional monists are able to defend their position up to a certain point, but are unable to give a convincing answer to the "filled in space problem". The same reasons that I gave for why we had to come to this conclusion can be partly levelled against an unqualified version of relational realism. A qualified version would, as I have stressed, need to account for the intrinsicality issue.

I have made the first step in that direction by pointing to the role that manifestations play. The general idea is that it is the manifestation aspect (singularity) that keeps the *relata* from disappearing into the relation, and that prevents the dispositional monist from falling prey to the two intertwined main charges – the passing-powers-around problem and the identity-problem. In the following chapters I will try to show how dispositional monism can be merged with relational realism in a more specific way. However, relational realism also has problems of its own, problems that are not related to dispositional monism as such. These problems will therefore also be addressed in the chapters that follow, including a more detailed elaboration of levels and bearers (objects).

4.5.1 First problem: how to limit potentiality

We have seen that the dispositional ontology can give an account of why we can have *de re* potentiality. This is one of the main and truly important benefits of dispositionalism. If we assume that the world is fundamentally dispositional in nature, we have a "truth-maker" for the modal term propensity and for all the statistics used in science. (One may see statistics as a methodological and practical answer to the fact that 'the world *is* dispositional'.)[18] If there is something like propensity, and not only necessity and contingency, then there are also some relations in the world that relate in a way that lies in-between necessity and contingency, which is exactly what we should think that dispositions can do.

The status of *propensity* is especially important for the naturalness view that I seek to develop through this book. The reality in 'a reality that allows us both to fail and to succeed in our efforts to treat something in accordance with it' (see subsection 1.2.1) depends on the modality of propensities. But this view of naturalness can only be granted if we can somehow restrict potentiality in such a way that it does not resemble logical possibility or a possibility span that has a similarly absurdly wide range. However, just such an outcome seems to be implied by the relational realist view developed in the previous chapters. On a full-blown relational view, it seems that any given object might have almost any imaginable disposition.

Although C.B. Martin doesn't seem to think about the range of potentiality as a problem, we can use his example to illustrate why it certainly could be a problem given certain assumptions:

> The readiness for a quark for certain kinds of manifestings with certain kinds of interrelations and interactivities for quarks and leptons constituting a golden-horned unicorn could fully exist even though nothing like a golden-horned unicorn ever existed. The quark actually has the readiness for it – it is ready to go.

(2007, 2)

A different example illustrating the same is to say that hydrogen (H) already had the dispositions to create the Empire State Building at the time hydrogen came into being. According to this position, it seems that *given* the right relational partners, you can ascribe the dispositions of "constituting a building like the Empire State Building" to H. This seems to be contra-intuitive, however. Although it is anticipated that H was the first element created after the Big Bang, and that the universe developed in such a way that we as a matter of *historically evolved fact* have something called The Empire State Building on planet Earth today, we might well be reluctant to ascribe such properties to H. If H has such dispositions, or quarks have this readiness, one might ask what kind of dispositions they do not have. None, it would seem.

Consider a pistol resting on the table. Let's say that for the moment it is manifesting the power to lie in a particular way on a plane and hard surface, while it is not manifesting its disposition to fire off bullets. What other dispositions are not manifested? Does it also have the capacity to grow wings and fly? Could we not provide dispositional partners in relation to which a disposition like this could be manifested? This seems to be no less reasonable than what Martin suggests for the quark. If the dispositions of a thing depend on the relations it has to every other thing, it seems that any thing can have any disposition given the right dispositional partners (or conditions as many would like to call them). According to this position, relationalism seems to jeopardize the very core of our project, which is to preserve a *range* of potentiality that might be called 'natural'.

The ontological problem with this wide-ranging potentiality is, as I said, that it outcompetes one of the major arguments in favour of the disposition ontology, which is that it supports *de re* potentialities. Despite the fact that one may say that logical possibility is categorically different from any other type of possibility, there does not seem to be a practically significant difference between the kind of *de re* potentiality displayed in, e.g. Martin's example and in logical possibility. There seems to be no way to define what something *is* in a reasonable way, since any thing seems to harbour almost any (dispositional) property.[19]

Argued for differently, Martin's statement (and the Empire State Building example) seems to recover the feature of Humean ontology captured by the phrase 'anything may produce anything else' (given the right circumstances). Also, this shows that relationalism can be even less restrictive than Armstrong's unlimited combinatorialism. (See Armstrong 1989 and Mumford 2007.) Under this regime, there are no ontological restrictions to the nature of a thing, and the range of its manipulability will be limitless. The compossible range that would ontologically be at our disposal would be absurdly wide, in keeping with the most optimistic techno-scientific scenarios of a limitless space for human intervention – exactly the position that I am trying to disprove. As I have previously described, we have today an ethico-ontological regime wherein limits are seen as either contingent or necessary, and where *ethics* therefore is seen to be the only way to '*restrict compossibility*' beyond. It would therefore be hugely important whether our *ontology* shows that *there is* a limited range of manipulability, and that this range also applies to 'the nature of the thing'.

4.5.2 A preliminary solution; the level-specificity of dispositions

One avenue into grasping the latent limits of dispositional potentiality is to take a closer look at how dispositions are and must be level-specific.

The identity of a disposition is determined by what its bearer is able to do. A hand *grips*, a nerve *signals*, a molecule *reacts*. A simple question may follow from this: what is a disposition a disposition for? A disposition is of course a disposition for something in particular. A disposition for signalling in the braincells is not a disposition for gripping (a hammer) or hitting (someone in the face), even though signals in the brain are involved in such processes. There is no signalling unit in the brain that can be marked off as "hit Lars quite hard on the right side of the cheek if he says that you have a big toe". Neuronal networks make it possible for me to hit Lars in the face, or to think (as I am doing now) about neuronal networks, but that does not mean that we can say that they dispose towards this. Neuronal networks dispose towards different types of *signalling*. The manifestation of neuronal activity will be some kind of receiving and sending signals, not thinking a specific thought. Thinking this or that specific thought is done on a different (relational) level.

When bearers come together they jointly manifest something that has *further* dispositions due to the novel relational whole that the manifestation *qua-facely* meets. Thus: the dispositions that neurons have to signal are dispositions that are made possible by the relational whole that the neuron is a part of, while the dispositions that make it possible for the "brain" to think are made possible by the relational whole of which the brain is a part.[20] These relational wholes are different. Committing oneself to a realist view of dispositions means that dispositions are real in virtue of what they do or can do, *which means that they are real in virtue of the specific level on which they actually do or can do their specific thing*. It is the relational whole that the being in question is a part of that enables it to have the dispositions it has. If you put "a single neuron" in water you will surely realize this.

When C.B. Martin (and John Heil) argue against any level-view, they do so with the help of the reciprocal-partner-view, saying that the parts are always interactive parts, something that for them explains why wholes always seem to be more than their parts (Martin 2007, 36ff). But this is not sufficient because it leaves unanswered the question: interaction between what – and in what sense? The interaction performed by particles is simply not the same action that is *needed for a horse* to pull a barge. Particles react; they don't pull. Dispositions on lower levels (assuming that such levels exist) cannot do what would be required for those dispositions at higher levels. Given this understanding, it would be absurd to say something like: a quark has a *disposition* to create a unicorn. The dispositions required for creating unicorns, horses or whatever are only to be found at higher levels, and to deny that there are different levels in nature is therefore not coherent. If these are just linguistic differences and *talk*,[21] then '*reacting*' and '*spinning*' would also just be talk or linguistic gestures. The only argument that Heil and Martin seem to have for saying that talk about the constituents is not just talk and linguistic gestures, in their view, is that they are fundamental, and as we have seen: even to argue that there are such things as fundamental constituents is controversial (see section 3.2).

According to the account worked out here, the answer to the question "what is a table?" should give descriptions of the dispositions *at the level* at which the table is a table (cf. Eddington's two tables). However, as I tried to show in Chapter 2, we are often pulled towards reductionist accounts of the table: i.e. it is tempting to say that the table *is* a particular combination of molecular structures made up of atoms, etc. On the Eleatic account given here, *the table* could not really be "this or that atomic structure", however complex, because *tables do* different things than atoms. It is the doing that makes the difference. If something *is what it does*, it follows that this reduction is invalid. Glass is fragile; molecules are not.

When we talk about dispositions – the actual and potential behaviour of things – we always already take levels into account. This is why it is impossible for genes to be egotistic, as Richard Dawkins (1976) claims and which many have pointed out. The underlying reason for why this is the case is, again, that the doings of things do not primarily descend from some kind of real *essence, derivative power* or *natural kind* on the levels below, but from the relational net in which some being is embedded. This theory clearly assumes that levels of nature are a part of the realm that we call reality. It is also a part of the argument (involving relationalism, the Eleatic stranger, and the relation between dispositions and their manifestations) that I launch against reductionism in this book. A more systematic and thorough theory of how dispositions, manifestations and levels are interconnected will be discussed in section 4.6.

If dispositions are level-specific, we may partly avoid the claim that bearers/objects have an absurdly wide range of dispositions, and therefore an absurdly wide nature and identity. This is an issue that I will come back to in more practical terms in Chapter 5, where (not the least) the historicity of dispositions is taken into account.

In addition to the specific argument put forward here, I suggest that we specify and explicate the following issues concerning potentiality.

Mere possibility/logical possibility concerns possible events, objects, properties and other phenomena that we can possibly think of without contradiction. Stones can fly, but a stone cannot both fly and not fly at the same time. If we identify 'The Possible' with what is logically possible, then potentiality will become a so called mind dependent entity entirely. The only thing that really exists independently of us would then be *actualia*. De re potentiality is something that cannot be observed and which therefore cannot pass the empiricist 'reality test'.

De re potentiality. The expression *de re* is, as we have seen, used when we want to say that the phenomenon we are talking about is 'in the thing', and not in our language or in any other cognitive representation. It does not mean that our phenomenon is necessarily reified, only that we are talking about something as if it is to be found in things themselves. In this case, it means that we are talking about potentiality as if there is real potentiality in nature – in the same way that we may say that there is necessity *in* nature. A real potentiality must, as Aristotle says, be something that can be realized. A potentiality that cannot be realized/ manifested is just a mere possibility (*Metaphysics*, Θ 4). It is possible for water to become ice. This is a possibility that is typically real. When we say that this is a possibility that is *de re*, we are saying that it is something that can be empirically examined. When we say that something is possible in the sense of being *logically* possible, we say that empirical examinations would be meaningless.

Can water dissolve fatty acids? Can a mule mate with a zebra and produce offspring capable of surviving? The space between what is logically possible and what is *de re* possible is vast, and we would have to think hard to come down to a meaningful distinction between the two. Science and technology investigate this area continuously, and it is the area wherein interesting questions about naturalness arise. (More about this in Chapter 5.)

Iterative potentiality. This expression is taken from Molnar (2003, 96), although he does not exploit the meaning in the same way that I do here. An iterative potential is a potentiality that needs a certain manifestation to become *de re*. Glass (that is fragile) has the *iterative* power to cut. A piece of paper has a *de re* potentiality to be folded, and an iterative potentiality to be folded into an origami swan manifesting certain aesthetic (and other) features.[22] *De re* potentialities are triggered or "released", while iterative potentialities cannot be simply triggered. To be a full hospital surgeon at the age of four is logically possible, but it is not a *de re* potential. It is, however, iteratively possible. On the other hand, this particular iterative potential is not something that can be attributed to a fly. But it is not logically impossible for a fly to have the iterative potential of becoming a doctor. This is a reason why we should differentiate between logical and iterative potentialities. Iterativity is the next-step potentiality of things.

4.5.3 The second problem of relationalism

For the non-relationalist who has already established the idea of distinctly existing relata (in virtue of e.g. a real essence, categorical bases, etc.) the question may sound like this: 'despite the distinctness between the entities; are they nevertheless related somehow?' For the relationist it would, however, look something like this: 'Despite the relational nature of everything, is it nevertheless possible to pick out the *relata* and characterize them in terms of their being?'

In Chapter 3 I came to the conclusion that the dispositional monist should be advised to admit 'categorical' properties back into their ontology, where 'categorical property' should be understood as the ("sheer") manifestation of dispositions. Reclaiming 'categorical properties' might lead us to think, once again, that dispositions are redundant "placeholders". But this is, as I have argued, not the case: 'manifestations' belong to the very core ontology of dispositions – essentially being manifestations of dispositions. Relationality is, as we have seen, also entailed in the manifestation, since any manifestation is relationally constituted. A manifestation is always a coming together of manifesting partners, as Martin says.

We may think of it in the following way. Manifestations congregate the relational partners, while dispositions (by contrast) spread out into the relational whole, wherein the disposition can be had, and wherein dispositional partners sometimes "meet" in further manifestations, creating the potential for new partnerings, etc.

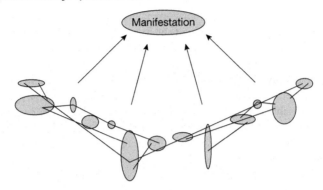

Figure 4.1 The manifestation aspect. Simple model representing the relational nature of the manifestation aspect of a bearer/thing (see text). Shaded elliptic/circular figures with no names are bearers, already related in their contribution to the manifestation.

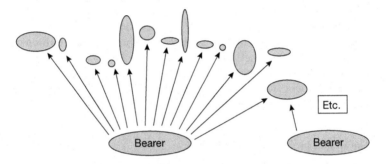

Figure 4.2 The disposition aspect. Simple model representing the relational nature of dispositions. Shaded elliptic/circular figures with no names are manifestations. The 'Etc.' just means that any disposition needs partners in order to be the disposition it is: "ready to go for its manifestation". (These two models are more thoroughly explained below, where they are combined.)

In the previous chapters I have to a large degree viewed the relation between dispositions and manifestations from the perspective of the disposition. I have tried to argue for the view that the identity of the disposition and the object depends upon the relational being of the disposition. I have had a specific problem connected to the way in which this should be formulated; I have said, "*partly* constituted by *its* relations", without saying anything about the other part, which *is* the manifestation aspect, and the role that it plays in bringing dispositions about. There is a particular dynamic between manifestations and dispositions that must be better understood, and it is this dynamic that in general keeps us from sliding into the "relata-disappearing-into-the-relation-problem" that befalls relationalism generally. This is what I intend to explain below.

Humean distinctness allows relations, properties (dispositions) and "objects" to vary independently and contingently of everything else, but this is exactly what the relationalist opposes. 'Relation' is primordially not a property of properties – a property that can be had or not had – it is rather something that defines the being of properties as such. This sounds fine until we realize that from this perspective there are suddenly no properties there anymore, since properties are totally relational. The issue can be formulated in the following way:

> [T]he identity of a property is determined by its relationships with other properties whose identities are determined by their relationships with yet other properties, in a set of relationships which at some point returns to involve the very property we started with. The identity of this property is what the set of relationships was supposed to settle. Yet the nature of this set of relationships is dependent on the identities of its relata, which *ex hypothesi* have not yet been settled.
>
> (Bird 2007, 12)

Bird and Mumford try to solve this problem by showing how a type of "relational *property* grid" will define its parts (Mumford 2004, 185; Bird 2007).[23] For reasons that I argued for in sections 3.5 and 3.6, and will argue below, I don't think that this is a good solution. To begin with I will therefore try to illuminate this problem by way of making our options transparent.

There are at least four alternatives:

#1 Under conditions[24] r, conditions r have D.
#2 Under conditions r, x has D.
#3 x has D under conditions r, s, t and v.
#4 x has D under all conditions.
     (Where x is the object).

In situation #1 the *relata* would have totally dissolved into the relation.[25] We need *relata* in order to even get started when we want to talk about properties. On this alternative, to even say "To be F is only to bear certain relations to all the other properties G, H, I and so on" (Mumford 2004, 185) is saying too much, since it (alternative #1) does not even allow us to pick out a certain property F in the first place. There must be some differences (F, G, H, I) already in the system in virtue of which it is possible to point out what is related, and those differences must be identifiable as something specific. If we can grant that a property belongs to some *thing* involved in the partnering – e.g. red-"able" belongs to the apple and not to the light or the eye,[26] we will by definition have some x (that has D).[27] If the property belongs or *adheres* "equally" to all of the partners, we will need very strong arguments to resist the conclusion that the *relata* disappear into the relation, because properties would then be properties of the relational system (the conditions), and not of the "objects" that are related. (We may, however, allow the view that the system is the bearer, for instance that the spin of electrons is not basically a property of *the* electron, but rather of the system as such.)

The dispositional monist rejects categorical properties because s/he thinks that they are redundant and that they import quiddities into the system. But what s/he gets in return is a theory that seems to lack a way to ensure the locus of the disposition and therefore also lacks a way to ensure that the *relata* do not disappear into the relation. His or her solution is to say that they are intrinsic, while being unable to explain why. If we redefine categorical properties as simply 'manifestations', we get a *locus* and we avoid the quiddity problem. It is the sugar cube that has the disposition to be dissolved, not the water; and it is the water that has the disposition to dissolve, not the sugar cube. *This is something that we can say because we can identify 'sugar cube' and 'water' as two different bearers, and we can identify these two bearers because they have two different manifestation aspects "filling in space", brought about by the combining dispositions on a level below.*

This means that we can say that dispositions are intrinsic in the sense that they (level-specifically) *belong* to some thing, but they are not intrinsic in the sense of being independent and non-relational. I have called this type of intrinsicness *adherence*.

Adherence is not a small thing. To localize dispositions is one of the main tasks in knowledge production. That stones are falling to the ground, that stars are moving in the sky, that leaves are turning brown, that summer follows spring, that the ball is red, that the Big Bang occurred (if it did) and that water dissolves certain things are all mutual manifestations which call for explanations where we try to localize the different bearers: bearers that we sometimes did not even know existed. What we are trying to do is to find the right adherences for the right dispositions.

Coming this far we are confronted with the choice between alternative #2 and #3, since alternative #4 is non-relational altogether. Alternative #2 says that x has D only under conditions r. So altering the conditions would mean that the *disposition* would cease to exist. Since the world is changing constantly, we would have to say that the properties of things come and go in parallel with the changing conditions, on alternative #2. The very existence of the disposition would thereby be as susceptible to changing conditions as the manifestations. Our ontology would thereby be totally relational again. Dispositions and manifestations would collapse into each other, and the whole theory would in addition lead into a kind of Megarianism.

The reality of dispositions is, as we remember, marked by the fact that they vary "independently" of the conditions. The glass is brittle independently of being dropped or not. The actuality of the manifestations is, on the other hand, marked by the fact that they are "actualized by the conditions". Thus, we have seen that for a dispositional *realist*, the distinction between the disposition and the manifestation is crucial. And therefore, without that distinction there would be no relational realism either. Alternative #2 does not therefore seem very attractive.

The alternative to alternative #2 would be to say that we are talking about the same *object*, even though conditions change. When we see change we see 'the same object' manifest different dispositions. In order to be able to differentiate between existence conditions and manifestation conditions it is therefore again necessary to have some notion of an object (x). The reason why we can say that the array of *actual* dispositions is much wider than the array of *actual* manifestations (see Martin 2007, 3f.) is that there is *a thing* (x) (having dispositions) involved. This seems to be agreed upon among the disposition/

power ontologists in the first place, but in the following sense it seems not to be:[28] Unless the dispositionalist can prevent reductionism, they no longer have *an object* that allows them to keep the distinction between dispositions and manifestations. If you say that a horse has the power to pull a barge, you need something to establish the horse as a real object having that particular power. If the power of the horse is *really* a power of the cells, and the power of the cells is *really* the power of the organic molecules, which is … – then we no longer have a horse, nor, consequently, the disposition to pull. "Macro-dispositions" such as dissolvability and the ability to pull, will in such an account not only be supervenient or epiphenomenal entities, they will not exist at all, because they will have no *real* object to which to adhere. If those who combine dispositional monism with a relational account approve of this reduction, then they are likely to go for alternative #1, which is some kind of structural realist ontology that leaves out the object category (x) altogether.

Thus, if I am right about my argument, reductionist accounts will not let us keep the necessary distinction between dispositions and manifestations – a result that would be a devastating blow for any disposition ontology. My claim is therefore, again, that any disposition ontology requires a particular account of levels in nature and their mutual irreducibility.

Alternative #3 is the proposal that D has some kind of 'resilience towards conditions' as such. D is relational in some *limited* sense. Under conditions, g, h, f, etc., x does not have D. This seems to launch a serious problem, however, because the properties/dispositions something have will depend upon what partners there are (in the universe). Let's say that Xa shares the same manifestation aspect as Xb. In this situation we *could* say that they would always have the same dispositions *because* they share the same base (manifestation aspect). Dispositions would thereby be reducible to a "categorical base", and all that we have said and argued for up to now would just fall apart. Alternatively, we could say that Xa and Xb could have had different dispositions, but that *as a matter of fact* they never have.

The reason for this is that Xa and Xb must belong to the same historically evolved universe. As long as they share the same manifestation aspect, they will also share the same universe containing the same partners (g, h, f, etc.), wherein the disposition-aspect is "had". Even though Xa is localized at the opposite side of the universe from Xb, and Xb is localized close enough to partner Xc (g) to jointly manifest something (w) with this partner, Xa would still have the disposition to w even though it never comes in contact with Xc (g), so long as they share the same *historically evolved universe*. The view that we can have, e.g. the same categorical properties but different laws (e.g. Armstrong and Lewis, i.e.: same manifesting aspect, but different dispositional aspect) is to my mind not possible. And the reason for this is that I trade on the assumed fact that the universe is created through the course of time, and that everything that exists, exists in virtue and in terms of the *particular* trajectory that this historical evolvement has taken (see section 5.2). Either you are on the inside or on the outside of this universal trajectory. The manifestation aspect and the dispositional aspect are *both* created by this trajectory. So if the two things Xa and Xb sharing the same manifestation aspect were to have had different dispositions, they would also have to have had different manifestation aspects. If a stone could suddenly *fly* by itself, it would simply not be a stone anymore. If a new partner could have occurred "in the system", and were to have done so, it would not have made a difference only to Xa. It would have made the *same difference* to Xb too. *But it would make a difference!* Both would have gained a *new* disposition (no matter how far they existed from each other in the universe). This is extremely important because it secures the assertion that the disposition itself is relational and not only the manifestation. Even the *having* of disposition X depends upon other dispositions in the universe. The point is that the existence of those other dispositions is determined by the historical evolvement of the universe, an evolvement shared by anything that exists in the universe. The argument coming from modal realists (Lewis) is therefore absurd on this account. There would simply not be a neighbouring world where Xa and Xb did not share all the properties of the other. This view is last, but not least, important if we are to argue against alternative #4.

In alternative #4, the fact that x has D is totally independent of conditions as such. This is the "wholly intrinsic view" or the categorical monist position held by Armstrong and others. It requires that having dispositions must be fully explained by something other than relations. Although you don't have to be a Lockean essentialist to hold this view, it seems that this type of intrinsicality has to be somehow positively argued for. It must contain something more than the nominal characteristic '*non-relational*', or 'un-conditional'. As we have seen, the most common thing to do in this philosophical situation is to defend this view by referring to some micro-properties/minute parts that can somehow be labelled non-relational.

One may therefore say that the proponent of #4 would have a strong liability to accept reductionism, and further that #1 and #2 do not seem very attractive, and that the best alternative that allows one to counter (the strong liability to accept) reductionism is therefore alternative #3.

In *effect*, #3 and #4 would not actually appear very different. But the difference *is* quite decisive, since they will *explain* the dispositions in a different way. I would say that the position held in #4 trades upon something that its proponent is not able to recognize, namely the historically evolved conditions that all x's share. It is the *stability* of these historically evolved conditions/partners that makes it possible to think positively about #4. It is the stable durability of the partners (see section 4.6, §4) that makes it possible to overlook the relational nature of dispositions/ properties, and hence to claim that these properties are intrinsic (i.e. in terms of being non-relational) and therefore are also reducible.[29]

In the figure below and in section 4.6 I will try to sum up the view that we have reached thus far. The reader may note, however that Chapter 5 also contributes to a completion of the specific ontological view developed in this chapter.

However, before doing that I would like to sum up this chapter in terms of a more complete visual model, followed by an appending comment.

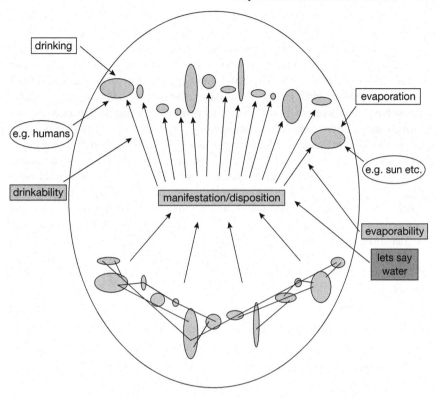

Figure 4.3 The dispositions/manifestation aspects in one i.e. a "Thing".

Hydrogen and oxygen together with other dispositional partners manifest something that we call H_2O. The manifestation, together with its further dispositions, is *water*. H_2O is the name for the *manifestation (aspect)* of the *partners* on the level below. *Water* is the whole bearer – the manifestation of the coming together of H and O *and* the dispositions of this actual manifestation. To call water H_2O reduces water to the manifestation of H and O (+ other manifesting partners). It reduces *water* to less than it is, because it equates water with its manifestation aspect and this aspect does nothing in itself. If it does something, it does something in togetherness with "other manifestation aspects", and we call these enabled abilities to do things dispositions. The "properties" of the manifestation aspect *are* the dispositions, and they are relationally had! The manifestation and the dispositions are *always already* a unit – a two-sided unit as Martin and Aristotle would say. This unit has so-called novel properties if we compare the unit with the mereologically computed sum of the partners that brings the manifestation about. This novelty ("emergence") comes about because the new manifestation is a part of a "new" whole, one that the manifesting partners that brought the manifestation about (existing on the level below) are not a part of *in the same way*. This situation is represented in the diagram by humans and the sun. Humans and the sun do not get into the same partnering relation with oxygen and hydrogen taken in separation. Oxygen reacts with other atoms; water is drunk (which true enough brings about metabolic reactions on lower levels etc.). Relational partners as such co-constitute the possibility for this new unit to have the dispositions/properties that it has. I say *co-constitute* because it would not be possible for water to have these (novel) dispositions had water not been manifested as H_2O by the manifesting partners in the first place. Again, dispositions are therefore not *determined* by the partnering instantiated in the manifestation; dispositions are relational in a way that stretches beyond their manifestation aspects. Dispositions are in this sense also "intentional". For water to be evaporable there must exist something such as the sun, which has the partnering disposition to bring about a certain temperature. The dispositional partnering of (e.g.) the sun is not *entailed* in the partnering going on between H and O.

Relational realism therefore makes dispositions irreducible despite the fact that they depend upon a "categorical" aspect that is brought about by the manifesting partners from the level below. This manifesting aspect 'fills in space' and makes it possible for the disposition to *adhere* to the bearer without being intrinsic (in terms of "independent") to the bearer. This prevents the *relata* from disappearing into the relation.

4.6 Towards a relational account of dispositions

In this section, I will attempt to sum up the theoretical commitments that we have reached thus far. Some of the commitments that I will explicate also include or trade upon new conceptual elements that will be clarified in Chapter 5.

§1 *Levels.* There are levels in nature that are real. Each level is made possible by the manifesting dispositions of the entities on the level below. Those manifestations constitute new dispositions that always already relate to a certain whole of partners. This whole is what I have called the '*qua*-whole'.

§2 *Neutral monism.* For each dispositional aspect there is a "categorical" aspect that can be traced back to the level below. I have called this categorical aspect the manifestation aspect. What we normally call an object and what the dispositionalist calls 'bearer' is the *combination* of the manifestation aspect and the dispositional aspect at a certain level. These aspects are not causally connected, but formally connected. Dispositionality is an aspect of manifestations and vice versa. This is in accord with Mumford's neutral monism and partly with Martin's two-sided view, as well as with the hylomorphic view of Aristotle, although there is an emphasis on the formal aspect of the relation between the two aspects. Water consists of a certain kind of manifestation of some dispositions that exist on a level that makes possible a certain array of dispositions (that can be further manifested, etc.). One may focus on the manifestation and manifesting partners on the level below – for instance: 'aggression was caused by adrenaline levels in the body' – or one may focus on the dispositional level of the whole object in question, e.g. "aggression was caused by the perceived threat X".

§3 *The dispositionality of the "categorical".* The categorical aspect is not categorical as such; it is just categorical (i.e. unconditional) in relation to given dispositions. For water to have the particular dispositions that it does, there must exist something that we call H_2O in an "unconditional" and manifested manner. On the other hand, this un-conditionality is just un-conditional in a level-specific sense, since this manifestation (H_2O) is (seen from the level below) conditioned by the mutual *manifestation partners* that bring *it* about. This is how the levels are also "physically" *related* "all the way – up and down". There are no categorical *properties* as such. This view might therefore also be labelled dispositional monism/pan-dispositionalism, although that would be slightly misleading. The view given here is consistent with Aristotle's "mild relativism" in the sense that what *matter* is – for a given *form* can itself be form for another matter (*Metaphysics*, Θ 7). Considering *water*, the *manifestation* partners are H and O (and other), while the *dispositional partners* are e.g. certain animals (e.g. drinkability), boats ("resistance" making floatability possible) etc. Considering hydrogen its dispositional partner is e.g. oxygen while its manifesting partners are electrons, protons and neutrons, etc.

§4 *Enduring manifestations.* The phrase 'the categorical aspect is really dispositional, seen from the level below' is more than an epistemic assertion, since this "categoricality" amounts to what I have called *manifestations of dispositions*. Manifestations of dispositions are what are created when two or more dispositions come together in their manifesting partnership. As I have said previously: much is said about dispositions, while comparatively little is said about their *manifestations*. Manifestations can have different characteristics:

(i) "self-destructive" manifestations. The manifestation can destroy the bearer of the disposition in the moment it is manifested (a vase breaking) or;

(ii) the manifestation can endure in different degrees. Some dispositions are manifest discontinuously (e.g. speech, a gene coding). Their manifestations are on and off, but the reason such a manifestation is off is not that it has "substantially changed" its bearer [*(i)*]. If it had, it would not be able to re-manifest. The dispositions that are endurable but discontinuously manifested are those that we pay most attention to, because they are the most dynamic ones.[30] Endurably manifesting dispositions that manifest continuously are those that we often call background conditions (together with *iii*). A deeper look into this field would reveal things such as manifestation patterns, cascading manifestation trajectories, etc. (e.g. ontogenesis). The enduring manifesting dispositions always seem to exert some energy (or are exposed to other "powers at work") while manifesting, something which brings the bearer into some kind of change or one may even say decay (cf., the second law of thermodynamics),[31] except from perhaps the strange phenomena that we call

(iii) Basic forces and constants. This third category is one that I barely dare to mention, because I know too little about the finer points of the topic (physics). However, I will simply mention it and leave it up to the reader to judge

whether or not it can be deemed a category on its own or whether it belongs to *(ii)*. The constant charge of, e.g. a dipole such as the electron, despite its continuously emitting electromagnetic rays, the gravitational force, etc., does not seem to destroy or decay its bearer (whatever that might be) while manifesting. Such properties nevertheless seem to be dispositional properties manifesting endurably.

Enduring manifested dispositions make *regularity* and iterative dispositions possible. They make up the "categorical basis" for the dispositions that are given on a certain level. The enduring manifestation of the liquidity-state of water is made possible by a certain group of constantly manifesting partners, which also make possible a number of other dispositions, each with its possible different type of discontinuous manifestations (i.e. water manifesting in a solid state will make up a different object with different dispositions than water manifesting in a liquid state). A thing "consists" of a special combination of those continuously manifesting dispositions on the lower level and dispositions that are further manifested, continuously or discontinuously. When some dispositional partners continually manifest they may also facilitate the possibility that a single new partner manifesting will bring about vast changes in the bearer (e.g. self-destructive manifestations). From the perspective of this account, there is no conflict between a process-view (e.g. a là Whitehead) and a typical 'object view'. Processes will typically be manifestations that change continuously. Such changes could also be due to feedback loops etc. (biology, cybernetic systems).

Processes can also be viewed as continually manifesting (running water) – and the process, when it manifests, will then give rise to new dispositions. (A very short-lived irregular manifestation could also be called a thing or a process, but is often called a phenomenon or incident. Further dispositions are difficult to establish in such instances of course since the manifestation lasts for such a short period of time, e.g. the creation of the heaviest elements in the laboratory.)

§5 *Enduring manifestations and the historicity of dispositions.* The account given here is that the different levels that exist in nature have been created by enduring manifesting dispositions. Nature consists of many layers of enduring manifesting dispositions that have been created over the course of *time*. The universe has a history. At each level there is a structure of enduring manifesting dispositions, which make up the possible ground for new enduring, discontinuously or self-destructively manifesting dispositions.

Enduring manifesting dispositions have arisen in the course of time and involve a particular history of events and a particular distribution of dispositional properties. The Humean phrase 'anything may produce anything else' may therefore be considered to be correct, but useless. The history of the universe might be "contingent", but this does not make the particular dispositional facts contingent. Thus even though the history of the universe is itself contingent, it's also a fact that I cannot survive from eating and digesting anything I wish (e.g. metal or wood) (see Mumford 1998, 236f.). And even though the history of the universe is itself contingent, ice *in fact* floats on water; it does not sink. One may call this the *facticity* of a certain state in the historical and ongoing development of the universe. Through the course of the history of the universe, "possible worlds" have come and gone, but at each moment there has only been one factual "possible world". We live in an "existential" universe. Time opens up and locks down possible trajectories. Since the "dispositional situation" is always in a state of relatedness, a change in one part of the system will involve changes in other parts of the system. There is no change going on outside the system. Or as Mumford says:

> If something is not a part of the web, it would be difficult to see how it could do anything. Having such a property would make no difference at all to what other properties did, did not, or could possibly have done. What would such a property be? What would fix its identity if not the relations born to other properties? The only answer seems to be a primitive property essence, a quidditas.
>
> (2004, 183)

As a matter of fact, the historical course of which we are a part has led to the particular situation in which there are observers such as humans, a situation that, as a matter of fact, excludes the possibility of water sinking when in its solid state. (Or rather, the other way around: if ice were heavier than water, the oceans would have been ice and the earth would have been inhabitable, and we would not be here.) This fact is neither contingent nor necessary.[32] Full contingency would only exist in a universe in which the properties were discrete and loose.[33] Given this factual and cascaded history there will be, as a matter of fact, properties and bearers that cannot exist alongside one another. This *de facto* restricts the partners of given dispositions. But as I have previously conceded, it is not possible for us to formally predict the future of the universe. Therefore, we cannot know the full range of the dispositions of the objects that we consider, since we cannot know which partners might occur and furthermore locally join (sometimes in continuously manifesting objects) in the course of time. But as a matter of a historically evolved fact, I can know that I don't have the disposition to fly or the disposition to re-grow an arm that has been cut off. If I had these properties, I would not 'be the one that I am'. *These are historically evolved dispositional facts (HEDFs)*. This description is very important for 'naturalness' and the further development of this concept (more on this in Chapter 5).

§6 *Identification.* The manifestation aspect "picks out" the entity as something specific (H_2O), but it does not identify *what* it is. What it is relates to what it can do, for instance put out fires. The manifestation aspect can initially only be picked out due to our knowledge of what the something does or has the capacity to do.[34] (As in neuroscience where activity areas in the brain are mapped through knowledge of the activity on the level above, e.g. 'feeling sad'.) In other words, it could not have been done the other way around because of the relational level-effects. (See point §7). Picking out a property and ascribing it to the object to which it belongs seems to be a hermeneutical process. That this is so would also programmatically be consistent with the neutral monist view. Failing to see that this is a hermeneutical process makes reductionism look plausible. Reductionism is plausible because ex *post facto* reasoning is possible.

§7 *The disposition–manifestation relation.* On the relation between manifestation and dispositions you could have had the same manifestation ("categorical base") but different *dispositions*. But you do not because the categorical base and the disposition are part of the same HEDF (see subsection 4.5.3 and section 5.2). The manifestation aspect *determines* neither the dispositions nor the further manifestation of these dispositions. We cannot "read" the disposition or the further manifestation (how some thing will manifest) from our knowledge of the manifestation aspect because the dispositions are not determined by the manifestation aspect (the "categorical" base) – they depend equally on the dispositional *partners*. (For an indirectly supportive argument, see Martin 2007, 89.) But given that something has exactly the same "categorical base", it will have the same dispositions (in the same historically evolved universe).

Therefore we will have:

A *Same categorical base, same dispositions.* This does not, of course, mean that a thing or process would have the same dispositions *manifested*, because that would depend upon the situation that it is in. All water has the same dispositions, but water behaves differently since different water in different situations manifests different dispositions. This partnering cannot of course be predicted from pure knowledge of the "H_2O base", neither in space nor in time.
   The other way around, we *can* have

B *Same disposition, different categorical base.* Multiple realization is the result of the fact that the same bearer (of course) can manifest different dispositions and not that the same disposition can manifest differently (subsection 4.4.1). At any place at any time the manifestation of the particular partnering between H and O will have the same dispositions (A). But it is still organisms such as, e.g. humans that make water have the disposition of being drinkable. Water being drinkable is partly independent from water being H_2O. It could have been XZY. Water being drinkable is a relationally evolved disposition occurring on the level where something like H_2O could be something like 'drinkable'. Drinkable is an *emergent* property that cannot be predicted from the manifestation aspect. But since we have (A), it is not strange that we would believe that the base determined the disposition.[35] This is also why arguing after the fact seems to be such an innocent thing to do, while it is clearly not. The relation is contingent and depends upon a certain historical development to be a historically evolved fact.

§8 *To change an object.* Any manifestation will change the object because to manifest something is to be exposed to other dispositional powers that will *eventually* bring about changes (with the possible exception of §4 (*iii*) – basic forces and constants). Manifestations in themselves will also exert some energy and "decay" in any case. When an object manifests a certain disposition, it will bring about changes in the particular way we find the object to be constantly manifested. (Objects and processes are not mutually exclusive.) Taking a certain thing, e.g. a fruit fly, into the laboratory (new conditions) does not change the object in the first place; it just changes which dispositions are manifested. When some given disposition is manifested, then the constantly manifesting "base" of the fruit fly *may* change. This will eventually change how the bearer is manifested further, etc.

Another way to change the object would of course be to change the manifesting partners "directly" (by e.g. inserting a gene). This is regarded as being more efficient. However, it should be conducted with the expectation of surprising effects, since again the categorical base does not determine the disposition.

§9 *Levels and objects*. Dispositions belong to objects. The *level* "picks out" the object bearing the disposition (i.e. 'This is a human being and not an assembly of organs, but this is not a society either an individual living being that (has the further capacity) to make up a society'.) The normal way to establish the ontological reality of objects is by referring to some notion of intrinsicness. But here too, levels play a crucial role. If levels are real, then objects are real. Saying that water *is* H_2O is a category mistake in the way that it ascribes the being of something to the wrong level (the wrong object). H_2O is the *manifestation* of the dispositions on the level below. Water *is* not (only) this manifestation; it is this manifestation and its dispositions, *together*. We believe that we can determine what *water* is by defining it as H_2O and thus describe its being by pointing to the "intrinsic" molecular properties of H_2O, but those properties are no longer "H_2O properties" because these H_2O properties have manifested themselves into a relational whole where those properties are no longer intrinsic *in this sense*. This relational whole makes "H_2O" do different things than it would in a *postulated/ fantasized* "pure" H_2O state.

A horse is an object that is constituted by: (1) its dispositions ("able to run", "able to pull", "able to mate", etc.); and (2) its categorical base (muscles, brain, skin, etc.). If this organismic *level* does not exist, "runable" does not exist either. Attributing dispositions demands a level-theory. A horse (*qua* horse) is not constituted by cells; *muscles* are (among other things) constituted by cells. The manifestation aspect of a horse is (I would say) its functional parts (eyes/skin, inner organs, etc.) manifested as a whole. Picking out cells, genes, molecules, quarks, etc., as the categorical base of a horse is a category mistake on the account developed here. The cells do not have the disposition to pump blood or to protect against cold weather. The right manifesting partners of a horse are its organs. The horse "consists" of many levels, but it is only one level that has the character of being the categorical/manifestation aspect of *the horse*. When we think that we can manipulate the horse *directly* on a nano-level, we are simply misguided. Our manipulation will have to trickle through all the levels before it reaches the qua-face of The Horse. Since we anticipate here that each level has its own *relational dynamic*, we should also expect that the *journey* from the nano-level to the horse-level will be long and unpredictable. The deeper we manipulate, the more we will see unpredictable and unintended effects. Certainly, on a reductionist account we would not see a rational reason that would explain such effects.

The view argued for here is formally a dispositional monist view (i.e. no categorical properties in the traditional sense). However, by highlighting the manifestations of the dispositions, a view has emerged that can be defined as *neutral monism*, where "categorical features" also have a place, and where "intrinsicness" can be accounted for without throwing relationalism overboard. This gives us a description that in general can explain why a headache pill works but does not fully work, or does not work all the time. Both totally holistic and totally reductionist accounts have got it wrong. A headache can occur for many qua-face relational reasons (but also for biochemical reasons[36]). Treating it biochemically *works* because mental activity has a "categorical base", but it does not work fully over time if the reason for having the headache is qua-face relational (e.g. stress). The pill also has unintended effects because it is put into a relational web of manifesting dispositions, where it changes some manifestations that eventually will dispose the patient to other relational effects.

4.7 The nature of things

The nature of a thing *is* its particular capacity to behave in a certain way. According to the proponent of dispositionalism, this behaviour is real. For macro-objects this realness is quite accessible to us. I know quite a lot, for instance, about the nature of ordinary wheat flour, the nature of a stove, the nature of building materials made from pine trees, the nature of cats, the nature of magnets, the nature of hens and the nature of light bulbs. These natures are what the passivist has problems accepting as real. Such an interlocutor says that my knowledge of these natures is contingent upon the way in which I *relate* to these things. To access these things as they really are, s/he says, we would have to look at them in a mind-independent way. A mind-independent way is one in which I would regard them as being something that they allegedly are in themselves, '*independently of everything else*'. What is wheat flour independently of everything else? According to the reductionist, the being of wheat flour is that which makes flour the flour that it is. And that which makes wheat flour wheat flour is its constitution – the reason why wheat flour behaves the way it does is due to its constitutive parts the reductionist say. What we call the nature of things is therefore just secondary epiphenomena determined upon or contingently aggregating from these parts. Furthermore, the way that I perceive this behaviour is even more unreliably a result of how I relate to the object.

This overall view is what I have tried to argue against so far in this book. I have also argued against constructivism, which can be regarded as an anti-thesis reflex of the reductionist view, namely that the nature of things is such that everything is relative to the perceiver and that the "things" that we talk about have no being of their own. I have argued against constructivism by saying: (1) that there *are* things; and (2) that our observation of them brings about certain manifestations of dispositions in the same way as *other things* bring about certain manifestations of dispositions, dispositions bestowed by the *things themselves (in terms of inherence)*. The dispositional view (developed here) does not support a relativistic epistemology. Perceiving some object or process brings forth certain manifestations of the object. This partnering between the object and the perceiving subject is not *principally* different from the partnering that occurs between, for instance, water and sugar cubes. In both cases, the partnering brings forth certain manifestations. Perceiving the same object from a different angle does not mean that the *object* changes as such, only that *other* dispositions of the *same object* are manifested. In the same vein, a different temperature on the "water" (ice) does not change the object (directly); it only brings forth a different disposition. Objectivity is thus sustained even though we are *in medias res*. In my view, this follows quite unproblematically from the dispositional theory itself, and it challenges the way in which we have been thinking about the beings of the world and how to access their realness for the last 400 years.

In arguing for this view I have also argued that dispositions must go together with bearers (objects) and levels to be real, and that a reductionist account in the context of a dispositional monist view would be self-defeating. I have argued that dispositions "create themselves" in a certain way, that they emerge from a whole of relational partners and belong to bearers that belong on a certain level. What things do is what makes them what they are, and what is done is done by bearers that exist on a certain level. Dispositions on one level are no more real than dispositions that belong to another level, because dispositions are not a net result of what dispositions do on a lower level, on *any* level! All of the emphasis that analytic philosophers, especially, put upon difficult physics (in order to keep up with philosophers and scientists who adopt a reductionist ontology) to my mind represents a grand circular failure. Recognizing dispositions and the level-specificity that comes with them, by contrast, makes possible arguments that support the reality of things like stones, hens, humans, trees and perhaps even landscapes.

If these things are real, then we need to treat them and comport ourselves in relation to them as though they were real also. How can we determine what such things are? Simply by understanding how they work; simply by understanding what kind of level-specific dispositions they have. An ecosystem, for instance, has certain level-specific dispositions such as the disposition to interact with the climate and to transfer nutrients and energy through the system. A plant such as wheat also has certain dispositions, which are relationally constituted. We need to understand how these dispositions relate to their partners so as to interfere "naturally" with the parts of the system as well as the system as a whole. (See Chapter 5.)

As I said in Chapter 2, I don't think that the scientist really goes by a complete reductionist ontology, because *procedurally* s/he needs to move heuristically between the levels, but I also said that the scientist, when *explaining* what is going on, often retains a reductionist ontology. The reason why s/he does this is complex, but we may assert that it is partly due to the many benefits of reductionism (monetary and others), but also partly because s/he does not seem to have a viable or compelling alternative (other than airy "holistic approaches").

Notes

1 As Schiller once said, "Nothing is cheaper and commoner in philosophy than monism [holism]; what, unhappily is still rare, is an attempt to defend it, and critically to establish its assumptions" (1897, 62).

2 See e.g. Dorato (2007). I have also cited Mumford, Martin and Bird previously. See also the next chapter. Extrinsic/"relational" dispositions that play no causal role are called Cambridge properties (see e.g. Mumford 1998, 122). It will become clear that these are not the type of relational properties we are talking about here, since we are not *starting* with the assumption that properties have to be independent to be real in the first place.

3 There has been a debate about this question in *Philosophy and Phenomenological Research*. The debate seemed to be kicked off by an article written by Langton and Lewis in 1998 in the same journal. (See esp. Sept. 2001 which is dedicated to this issue.)

4 Naturalness, the nature of things and processes, would disappear down the same black hole.

5 For a closer examination of this case see Mumford 1998: section 6.5.

6 See also Franklin 1986, 62.

7 For a thoroughgoing disposition-based criticism of this view, see Mumford and Anjum 2011.

8 This is, of course, not a novel idea. For an oversight, see Bunge 1959, chs. 4 and 6.

9 I am not certain whether this is the last word when it comes to the status of background conditions. We might define background conditions as those 'causal factors' that have an impact on a certain causal event, but are not reciprocally affected back by the same event, e.g. the gravity of the moon might influence the foraging of blue mussels, but this foraging does not influence the gravity of the moon. But in general we should be sceptical about doing away with dispositional partners by masking their all-pervasive existence by differentiating them into 'background conditions', 'triggering factors', etc.

10 The composition of causes: "[T]he joint effect of their causes is the sum of their separate effects" (Mill 1843/2002, 268).

11 Heteropathic laws: "[W]here a concurrence of causes takes place which calls into action new laws bearing no analogy to any that we can trace in the separate operation of the causes" (Mill 1843/2002, 269).

  Molnar leaves the impression that Mill would classify all cases as an instance of "composition of causes". This is not the case. Mill tries to eliminate what he calls heteropathic laws, but admits that there are some stubborn cases.

12 This expression is taken from genetics. Molnar has it from Dupré (1993). Polygeny: when different powers join to create a single manifestation. Pleiotropy: that one gene (object) contributes to many traits (Molnar 2003, 194).

13 It is true that Mumford and Anjum (2011) have developed this view in a slightly different direction in their Vector Addition Theory, but I am not sure if this makes the difference that is necessary to avoid the real problems that we encounter in the 'combinatorial puzzle'. See discussion that follows.

14 Here, I would claim the following: if laws really trade upon dispositions (e.g. Mumford 1998, 230; 2004; Ellis 2002, 59; Bird 2007, 43), and dispositions are singular contributors as Molnar and Mumford suggest, then actually I would prefer the opposite view – given that we describe laws as descriptions of how things *relationally act* and not how things act singularly. Or rather, the two views might be merged: laws can only trade on dispositions if dispositions are understood relationally. 'Laws' would then be describing a group of cases where dispositions work together in a regular way.

15 Constituents? Martin typically provides the classical philosopher's answer: "The ultimate constituents are best left to theoretical physics to detect ..." (2007, 39).

16 I am not sure if Luke Fenton-Glynn holds the same position as I do, but he seems to have the same worry as I do when he says that: "Interaction between causes in the production of an effect leads to non-linearities in composition, ensuring that the overall influence of a set of causes isn't factorizable into separate and independent contributions attributable to the individual causal factors" (2012, 10).

17 This contrasts with Mumford's view, which is that the manifestation is directly a new *property* (i.e., passing powers around).

18 Recall Hume who had the idea that everything that is not necessary must be contingent, and that Humeans have struggled with 'possibility' in general, wanting to show that potencies can be dealt with in terms of actuality and logical possibility. The heavy price that empiricists such as Hume are willing to pay is that they cannot distinguish between what is logically possible and what is possible in any real sense. (Not everyone thinks that David Lewis's solution, which is to argue that possible worlds are real, is the right way to go!)

19 This is not the same question as the identity question of dispositions, since this has to do with the identity of objects.

20 This is analogous to intentionality. Thinking is always thinking *about* something, and it is the specificity of the thoughts, the *specific* intentional content, that make *thinking into thinking* (i.e. I am now thinking about the "sun that finds the landscape so beautiful that it refuses to disappear down the horizon in the summertime": where are the neurons *determining* this thought?). This "something" is never contained in the brain or the "thoughts themselves", but is something that ascends in the space between the outer world and the mind – and which therefore cannot be reduced to either of the parts. In this sense I agree with Molnar (2003), who argues that mental intentionality is only possible because dispositions in general are intentional (that is: "directed towards something outside themselves", or rather outside of the bearer, I would add, ibid., 63).

21 See Heil 2003, 216–217. Cf. Locke's distinction between real and nominal essences.

22 This example is from Bird 2006, 501. Bird does not make the same distinction between *de re* and iterative potentiality, however.

23 I have not laid out Bird's quite technical solution in this book, because I think that it does not solve the problems that I claimed that the dispositional monists and Mumford face (see sections 3.3–3.5). Mumford says that his relational view is not problematic in relation to the regress problem, or what I would call the problem of 'relata disappearing in the relation', as long as there is a final set of properties. I don't agree with this and I also think that his promising start is not sufficiently worked out.

24 I could have used 'partners' instead of 'conditions', but the partnering idea belongs to a more specific and restricted ontology, and it is more important here to formulate the issue widely than to use the language that I would ideally prefer.

25 Every thing must go, as Ladyman and Ross (2007) say in their book on structural realism.

26 More accurately: a spectator with a certain ability to see these wavelengths as red.

27 The structural realists don't accept objects as a part of the ontology in the first place, and are therefore somehow not hit by this argument at all. This is not important here, however, since we would like to hold onto a disposition ontology, which definitely seems to require such "entities", i.e. bearers.

28 John Heil and in part also C.B. Martin hold a dispositional account and a reductionistic account simultaneously (see e.g. Heil 2003, 143ff. up against ch. 12) and Brian Ellis concedes "[D]ispositions of things depend on the intrinsic causal powers or capacities of their most basic constituents" (2002, 66).

29 A useful comparison to the view suggested here could be J.S. Mill's view on laws. He thinks of laws in a partly relational manner; that they are "invariant" or constant because of the *other* "invariant" and constant laws. The "invariant" laws are held together by each other

> From these separate threads of connection between parts of the great whole which we term nature a general tissue of connection unavoidably weaves itself, by which the whole is held together. If A is always accompanied by D, B by E, and C by F it follows that A and B is accompanied by D E, A C by D F, B C by E F and finally A B C by D E F; and thus the general character of regularity is produced, which along with and in the midst of infinite diversity, pervades all nature.

(Mill 1891, 206)

It is at least a view where things have their dispositions (laws) in relation to other dispositions, and where there is nothing outside this system.

30 This must not be confused with what Andreas Hütterman calls discontinuously manifesting disposition, or DMD (Hüttermann 2007). His concept of a continuously manifesting disposition (CMD) is also completely different from what I call enduring manifestations.

31 The walls in a house have some dispositions that constantly endure, but the walls 'are falling down' (if they are not maintained). Similarly with mountains, the sun and the galaxies. Life processes are of course special in the sense that they are able to feed themselves with new energy. This exertion of energy, when manifesting, changes the object little by little, or sometimes a lot (tipping points). Objects are therefore in constant change. I believe that the essences that we intuitively ascribe to things are due to a relatively stable constellation of mutually manifesting partners on the level below. As long as the manifestation of the dispositions does not destroy this 'relatively stable constellation', we will have objects that are "susceptible" to essence ascriptions (essentialism) and nomothetic explanations.

32 Against necessity and determinism I will again invoke the claim that the level below/ categorical base/micro-properties, or whatever we might call it, cannot determine dispositions on a higher level because of the relational nature of dispositions. (See section 4.6, §7.)

33 Helen Beebee maintains that even though we cannot give a reason why the universe is regular we can still "explain particular phenomena by saying something about their causal history, for example" (2006, 525). I believe that this is completely correct, but I don't think that she is able to arrive at this conclusion if everything, all the time, is loose and separate (which she, as a Humean, is generally committed to saying). Relational dispositionality ensures that there is a limited span at every point in the 'history of possibilities', and this also makes up the possible condition for the *explanation* that she is talking about. I am, however, sympathetic to the possible viewpoint that the account given here can infact incorporate the main and basically Humean intuition that she is trying to argue for in this article.

34 This view is partly consistent with the view that we saw Aristotle had in section 2.1, although the "form" is not what it is in virtue of the *telos* of the substance ("The nature of a thing is its end and its purpose" (*Phy.* 194 a30)), but rather in virtue of its relational partners.

35 In section 2.4 I referred to an article in *New Scientist* to illustrate what I meant by the 'Lockean reality principle'. It should be clear by now that I agree that the "*neurotransmitter called GABA*" – in this case a manifesting partner for depression – plays a role. What I would disagree with is when someone says that this "categorical base" *determines* that depressed people see the world differently and that this would be the only way to pick out the fact that they do so. This makes a significant difference, especially if we think that we can cure the "deficient" way that the depressed person perceives the world by manipulating the neurotransmitter.

36 Although measured biochemical "causes" may camouflage relational partnering, e.g. in the case of ADHD. One might measure a chemical imbalance by reduced dopamine levels. But the cause may still be related to stress in early childhood conditions, stress that *eventually* brings about the measured 'chemical unbalance' (e.g. Crittenden and Kulbotten 2007).

References

Aristotle (1998) *The Metaphysics* (trans. H. Lawson-Tancred), Penguin.

Armstrong, D. (1989) *A Combinatorial Theory of Possibility*, Cambridge University Press.

—— (2005) "Four Disputes about Properties", *Synthese*, vol. 144.

Beebee, H. (2006) "Does Anything Hold the Universe Together?", *Synthese*, vol. 149.

Bird, A. (2006) "Potency and Modality", *Synthese*, vol. 149.

—— (2007) "The Regress of Pure Powers", *The Philosophical Quarterly*, vol. 57 (229).

Bunge, M. (1959/1963) *Causality*, Meridian Books.

Crittenden, P.M., and Kulbotten, G.R. (2007) "Familial Contributions to ADHD: An Attachment Perspective", *Tidsskrift for Norsk Psykologforening*, 44, 1220–1229.

Dawkins, R. (1976) *The Selfish Gene*, Oxford University Press.

Dorato, M. (2007) "Dispositions, Relational Properties and the Quantum World", in M. Kistler and B. Gnassounou (eds.) *Dispositions and Causal Powers*. Ashgate.

Dupré, J. (1993) *The Disorder of Things*, Harvard University Press.

Ellis, B. (2002) *The Philosophy of Nature*, Acumen.

Fenton-Glynn, L. (2012) "Getting Causes from Powers" (review), *Mind*, vol. 121 (484).

Franklin, J. (1986) "Are Dispositions Reducible to Categorical Properties?", *Philosophical Quarterly*, vol. 36.

Heil, J. (2003) "Levels of Reality", *Ratio*, September.

Hüttermann, A. (2007) "Causation, Laws and Dispositions", in M. Kistler and B. Gnassounou (eds.) *Dispositions and Causal Powers*, Ashgate.

Kepler, J. (1609/1992) *New Astronomy* (trans. W.H. Donahue), Cambridge University Press.

Kim, J. (1999) "Making Sense of Emergence", *Philosophical Studies*, vol. 95.

Ladyman, J. and Ross, D. (2007) *Everything Must Go*, Oxford University Press.

Langton, R. and Lewis, D. (1998) "Defining Intrinsic", *Philosophy and Phenomenological Research*, June.

Laughlin, R. and Pines, D. (2000) "The Theory of Everything", *Proceedings of the National Academy of Sciences*, January.

Martin, C.B. (2007) *Mind in Nature*, Oxford University Press.

Mill, J.S. (1843/2002) *A System of Logic*, University Press of the Pacific, Honolulu.

Molnar, G. (2003) *Powers* (ed. S. Mumford), Oxford University Press.

Morrison, M. (2006) "Emergence, Reduction and Theoretical Principles: Rethinking Fundamentalism", *Philosophy of Science*, vol. 73.

Moss, L. (2004) *What Genes Can't Do*, MIT Press.

Mumford, S. (1998) *Dispositions*, Oxford University Press.

—— (2004) *Laws in Nature*, Routledge.

—— (2007) "Power, Dispositions, Properties: A Causal Realist Manifesto", in R. Groff (ed.) *Revitalizing Causality: Realism about Causality in Philosophy and Social Science*, Routledge.

—— (2009) "Passing Powers Around", *The Monist*, vol. 92.

Mumford, S. and Anjum, R.L. (2011), *Getting Causes from Powers*, Oxford University Press.

Pritchard, D. (2006) *What is this Thing Called Knowledge?*, Routledge.

Schiller, F.C.S. (1897) "Reply: Lotze's Monism", *Philosophical Review*, vol. 6.

Woodward, J. (2003) *Making Things Happen. A Theory of Causal Explanation*, Oxford University Press.

5 Rethinking naturalness

5.0 Introduction

This chapter consists of two elements. The first element deals with – once again – the question of potentiality; but this time in a way that relates this question directly to the question of naturalness. The second element deals with the questions related to environmental ethics, science and technology that we raised in chapters 1 and 2 in the light of the theoretical commitments made throughout chapters 4 and 5.

What I will not do is to present some kind of 'ethics of dispositions', i.e., a theory about why it would be *good* to take the nature of things into our considerations. There are two major reasons for this. One is that I do not want to add a further element into this book, an element that would be controversial and contested. What I have said thus far is already strained with enough claims as is.

The second reason is that I have come to the conclusion, also anticipated in Chapter 1, that such a theory is not strictly needed. What I conclude in section 5.7 is that the account given here is *enough* to make the case that instrumental action indirectly grants the beings in question 'intrinsic value'. Strangely enough, we have a situation in which person A, acting in accordance with pure instrumental rationality, and person B, acting in accordance with a deep valuation of some being(s) in question, come out very similarly.

5.1 Logical and *de re* possibility

We have seen that dispositions can be formally expressed as conditionals. 'If I were to put this sugar cube into water, then it would dissolve'. Or: 'if gene A were to be expressed, then gene B would be silenced'. Formulating a conditional is a way to express a hypothesis about what will happen *if*. The process of making workable hypotheses is a familiar process to any scientist or engineer who wants to explore reality or develop certain technologies. Sometimes these conditionals might *seem* impossible (e.g., Drexler's idea about nano-robots/molecular assemblers). But by systematically and carefully changing present conditions with the help of laboratory facilities, we may explore a certain object in new ways – whereby, of course, new dispositional properties can be discovered and manifested and functionally put to use. Through the manipulation of the conditions (i.e. the dispositional partners), we may explore the wider range of the dispositions of things. This exploration sometimes gives rise to the production of an "IF–THEN unit", which we call a technology. "IF–THEN units" of this sort are apparently possible in a dispositional sense *since they obviously work* somehow. This is not categorically different from, let us say, the process of photosynthesis, which evidently also works according to schemes of the type "IF ... THEN ...", which eventually are not expressly restricted by anything more than the rules of logic. Wherein, then, is the restriction to be found that defines the real possibility of dispositional potentialities as distinct from mere logical possibility? Is there truly a difference between *de re* potentiality and logical possibility? The following theoretical differences are highlighted here:

#1 Logical possibility does not have the same relationship to potentiality and manifestation. In the case of dispositional potentiality, you will for instance have a massive number of cases in which the manifestations of two dispositions temporally exclude one another (Mumford 2004, section 10.8). A given disposition might never be manifested due to some other dispositions being constantly manifested. Within the gravitational field of Earth, the *manifestation* of gravitation excludes the manifestation of objects floating freely in space. The manifestation of a gene G coding for the production of enzyme X might obstruct another gene H from coding for the production of enzyme Z. The examples are truly countless. *Logically*, however, most of these manifestations do not exclude each other. Since logical possibilities do not depend upon a manifestation's being a real possibility, there are never cases in which logical possibilities exclude each other because of their manifestations.

#2 I have previously argued that I believe that the world of dispositions is given by the historical funnel of the universe (subsection 4.5.3). A sugar cube dissolves as a matter of fact in water, and this is due to the historically produced properties/dispositions that water and sugar have. There is no metaphysical (time-independent) physical or logical reason that can be given for the fact that water dissolves sugar; it is a fact, but it is neither a necessary nor a contingent fact. But let us now swap our boring sugar cube with a 44-magnum gun. Let us also anticipate that we observed (under the same conditions) that the gun was actually dissolved in water within twenty-five seconds. Would we still call this water? If the identity of a thing is defined by what it can do and water is suddenly able to dissolve a 44-magnum gun in twenty-five seconds, we might start to wonder whether it is really water or if it is some extremely caustic acid that looks like water. However, if we were to say that water has the properties that it has independently of everything else, and that it is the laws or the way these independent properties combine that determines their behaviour, we would be able to say: 'Nothing strange here: water can dissolve a 44-magnum gun in twenty-five seconds, and it is *still water because it has still the same categorical properties*. It is only the laws that have changed.'

This is not how a dispositionalist would describe the situation. Stephen Mumford – and I, in the account given in the previous chapter – would, for instance, argue that properties/dispositions and their identities are interconnected in a very fundamental way (Mumford 2004, 182ff.). What water does is related to other properties, which are further related to other properties, etc. And there is nothing outside of this system, as Mumford says (ibid., 183). We would therefore not be able to change the properties of water without also changing a lot of the other things that are contained in the same universe. Water is not water independently of other things, or independently of what it does. The concept of logical possibility or total contingency requires full compossibility between properties, something that excludes the idea of interconnectedness and identity throughout this historically evolved web.

For these and other reasons, it should be clear that there is a difference between logical possibility and real potentiality. We can imagine that something is logically possible, but our imagination will stop at what is physically possible; this border is guarded by what we normally call "the necessities of nature".

The question is whether or not there are reasons to believe that there is even something real in what I provisionally have called "less than physical necessity". There must be, if the concept of naturalness is to have a counterpart in nature as such. There must be something about the real world that makes it possible to act both in keeping with and in contradiction to it. Real potentiality must not be contrasted with logical possibility alone; it must in our case contain a feature that can give rise to yet another distinction.

5.2 HEDFs

Within the scientific community it is believed that during the first second of the Big Bang 13.8 billion years ago, electrons and then (when quarks glued together) protons and neutrons were created. During the first part of this "sequence" the universe expanded rapidly in a 'cosmic inflation'. This allegedly "smoothed" the expansion of the universe to the extent that we can now observe similar background radiation all over the (known) universe. However, it was not smoothed to the extent that stars, galaxies and quasars could not be created one billion years later. Concerning the chemical elements, it is assumed that hydrogen was created during the first second. Helium, lithium and deuterium were created within the next three minutes. The other elements such as carbon, nitrogen, oxygen and iron were created a billion years later, when the formation of stars and quasars made possible the necessary pressure and temperature conditions.

The cosmology of the Big Bang is not something that I *know* and really understand; it is rather something that I have read about in my efforts to get some kind of grip on what is assumed to be the history of our universe. In what follows, I therefore do not focus too closely on the contested facts, but rather try to convey general features that seem to be agreed upon in the varying portraits of this history.

What is worth noticing first and foremost is exactly the point that the universe is said to have a history. (This would even be true for the constants of the universe.

Barrow 1996, 137[1]). For example, the heavier elements were created by hydrogen and helium in the "wrinkle- and gravitation-created" stars, 12.7 billion years ago. On the one hand, some "wrinkles in the universe" (ultimately due to some quantum fluctuations) had to exist, in order for stars, etc., to be made – something which, as we saw, made possible the creation of oxygen, carbon, iron and other elements that have turned out to be vital for life processes. On the other hand, had the wrinkles been too "rough", then the Big Bang would probably have ended in the big crunch. But due to the cosmic inflation, which took place 10^{-43} till 10^{-34} after the Big Bang, this did not happen (Greene 2004, 305). Had these events not occurred, and in this order, I would certainly not be here writing about it now. The *conditions* of the Big Bang *have been*, but still prevail by creating the context and setting necessary for survival and life as we know it today.

What is also worth noticing is that the history is always told in terms of describing the conditions under which the different "steps" could take place, for instance, temperature is a condition that is always of utmost importance. Everything that happens and is created happens and is created in relation to "everything else", but in steps, it seems. The history is a history of an evolution wherein conditions create the conditions that allow something new to come about. If this is so, it fits very neatly with the disposition theory and the iterativity of dispositions, through endurable manifestations. The manifestation of a disposition always creates conditions for new dispositions to occur. This is how something can develop and have a history that creates novelty in the first place. What we call novelty is, as I have argued, made possible by the fact that dispositions are relational. Whenever dispositions are manifested, there will always be a chance for novel dispositions to come into existence and manifest the new qua-whole that eventually and inevitably will "encounter" new partners. If these partners come together in a way that manifests the dispositions continuously, we will probably call it an object (or a process); and we will understand it as an object (new qua-whole) that will also be capable of bestowing further dispositions, which, given certain partners, will manifest within yet another qua-whole, etc.

Is *contingency* the word that could best describe this process? About this question I have noticed the following. Researchers try to figure out why the Big Bang started as it actually did by imagining other possible ways for events to have unfolded. There seems to be no ultimate reason for the actual trajectory that it took (Barrow 1996, 101).[2] The likelihood of a universe with human observers is very small, yet here we are gazing back in time (ibid., 140). This phenomenon famously has a name: *weak anthropic principle*. The background for making this into a principle is of course the idea that the development of the universe is thought to be basically contingent. It is against the background of contingency that the likelihood of the conditions that we see today is measured. The alternative would be to see it as an unfolding of necessity. The fact is, however, that necessity does not seem to apply. From a set of premises (initial conditions) we cannot predict the actual development of the universe.[3] This rules out any (strong) necessity-thesis.[4] But still: is it contingent? I would argue no: it is neither contingent nor necessary. It was not necessary that carbon develop, relative to the fact that wrinkles developed during the cosmic inflation; many other conditions had to be in place as well – highly unlikely conditions, we might add.[5] But when those conditions were right, then, as a matter of historically evolved fact, the dispositions of helium and beryllium manifested what we humans call carbon, which then had dispositions in its encounter with the "new" dispositional partners. *That* was not contingent, at least not in the Humean sense.

By the same token, we might argue that the development of the ingestion system of humans was "accidental" in the sense of not being designed or determined, but the fact that I actually have the system that I have makes it impossible for me to digest, let us say, a marble stone. The propensities or dispositions of things are in *this sense* not contingent. Given the historically evolved relational fact that my gut is the way it is, I cannot digest marble stones. On the other hand, it is not necessary that my gut became the way it is from the fact that the universe had developed conditions for the possibility of life, etc.

The point is not to make big claims about cosmological questions, but rather to underpin the view that the real compossibility of the universe is restricted in a very fundamental way that on the other hand is not due to laws or essences bringing about the specific dispositions that things do – as a matter of fact – have.

We may consider a different example to make this even clearer. The triplet UAU (CodonA) does not in fact code for tyrosine (amino acid B) because of its particular molecular make up. There is nothing in its molecular structure that necessitates the fact that it codes for tyrosine. UAU codes for many other amino acids as well, depending on the context (Laubichler and Wagner 2001, 63). The connection between these two levels is *dis*entangled, if by 'entangled' we mean that the lower level (UAU) determines which amino acid has to be produced. We cannot answer the question "Why does UAU code for tyrosine?" by saying "Because of the molecular composition X". The answer must be sought in the *history* brought about by a myriad of different evolutionary pathways wherein different relationally constituted dispositions (such as UAU-tyrosine) did and *could* occur, step by step.

The history and the parts involved in the history might be called contingent in the sense of not being necessarily determined, but the fact that *this* deoxyribonucleic acid (DNA) codes for *this* amino acid, in *this* and *this* way, is not therefore contingent. The DNA does not do this in a contingent way, in the sense that you might as well make it code for something else in the same specific situation. It's not like a word (sign) for which one day we could potentially decide a different signification. The codonA is caught in, and is constituted by, a relational web wherein this codon as matter of fact codes for tyrosine (given relational manifesting partners a, b, c, etc.). What it does is therefore both non-contingent and non-necessary, but it is nevertheless a fact that it does the things that it does. It is a historically evolved dispositional fact that no-one can bypass or evade. We are prisoners of the historically produced web of the universe. The potentiality of a *certain* deoxyribonucleic acid (DNA) molecule is enormous and broad, but given a certain historical evolvement, this potentiality becomes strongly restricted – as a matter of historically evolved dispositional *fact*, our "codonA" will manifest such and such in a way that gives it further specific dispositions (and so on).

The relational ontology that has been highlighted in this book gives us a special advantage when it comes to the understanding and interpretation of this situation. From the perspective of the relational account, we should not really say that the HEDFs *restrict* the particular "DNA-unit", but rather that they define it. It is not as if you have the gene and subsequently the HEDFs restricting it.[6] It is due to the particular history of evolution that the particular DNA-molecule has its particular dispositions (see subsection 4.5.3 iii). Its identity is created historically. This means that the identity of the molecule is not unchangeable and fixed, which it would have to be if we were essentialists – but that does not mean that the identity can be changed arbitrarily (as Hume would say), either. *Its identity is simultaneously held together by the continuously manifesting partners on the level below and by there being the specific mutual manifesting partners on its qua-face level.* This is of course again a conclusion that rests on the Eleatic principle of pegging realness to dispositions.

5.3 Possible-I and possible-N

Apparently humans can, as I said, carry out experiments and reveal new and sometimes also surprising dispositional properties of different phenomena. We are able to put things together in a way that the HEDF-totality did not do, e.g., we can insert a flounder-gene into the genome of a plant. Humans can also transfer experimental set-up situations into a more permanent working system – "IF–THEN units" we often call technologies or systems of technologies, as noted earlier. By changing different manifestations and manifestation conditions, we can facilitate or mask the manifestations of different dispositions. This is basically what is done with a technology or in an experiment wherein we arrange the conditions such that they become ideal for the particular bearers to manifest the dispositions in question. Such an arrangement, however, *demands "external" construction and energy* in order for it to be constructed and maintained.[7] Such systems are constructed in such a way that if those powers were retracted, the system would fall apart and retreat into a being where 'normal conditions' dominate.[8] (Mumford uses the phrase 'normal/ordinary background-conditions', although in a different context (1998, 87ff.).)

J.S. Mill covers the main meaning of this concept with his expression "what nature spontaneously offers" (2002, book 3, ch. VII, §3). An experiment or a technology investigating, rearranging or exploiting the wider range of the dispositions spontaneously offered is always compared to the possible-N (retreat) situation. The laboratory conditions typically deviate from *something*, or else they would not be called 'laboratory conditions'. What is this something? I call this something possible-N. The possible-N is that for which anything else can be called ideal conditions (although I believe the expression 'ideal conditions' is ontologically inaccurate).

We have seen that there are many suggestions as to how we should understand the term naturalness. The term is notoriously ambiguous and filled with "intuitive" opaque meaning. My solution to this problem is to use the more specific term possible-N to denote what I define as being the meaning of 'naturalness'. This is a technical term that has few further connotations, normative and ontological. This gives me the opportunity to define this concept in relative independence from the variable semantic associations of 'naturalness'. Possible-N is compared with possible-I. Possible-I does not mean unnatural but points to the fact that nature does have a "wider range" than what we find to be possible-N. Within the range of the "physically possible", there is a more *restricted* range brought about by the *actual* history of the universe (possible-N). It is physically possible for me to jump from a skyscraper, but the actual course that the historical development the universe took has not given me dispositions to survive such a fall. It is physically possible for me to smoke cigarettes, but the particular evolutionary development that my ancestors took did not equip me with dispositions that could make the impact of smoking un-harmful for some of my bodily functions. The natural world that I am born into is simply not captured by relations that can be described as either necessary or contingent. It is not so that whenever I cannot physically do something it makes no difference what I do.

What I want with these two concepts is obviously to place them within a theory that explains how we can change nature in a boundless number of ways, while at the same time the *same theory* can show us why and how not all of these ways is in consent with the way "nature is". What we do not want is a theory that points to what is simply possible or not, and then a *pure* ethical theory (or cultural/religious dogmas) that tells us why we should or should not make use of certain possibilities.

5.4 Containment and possible-I

What we have said about the distinction between possible-I and possible-N might seem promising, although at this point also too suggestive and premature. By aid of the expression 'contained use', we will see if there is a way to define the distinction between possible-I and possible-N in a more systematic and exhaustive way.

Contained use is an expression that designates a situation in which different organisms, chemicals, etc., are handled in such a way that they "cannot" escape the laboratory or a similar type of facility.[9] The material that is subjected to containment is directly extracted from the possible-N (e.g., different viruses) or it can be "material" that is novel (e.g., GMOs, synthetic organisms, etc.). The rationale behind what we call contained use is that we do not want the material to "contaminate" *something*, and it is this something that I call the possible-N (world).

The difference between possible-N and possible-I has, to my mind, been confused in the modern history of science. Science, broadly construed seems to assume that it is the possible-N ("reality") that is unveiled, while it normally uncovers both possible-N *and* possible-I. Often there has been – as I claimed in section 2.7 – an emphasis on the possible-I (through experiments), in the sense that it is believed that one *thereby* discovers the 'essence of nature', *and therefore the alleged possible-N itself* (e.g., Galileo Galilei and onwards). Such emphasis has been criticized by constructivists, who say that experiments in general are a way to construct the *truth* (see subsection 2.5.1 and section 2.8). This is, however, also a misconception. Things and processes have an endless range of dispositions that we can observe when these things are put into different partnering situations. Experiments typically bring about "a different situation": a situation wherein the same or other dispositions of the object are studied and uncovered. *Accordingly, experiments do not unveil the secret essential mystery of the world; neither does pure observation of the possible-N itself.* It is not as if the possible-I un-covered in a laboratory (*in-vitro*) is less *true* than the possibilities-N uncovered *in-vivo* (see section 2.8). Every object or process comes with a large and essentially indeterminate set of dispositions, any member of which depends upon its partners being existentially present for its manifestation. The main difference broadly speaking is that the partners are put in place and maintained by humans in the case of possible-I and by the HEDF-totality in the case of possible-N.[10] However, it seems that both the scientific realist and the constructivist hold on to the possible-N-reality as superior. What they *disagree on is the role that possible-I plays*, and what they both misunderstand, in my view, is the particular relation between possible-I and possible-N. The constructivists can only claim that the possible-I is *constructed on the basis of something* being possible-N, but are unable to *explain* why something that should be basically constructed nevertheless can *work* (cf. 'Miracle Argument'). What is it about possible-N that can make the constructed possible-I work? Why is it not the case that we can construct *anything* and make it work? Do we need to know what possible-N is to *construct* something? If so, what is exactly constructed and what is not? The answers to these questions have not been given by the constructivists. This makes their criticism of science and technology unsuccessful.

The scientific realist, meanwhile, does not understand or realize that the *lack of recognition* of the relevant difference between possible-N and possible-I leads to a reductionist approach (something that *de facto* rules out possible-N). S/he thinks that the *ceteris paribus* "necessities" found in the possible-I situation map *the real relations* found in possible-N, which of course is not the case according to the dispositional account supported and worked out here. When the realists find their distinct contributor causes in the laboratory they are not aware of the fact that this is "extracted" from a relational HEDF-totality in the first place. The realist thinks that the truth found in the laboratory *is* the truth about reality as such. That is how nature really works.

To call something constructed, the constructivist needs to appeal to something un-constructed, but since that is also constructed, the constructivist is not in the position to investigate and understand what the possible-N might be. In the case of realism, there is no relevant distinction between possible-N and possible-I – and therefore, *de facto*, no nature of wholes. This means that a realist thinks that what is true for possible-I is *also* true for possible-N. This mistake is a harmful mistake of potentially wide-ranging proportions.

What is the reasonable justification for contained use, and how can we differentiate between what is naturally possible (possible-N) and what is physically possible (possible-I)?

Since discovering something possible-I (*in-vitro*) is not discovering the essence of something possible-N, we can rarely make the possible-I work "naked" in the possible-N situation without transporting all of the constructed conditions into the possible-N world. We need to keep in mind that the possible-I conditions have been constructed with the exact aim of bracketing the possible-N reality for the sake of making the possible-I *work* (i.e., manifesting the preferred dispositions). Thus, to make the possible-I work *in-vivo*, one has to construct a *functional ferry* that can transport those conditions into the possible-N state. This whole package – the ferry containing the (contrived) conditions, along with the objects with their dispositions and manifestations – is what we call a technological application. We have to *contain* or protect the preferred causal relations by also transporting the partners maintaining or making these relations *work* as intended. There is no place on possible-N Earth that Galileo or any experimentalist would not have to bring his laboratory gear with him. However, there is no difference in terms of *truth*; the real difference is that the possible-I constructed knowledge is true about the possible-I situation, not about the possible-N situation. And the reason for this is, of course, *that dispositions are relational* and historically evolved. The relational partners have to be in place for the preferred dispositions to manifest. Against this background we might therefore say that any use of technology is always contained in a broader sense; the issue therefore concerns *degrees* of containment, not either containment or no containment. Not either natural or unnatural.

5.4.1 "The size of a container"

The question about unintended consequences concerns how inclusive we decide the container should be. Often we make containers inclusive enough to get the desired possible-I constructed function to work, but seldom do we make them inclusive enough for possible-N to "work"; we protect the possible-I from the possible-N, but not vice versa![11] Possible-I is contained from possible-N, but possible-N is not contained from possible-I. This creates an asymmetry that looks like Figure 5.1.

It is not physically possible for the possible-I to work without containment. Since technologies by definition are conditioned IF–THEN units, we cannot "let them out" and expect them to work. They need their *ceteris paribus* container in order to work. While this is almost a truism, one might expect that the reasoning would also apply the other way around. In fact it does not, the asymmetry says. It is *physically* possible for the possible-N to "work" even if possible-N is not protected from possible-I (It will always "work" somehow). But the fact that this is *physically* possible does not mean that possible-N *should* not have been protected from possible-I. For example, a car is a structural whole, containing conditions for the basic functions

Possible-N → [Possible-I],
Possible-I → Possible-N.

Asymmetry: The possible-I is protected from the relational effects of possible-N but not vice versa.

Figure 5.1 Asymmetry between possible-N and possible-I

to work. These *containments* are comprehensive enough to prevent it from being "absorbed back into" possible-N, at least for its "life-time" of twenty-odd years, given decent maintenance and the technological infrastructure of gasoline stations and car repairs, etc. However, it, in turn, does not fully *contain* all the *possible* impacts it has on possible-N. The car technology itself is not comprehensive enough to contain all these impacts on possible-N.[12] In many cases we accept this as a trade-off with other values, but that does not mean that there is no possible-N! Rather the opposite. If there were no possible-N, there would be no trade-off.

If one (for some ontological or other reason) thinks that what is physically possible is what *is* possible, one will of course not bother about how possible-I → possible-N, since, to one's knowledge, there is no possible-N. Persons who don't understand the nature of this asymmetry will call the effects on the possible-N unintended effects. Persons who do understand it will also understand that our intentions cannot excuse these effects. They are able to see the "fairness" in making the container inclusive enough to also protect the possible-N from the possible-I.

The asymmetrical gap between possible-N → [possible-I] and possible-I → possible-N is evidence revealing that naturalness has its counterpart in the real world – that it is a property that can also be ascribed to scientific objects.[13]

Another and complementary way of perceiving this issue is to say that the impact made by possible-I onto the possible-N is really a possible-N → possible-I relation. This way of seeing it highlights to a higher degree the relational aspect of the situation, i.e., that casual pathways are seen as mutual.

In an experiment, we seek to define what something does, i.e., what it is. In an experiment we may, for instance, observe that geneA codes for enzymeX. If this happens repeatedly, we will say that geneA has the disposition L – the ability to "code for" enzymeX. When this *defining* has been performed under given laboratory conditions we should, unless we are essentialists or Humeans, regard those conditions as part of the definition.[14] What happens when we put this into the possible-N world, is that the possible-N world starts to expand the *definition* of our geneA, in the sense that geneA begins to manifest "new and unpredictable things" (directly or iteratively). By putting geneA into possible-N (*in-vivo*), we will explore new dispositions of geneA that did not manifest in the laboratory situation (nor in the original possible-N conditions either). The dispositions of the lab-geneA might be turned off and other dispositional properties might be "turned on" when it is placed under possible-N (as well as different possible-I) conditions.[15] The required size of the container should therefore be measured in relation to the risk related to the possible-N induced definitions of geneA, i.e., considering whether or not we should contain the possible-I in a way that does not unleash the 'relational effects' produced by the possible-N in a way that is undesirable.

As we have seen, a Humean would not accept this claim of asymmetry, simply for the reason that there would be no way to distinguish between possible-I and possible-N in a world of contingently related properties. A Lockean reductionist might admit to the difference between possible-I and possible-N (in an inverted version), but would have no worries about the asymmetry. The behaviour of a possible-I unit is *necessitated by its parts* and the unit will therefore not *do* anything more than what is predicted in the lab (there is no risk-issue!). A given A will always give us B. The possible-N is already contained from the possible-I, assuming this ontology. Gene sequence A will always give us property B, and nothing more. There are no 'relational effects', says the Lockean essentialist.

These ontologies do have an advantage. And the advantage is related to containment. Because the larger the containment, the more *expensive* it will be. Admitting to the legitimacy of the asymmetry, which is an indirect admission to the legitimacy of naturalness, is expensive! I am not saying that this is not recognized. The environmental debate is often a debate over exactly this point.[16] How much should the producer and the consumer contain the possible-I when it is being used? How high a price should the commons (humans and other living creatures) pay for the individual or corporate usage of some possible-I ferry? Those who have the highest degree of containment (often due to standards set by governments) will lose in the competitive production system that reigns today. The production of something might benefit the human commons monetarily (if distributed fairly), but not environmentally or biologically. (However, some argue that a high profit is needed for reinvestment in better containment systems, while others say that this would be to start the argument from the wrong starting point. I agree with the latter. Reinvestment does not help as long as this situation is not ontologically understood and acted on in the first place.)

Hopefully, it is clear by now how the relationalist account of dispositions supports our theory of HEDFs and the possible-I/possible-N distinction. In what follows I will trade upon this distinction to say something more specific about the main claims that were partly anticipated in Chapter 2.

While the reductionist would be tempted to explain some behaviour in terms of essences determined by the inner constitution, the relationalist will admit relational causes on the same or upper level. The cause of the *new* behaviour of some gene (the function of the gene) could therefore be found in the environment, e.g., effects that impact how the protein is folding, or on how genes are turned on and off, etc. The relationality of dispositions explains how and why the *environment* can make (for instance) location-effects have an effect in the genome.[17] These "causes" are relational; taking account *only* of the "biochemical causes" would amount to a typical reductionist approach, wherein things like location-effects would be a mystery.

The substantial equivalence principle that underlies the regulatory laws of GMOs in the U.S. and other countries is an example of this non-relational view being effectuated through regulatory bodies. The principle says that as long as the GMOs are substantially equivalent with their "motherlines", they can be put on the market without any further tests.[18] A company that produces GMOs can establish substantial equivalence by comparing the *biochemical* profile between two samples. The principle thereby assumes that "if there are no substantial (i.e., *essential*[19]) differences on the level *beneath*, then there are no differences on the level above either".

Given what was said in chapters 3, 4 and previous parts of this chapter, this should hopefully sum up and substantiate the claims that I made in Chapter 2 about scientific ontologies in general and about essentialism and reductionism in particular. With the qualifications made in the intermediate chapters, it seems reasonable to assume now that proponents of a reductionist account would be more inclined to assume that these types of technologies don't need to be "contained" from possible-N, since proponents of this account will ontologically ascertain that:

1 The behaviour of the possible-N is a net result of its categorical base; and that
2 The laboratory conditions therefore uncover the *real* possible-N (essentialism).

Claiming this, however, would be tantamount to saying that there is no nature in nature, because it amounts to the claim that there is no relevant difference between possible-I and possible-N.

My main point in this chapter has been to defend the intuition that there is an important and relevant difference between the possible-I and the possible-N and that we should be 'careful with what we put into action based on our knowledge gained from possible-I'. But is this not a common intuition we all go by? To some extent it might be. The way that I represented the case above may be overstated. But again I will appeal to the area of science that is regarded as the "hottest" area today. Nanotechnology,[20] synthetic biology, converging technologies, brain science, psychopharmacological science, etc., are all areas whose practitioners and advocates, by definition, embrace a reductionist account. These are sciences that by "ontological necessity" transgress the "borders" between possible-I and possible-N in a way that does not square with the difference that I have described here. I will argue that the criticism raised in this chapter cannot be said to be very common and it would therefore be wrong to assume that this is just "common-sense" and that I have argued against a straw man.

Technologies based in these sciences always look workable, but only with a special homemade blend of necessity and contingency. Nanotechnology is, as we saw in section 2.8 in Drexler's debate with Smally, for example, based on the view that the being of things is fully distinct and can be fully re-compossible *if* we manipulate the things on a lower level (viz. an atomic level). On the other hand, it rests on the view that there is strong vertical necessity between the levels in the way that assumes that the behaviour on higher levels is necessitated by lower-level "essences". The gene-reductionist-thesis that genetic technologies in general go by states that genes can be compossible in any which way, but at the same time puts forward a thesis conceding that genes *determine* the behaviour of the organism. *The contingency between the elements on a certain level is combined with an idea about vertical necessity between the levels.*

To me it seems much more attractive to deploy the disposition ontology that can deal with potentiality head on, rather than to come up with idiosyncratic moves that oscillate between necessity and contingency in an attempt to deal with or do away with potentiality *de re*. We also have no other choice but to acknowledge that possible-I must be protected from possible-N, even though we can see that the technology "works". It is possible to manipulate the being of some object by altering the manifesting partners on the level below, but it comes with a price – the price of containment and/or contamination.

What we may gather from this is that truth is actually not essentially important when it comes to the undertaking of science. Endless assertions about reality can be said to be true. Facts about the world do not have a finite number on the basis of a non-essentialist dispositional account. An endless array of situations can be rigged and constructed and endless true propositions about the dispositional behaviour of some 'possible-I process' can be produced. More relevant and vital than truth is naturalness, or the relation between possible-N and possible-I. The Miracle Argument presupposes the idea that there is no difference between possible-N and possible-I, and does not therefore recognize that an immense width of truths are out there to be discovered and used by "successful sciences", and miracle technologies. But this is not a success or a miracle for the relational realist. Where our knowledge should focus is on how possible-I truths relate to possible-N truths. It is one thing to "discover" a causal relationship between vitamin D and absorption of calcium in our gut, but the real task is to understand which role this plays in the historically evolved web of interactions taking place in our bodies (see subsection 4.4.1).

5.5 It is possible-I, but is it possible-N?

The technological imperative 'What is possible to develop *should* be developed' is a yes-answer to the question 'It is possible-I, but is it possible-N?' If we don't side with this imperative, or we think that there should be suitable restrictions placed upon our explorations and exploitations of the possible-I, we immediately face serious difficulties. On what grounds do we even begin to restrict what we find to be possible-I? Do we have something more than ethical arguments to employ in this debate? My tenacious claim has been that we will have to start with the theoretical establishment of something similar to possible-N in order to find a suitable way to understand and frame for possible-I. The favoured approach to date has, however, been to restrict possible-I by way of "pure ethics".

In this book I have tried to develop an argument to convince the reader that naturalness is something that 'belongs to the world'. The typical way to treat naturalness has been to place this concept among those entities unjustifiably projected onto the world. To say that something is natural has been seen as being a classical layman's categorical mistake, one that can only be cured by enlightenment. A concept of naturalness will challenge the bifurcation between science and ethics. It makes it possible to do something with a reference to naturalness without having to refer to an ethical theory, but it also makes it possible to argue more consistently for the interests of non-human beings. While the "ethicist" has to deal with possible-I (e.g., cloning) on purely ethical grounds – on the grounds of a human-encountered ethics, born out of a passivist ontology, we can choose to argue differently.

The dispositions of some specific thing or some specific system are not possible to circumscribe. There is no finite description of nature. We investigate some of these dispositions in laboratories, which do not normally occur in possible-N. The whole and unlimited range of dispositions that is possible is exactly what I would propose to call 'Nature': What I have proposed to call 'Natural', however, is what I call possible-N. What we find to be possible-I is of course much more inclusive than what we find to be possible-N. When we investigate what is possible-I, we investigate what is physically possible. However, to propose that there is some given reality that can be characterized as possible-N means that there is a reality "out there" that is "less than" what we find to be physically possible: something that would allow us both to fail and succeed in our efforts to treat something in accordance with it. The difference between the two is, as I have said, not a matter of their relation to truth, but of 'what the universe spontaneously offers'.

Are humans a part of nature, but not the natural? Of course not. We are a part of the relational whole from which we evolved and which made and continuously makes us possible. When I want to lift a stone, there will be a way to lift this stone that is easier than any other way. In the same way, it can be argued that there are optimal (individual) diets, optimal ways to grow things, etc. But there is, of course, nothing that is optimal in itself. The big mistake, however, is to think that "since there is nothing optimal in itself", humans can decide the optimality of things. Optimal is a relational but real faculty, although not in the Aristotelian sense (cf. section 2.1). The reason that there is an optimal way to do things is due to the existence of something that can be called possible-N – facts that are relationally and historically constituted.

The relational whole constituted by the possible-N relations also makes up a starting point for human manipulations and makes it possible to say that these manipulations are *deviations from something that is not on a contingent course.* Deprived of this starting point we cannot ask: what would be the *best* or smartest deviations? Conversely, a starting point like this will simply make it possible to say 'I would not do it that way, I would rather do it this way, because this way deviates to a lesser degree from possible-N'. Furthermore, a benchmark like possible-N means that I can legitimately say publicly that 'I do not want X because I think it is too far from possible-N'. Some or many (I don't know) would not prefer to argue this way, but that is not the point. The point is that those who want to argue this way may not be easily dismissed.

"Technologies" that already assume in their functions that the properties of the world are fully compossible will not even comprehend what this deviation is about and will therefore not come into communication where this is or could be an issue.

It is not my task, however, to generally state that technologies which have a comprehensive deviation makes this technology bad (or good). The way in which people choose to relate to naturalness is a different question! My task has been to argue that there is such a thing as a possible-N that our actions can comply with or deviate from, and furthermore that technologies that do not presuppose that this is the case might be dangerous *just for that reason* (and not necessarily for comprehensive deviation reasons), since their proponents will not understand the meaning of the asymmetry between possible-I and possible-N.

If the reader agrees with me about this conclusion and the arguments that have led to it, I would say that my main goal has been accomplished: to establish a viable theoretical reason to believe that 'naturalness' is a term that can be rightfully employed in the layman's discourse as well as in the ethical and scientific discourse. My undertaking has been to steal naturalness from the ethicists, who in any case did not know what to do with it, and hand it over to science where it really belongs. It is possible for scientists to (roughly) describe the natures of things, for instance the nature of a salmon. It is a philosophical task, however, to argue that these descriptions refer to something real, and this is what I have tried to do here. This means that I think that it is possible to describe this nature in terms of the dispositional web of relations that constitute the nature of the salmon: a nature that has evolved through the course of the history of the universe. It is possible to take this as a starting point in order to see how the way that we treat salmon (in e.g. salmon farming) today deviates from the possible-N salmon and to ascribe some or many of the problems occurring in today's aquaculture to this deviation. If this was properly understood in the beginning I do not think that (as an example) the aquaculture research would have gone along with the way salmon farming developed in the first place.

5.6 Naturalness and dispositions

In this chapter, I will try to sum up some of the features that are relevant for the question of naturalness in general, given the ontological reorientation that has been outlined during chapters 3 and 4, and the previous parts of Chapter 5. I will also refer back to some of the major points that were established in Chapters 1 and 2. What we shall consider is the question of change in relation to the concept of naturalness for which I have argued thus far.

I suggest that we continue to hold on to our pol-ly hen as an example. Aristotle would definitely say that to change the hen into a pol-ly would be to change the nature of the hen in such a way that it becomes just matter for a human-imposed form (*telos*), and thus that it would be a thing that exists by *technē*, and not by nature. Some may react to this morally, and say that this violates the integrity[21] of the hen, by way of changing its very *telos* (see section 2.2). But this is exactly where these two concepts of naturalness, the Aristotelian one and the one proposed here, differ.

The change of the hen into a pol-ly hen is made possible by the changes that we (can) make at the levels below. This is a substantial change, according to Aristotle. If the life-scientist is a true reductionist s/he would say that the hen has no being that could give rise to something like integrity to start with (it is just an aggregate), and therefore no *identity* that could be changed in a way that could be called a violation. In the disposition ontology, there is no principle of rest and change inhabiting the beings, at least not in the teleological sense. Rather, what makes them irreducible is the nature that they have in virtue of hens' relations to other beings. Is this enough to account for the "Aristotelian intuition"?

If we follow the Eleatic stranger again, we would say that the identity of some given entity is defined by what it is doing or what it is able to do. But what the hen can do is also dependent upon its categorical base (see subsection 4.5.3 and section 4.6). A change in the "categorical base" will bring about new dispositions in the hen, and therefore change its identity, i.e., what it is able to do. To change the properties on the level below (the manifesting partners) *would therefore* definitely change the identity of the hen. However, the identity and being of the hen does not lie in its "categorical base" (or the manifesting partners making up this base), in the same way that changes in the "categorical base" do not determine the identity of dispositions. A change in the "categorical base" just brings about change, which is eventually determined as such-and-such *particular change* (identity) by the dispositional partners. Changing the dispositional partners, meanwhile, would just bring about different manifestations (that *eventually* or iteratively can bring about change in the "categorical base" – e.g., evolution).

The next step would therefore be to ask whether the hen has a being that *could*, on certain *ethical* qualifications, be violated. On a reductionist account, we have seen that this would not be possible. On the account developed here, the hen has its irreducible being in virtue of its dispositional nature that is relationally dependent upon certain types of change and cascading patterns of change (see below) in the first place. This means that even though the nature of the hen *can* be violated given certain ethical qualifications, this does not mean that every type of change and restriction brought upon the hen brings this "violation" about. Certain types of change are in accord with the nature of the hen, while other types of change are not.

However, the fact that things have a nature that *can* be ascribed integrity does not prescribe an ethical reason to act in a particular way. That something "has a nature" does not tell us what is good. This said, we may assert that the ascription potential seen here is no different from what we see in "human-centred" ethics, where the fact that someone is able to have her integrity violated is not enough to outline the specific ethical position in itself (G.E. Moore 2004, see also section 5.7). We should therefore *not* conclude that this would give us an *intrinsic* argument against, e.g., genetic engineering, which would be to say that this technology is untenable *in itself*, but it does not exclude the very possibility that such an argument could be launched either, given a certain ethical justification. In other words, if I argue ethically that the integrity of a hen should be respected it is possible to do this with the account developed here. On a passivist account this is not possible because the hen does not have being of its own in the first place. Therein lies the difference.

Establishing an argument for the fact that something *can* have a being that *can* be violated is different from saying something about the aspects that should be taken into consideration when we choose to change something. In what follows I will say something about what Aristotle called forced movement (see section 2.3). What I will say about this is purely descriptive and does not say that we should or should not restrict or manipulate in a particular way.

1. Same-level manipulations

What can be said about a situation in which we don't make our wild hen into a pol-ly hen, but place it in a cage? Hens put in cages "suffer" *same-level manipulations*. What we effectively do is to deprive the hen of some of the relational partners of its dispositions, thereby blocking the unfolding/manifestation of some of these dispositions. But is there not a crucial difference between the disposition and the manifestation in the sense that you can have the former without having the latter? Generally yes, but for living creatures it is of course not sufficient to only 'have the dispositions'; they also depend for their existence upon the manifesting of some of them (e.g., eating). For this they need some of their partners or viable substitutes.

However, we also know that during, e.g., the course of evolution these partners have changed continuously; nature is in constant change and flux. But what does that really mean? There are at least two points that must complement this assertion.

(i) The fact that there is constant change and flux between dispositions and their dispositional partners and the dispositions and the "categorical base" – species-wise – does not help the hen in the cage very much. It is still far away from possible-N for the individual hen to exist without its partners. This is a similar argument that I use against the contingency-thesis in general, i.e., even though the history of the universe is (or could be considered to be) contingent, ice *in fact* floats on water; it does not sink, and our hen needs a sand-bath now and then – even though this disposition has come about by a contingent evolutionary process. Similarly, it could have been the case, given what we said in 5.1 #1, that ice *could (logically) have* sunk, but as a matter of fact it does not. This is a HEDF.

It is a saying among laypeople and even scientists (e.g. in the climate change debate) that "nature changes all the time". For some, this fact seems to be enough to qualify the statement that we cannot morally or otherwise denounce changes in general, and this is right. But the reasoning is mistaken if we infer from this that any change is "neutral". The fact that nature 'changes all the time' gives us little or no valuable information about how to change nature in the right way.

(ii) If we agree to the theory of evolution by natural selection we should take the *pace* and *extension* of change into consideration. Changes that are too *fast* or too geographically *vast* will be out of pace with the time needed for species and systems to adapt. Processes taking place with and among living beings have their own pace, although different species can have different paces (i.e., a fast change will favour species that change quickly – e.g., viruses, insects, etc.). Therefore, if we want to keep the major system of relationally connected partners (of which we and our dispositions are a part) intact, we should keep this in mind (i.e. climate change is not a problem if the change does not happen too fast). I am not sure if we can literally talk of a *natural* pace for a certain system, but rudimentarily I think that we can say that such systems have dispositions (e.g., resilience), which make them *more* or *less* vulnerable to change (see Chapter 6).

A second point about same-level manipulation is connected to the iterativity of dispositions. Some dispositions are what they are in virtue of being a part of a (developmental) chain, such as the ontogenesis of an organism. In such a chain, the disposition has to be manifested in order to be a part of the further process that constitutes its being. The disposition that the zygote has for differentiation is only had in relation to the next steps in its process of development. (A zygote would not be a zygote and would certainly not have the ability to differentiate if it were not a part of this developmental chain.) The manifestation of this disposition is *necessary for the identity of the disposition itself*. In this case we can talk of the *teleology of dispositions*.

2. Lower-level manipulations

Although changes made to the manifesting partners on the lower level will always bring about changes in the bearer, and therefore to the dispositions on the higher level, dispositions on lower levels do not *determine* dispositions on higher levels. This has been one of the major claims of this book, a claim that the reader must be almost tired of hearing once again. Against the idea that lower-level constituents determine the dispositions on higher levels I have argued that dispositions are both relational and level-specific. Given that we accept this argument, we would have to expect that changes in lower levels will bring about new changes in each and every level, which the being in question consists of. A change made on a nano-level will *trickle all the way through the relevant levels*, with 'relational effects' at each and every level, before it reaches the biological, human and sometimes the social interface. The level-theory argued for here will, in other words, contain the claim that there is no way to 'jump the levels'. A "pure chemical substance" entering the body of the hen would have to be successively translated into a biochemical interaction, a cellular interaction and then into an organismic interaction, and then (sometimes) into an environmental and hen social interaction. If someone were to make it possible to change the electromagnetic force that binds the atom together, we would of course see enormously wide changes in the universe at all levels, *but each level would have its own level-specific change* (although in this case that would only mean 'cease to exist' in its level-specific way). This is why I have said that the deeper we manipulate, the more likelihood there is for 'unintended effects',[22] i.e., changing the genome of some given organism might bring about new dispositions that we cannot see in the laboratory or in controlled trials, because such altered dispositions might manifest only under special conditions that "cannot" be tested for because we would not even think about those possibilities. This argument is to my mind extremely important for the understanding of "deep technologies", which explains why I have spent so much time on the arguments devoted to the relationality of dispositions. It is also why I would be sceptical of the *ambition* to test whether or not a certain product *is* safe or not, especially if we start out with ("Humean") 50/50 probability distributions.[23]

When research is performed with the aim of altering the dispositions of beings by way of altering the manifesting partners on lower levels, it should be done with the assumption that there is a HEDF-totality there in the first place (as well as on lower levels, of course). In section 2.6 I talked about the fact that science is famously known to be organized in a way that in most cases allows the scientist to work within 'well-defined and narrow areas'. On a reductionist account, we should be able to just put this knowledge gained within this small area into action to produce the effect that we wish to gain. On the account given here, such a strategy would be ontologically counterintuitive, to put it mildly. The alterations made on the level below to produce an effect on the level above should first and foremost be understood within the whole wherein this change is assigned to make a difference. This nature (whole) should be studied in advance, in order to understand – or, rather, to anticipate – what kind of actual and potential effect such an alteration might bring about. That, however, demands that we acknowledge the possibility that there is a nature there in the first place.

Naturalness-wise we should not just protect the possible-I from the possible-N, but also vice versa. When I say 'should', I don't refer to an ethical 'should', but an 'ontological should'. With a reductionist ontology we would not need this 'should', because there is no possible-N – no possible-N that could be in need of protection.[24] It is only on a reductionist account that one would claim that the 'should' that I am talking about here is an ethical or a misplaced should.

The important question of efficiency should also be considered in the light of possible-N. We should keep in mind that protecting the possible-I – the desired dispositions – will bring about a (partly unpredictable) need for support in terms of labour (see Winner 1977, 100ff.). Technologies often come into existence because they are regarded as more efficient, but we have seen that that might not be the case in many instances if we take the acquired containment maintenance costs, unintended effects, etc. into consideration. The further we go down in the levels of nature, the more that various levels will be altered. This means that the changes will have wider implications, and more unpredicted effects.[25] Deeper manipulations need bigger containers, to protect both the possible-I and the possible-N (e.g. a nano-computer requires a more comprehensive container).

As I have previously argued, there is an asymmetry between possible-I and possible-N, and this might explain why we regard lower-level manipulation as more effective, although this estimation of efficiency *profits* from the ontologically unacknowledged change of the possible-N. Hence, the economical profitability rests on the assumption that possible-I $\rightarrow$ [possible-N] has no "costs" – either because one is a (Lockean) essentialist or because there is no systematic recounting of the causes of the costs that the commons suffer. We should therefore ask: how expensive/effective would this technology be (i.e., how inclusive would the container need to be) if we were to accept that possible-N needs to be protected from possible-I (something that we would not be ready to accept if we are essentialists)? It is on such grounds that it would be *fair* to compare the efficiency of a certain 'deep technology' with the possible efficiency of 'same-level plasticity technologies'. (The fairness that I am talking about here is what lies in the ontological 'should' above.) One may in any case ask whether it is true that the technological development propels efficiency, and I mean true efficiency, wherein the use of external production and maintenance energy and true containment is factored in.

There is a (non-strict) difference between altering the conditions that change how the manifesting partners on the lower level come together to manifest the bearer on the higher level and directly manipulating those partners. It is a difference between sinking a piece of wood down to 100 metres below sea-level so as to change the molecular structure of the wood and changing the structure on a molecular level directly.[26] One could say that the ability to change these partners directly has been one of the most successful achievements of science, although the principal and practical fallibilities of this method have been poorly assessed and understood.

5.7 New eyes on environmental ethics

I have previously argued that the distinction between is and ought, fact and value, is a distinction that rests upon certain ontological claims about the world, and that this distinction needs to come down from its high horse and make its justification in a more concrete and substantiated way. You might assume, therefore, that I would argue that one's ethical theory follows from one's ontology. However, as I have indicated before, I don't think that a revised is/ought distinction should make us abandon a distinction between ethics and ontology as such. There is nothing principally wrong in acknowledging what is natural in a particular case and choosing to act on an ethical principle that goes against this understanding. If we have no concept of naturalness, however, we do not (of course) have this choice.

Accordingly, the aim of this book has been to overcome the 'non-natural ontologies' in a way that may enable us to come out with something that we *could* choose to follow or not. True, having a concept of naturalness presupposes a concept of freedom. It is an act of freedom to choose whether we should act in accordance with some postulated 'natural way' or not. But the fact that it is *possible* to postulate 'a natural way' also rests on the plausibility of an ontology that is able to challenge the modal dualist ontologies. The freedom to choose to act in accordance with the way things naturally behave is not possible under a passivist regime.

This means that the "data" that the scientist presents into the public sphere should include an explanation of the role that the natures of his subjects play, e.g., a scientist developing psychopharma should explain the connection between the chemical substance developed and the nature of the (target) organism that receives it. The scientist should relate her findings to the psychologically constituted dispositions that she tries to cure with this substance. For instance, what is the nature of 'feeling sad'? Might there be a reason for why 'feeling sad' exists? I.e. is this a kind of feeling that corresponds to certain dispositional partners of the world we are living in? If that is the case, to what degree would 'this pill' help in relation to the nature of feeling sad? If the nature of feeling sad is seen as either contingent or necessitated by "its" parts, we will not be able to compare the effect of the pill with something that we could choose to follow or not.

The concept of naturalness that is worked out here is not one that is fixed by some theory of 'how nature *really* works'. Every system has different and conflicting dispositions (theoretically speaking) that can be manifested, and we have to understand this array of dispositions and their relatedness in order to be able to say something about how a certain system works as a whole. In fact, the very idea of finding out 'how the system really works' becomes secondary on the dispositional account. Animals such as humans will always find that there are many and different dispositions involved in any activity and that every kind has different and diverging dispositions. To say something like 'man *is* evil' does not go very well with the dispositional account (developed here). If we were to grant that we could find a way to define evil acts, I guess that we could say that man has a disposition to perform evil acts, but it would be a categorical misunderstanding to infer from this that man *is* evil. To say that man *is* evil one would need to invoke some kind of reified, non-relational version of essentialism. The urge to discover e.g., 'how we really learn' or 'how we really keep ourselves healthy' or 'what women really are' originates from an essentialist mindset that is not dispositional in spirit. It is my claim that we, according to the dispositional account given above, have not constructed a highway between is and ought, but rather, a leeway that allows us to talk about the natures of things and processes.

At the same time, I have also indicated that dispositions-activeness is **enough** *for disclaiming the traditional passivist metaphysics* and it is enough for those who want to **differentiate** their behaviour towards other (sentient or non-sentient) beings. 'Being active' in a dispositional sense does not mean that things are teleologically driven, but that is of secondary importance.[27] The urge for further and stronger requirements is, to my mind, reminiscent of Aristotelian teleology.[28]

The way that my argument goes in this book does not follow the traditional route wherein certain traits or properties are picked out as particularly relevant for ascribing value to certain beings, or including them into the moral community. This, which I have called the *criteria-of-distinction*-route (1.4.2 B.), leads (to my mind) to a lot of disagreement related to confining the different properties, such as speech, reason, suffering, having interests, etc. Environmental ethicists have a tendency to venture into such quarrels over property-based distinctions, notably those engaged in quarrels over points such as "Are invertebrates a part of the moral community?" (Singer 1975, 179). The aim of bringing naturalness and dispositions into this area of interest is to show that we don't need anything more than *activeness* in terms of dispositional natures. We don't need Aristotelian teleology and we don't need any criteria of distinction.[29]

It is important to repeat again that I am not discussing the ethics of naturalness; I am discussing the possibility of naturalness, and what changes 'naturalness' would be able to bring about in how we theorize and understand the relation between humans and non-humans. In my view, it could generally facilitate and host all sorts of motifs on a scale from the instrumental to the religious. An argument motivated by a religious belief *can* point to the naturalness of a certain being or process. At the other end of the scale I can say that it would be instrumentally better to do X and point to the natural behaviour of F. This means again that, although 'naturalness' is able to change some of the content of each and every motif, it is not the case that 'naturalness' can dictate any motif in particular as the passivist ontologies in certain respects do.

I have signalled that I think that the account developed here is also relevant for how we see and deem *instrumental rationality*. I will try to elaborate upon that as follows. Instrumental rationality contains the simple idea that the most efficient way 'is the best way'. Alternatively, some would perhaps formulate it thus: in the exercise of instrumental rationality the *only consideration* is what the most efficient way to perform X is. Instrumental rationality presupposes *the value of efficiency as a value in itself, not as a particular strategy to obtain certain non-instrumental goals* (see e.g., Ellul 1964). For me, instrumental rationality looks very different in a world with active beings bestowed with natures as opposed to one with beings that are totally compossible and fully at our disposal. Agents who recognize the dispositional nature of things while instantiating instrumental rationality will perceive the question 'What is the most efficient way to perform X?' differently from those who engage in instrumental action guided by a passivist ontology.[30]

To lift a stone with a certain particular shape can be done with raw power or prudence. Raw power amounts to more energy disposal, and therefore less efficiency. The more we know about the dispositions of things, the more we know about how to *go with* the dispositional whole in question. Even Francis Bacon's dictum "knowledge is power" would have a different flavour under this ontological regime. It is therefore, in my view, due to the passivist regime that the so-called instrumental rationality has been viewed as a big problem. Optimizing instrumental rationality should be about finding the most efficient way for things to work. If things 'have their own way to relationally work' *already*, there should be no doubt which way would be the most efficient, given sufficient knowledge about their relationally constituted level-specific dispositions.[31] The reason why the passivist regime looks more efficient is, as I claimed in the previous chapter, that the cost of not protecting the possible-N from the possible-I is not counted in.

Prudence and *re-cognition* would, under the dispositional regime, be vital for efficient comportment. Prudence and instrumental rationality would actually converge, because prudence would make us see what kind of "efficiency" lies in phenomena themselves. Prudence, and taking a 'second look', refers to the fact that a dispositional account would not be able to offer certainty (in the same way as an essentialist account would), because we could never give a finite description of the range of dispositional possibilities. To take a 'second look' would therefore be epistemologically and scientifically advised.

By combining re-cognition with relationalism and the idea of level-specificity, I believe that we, pragmatically speaking, have a stronger general 'defence for nature' than do proponents of a traditional 'intrinsic value ethics' account. The reason for this is that the intrinsic value account often is an answer to the current passivist-based ontological account, which is an account that has a lot of financial, scientific and prestigious support – something which leaves intrinsic-value proponents on the outside of the core debate. The view developed here is typically 'a third alternative'. Such an alternative is or should be able to break the stand-off between two alternatives that is fed and sustained by each being a critique of the other. The lack of a third alternative in the environmental debate has meant that the holder of the passivist view has been able to defend their own position by way of confronting 'the rival view' for generating mind-dependent claims that are really 'dogmas of purity and danger', and in so doing regard their own position as neutral and inescapable.

It has been a goal of mine in this book to try to show that the area of descriptions should stretch into areas that are traditionally thought of as ethical, and that the area of environmental ethics should become more confined. The legitimate area of environmental ethics under a passivist ontology is vast; it is more limited under a disposition ontology. The reason for this is that there are fewer conflict areas between instrumental interests and traditional environmental ethics interests under a dispositional regime. In effect, this means that disagreements that look as though they are ethical might actually be ontological. Disagreements over modern biotechnology might be disagreements over the ontological presuppositions that underlie the technology, rather than an ethical disagreement. Disagreements that look like a lack of willingness to accept intrinsic value for salmon might actually be disagreements over the ontological assumptions that underlie the description of the welfare of salmon in general. If we could agree upon a common description, we might also easily agree on how to treat other beings such as salmon. We might even be able to abandon the whole debate about intrinsic value and call it failed or superfluous.

Such a view could be justified in the following way. To see things and treat them in accordance with what they are points exactly to the general meaning of intrinsic value. Intrinsic value is not a property that comes in addition as an extra evaluative property that inheres in the substance. That is not what is meant by seeing the thing as it is.[32] The core question of intrinsic value is whether other beings can be treated with respect,[33] or with some similar attitude that transcends their (passivist) instrumental value. But what does 'respect' mean? When we claim that something is not treated with respect, we usually claim that the something is not being treated according to "its nature", or its being. For instance, when we say "You should respect human rights" we mean "You should respect a certain description of what humans really are". Ascribing 'intrinsic value' to others presupposes a conception of what they are – what I here have called their nature – and thus, in reality, it also presupposes an ontology to support the specific concept of naturalness that is mobilized. This goes for atoms as well as stones, animals, landscapes and other humans. There might be legitimate ethical justifications for saying that one type of being (e.g., humans) are more worthy of being treated in accordance with their (relational) nature than other beings, but such arguments would not be in a basic conflict with human interests as long as intrinsic and instrumental values do not, in principle, part company.[34]

On this occasion one may pose the question of whether or not ethics is more local and anthropocentric than even the biocentric ethicist normally thinks it is. Maybe our ethics truly *is* developed for humans only? Maybe our ethics generally is guided by our ideas about what humans really *are* (philosophical anthropology) and maybe this starting point does not simply work for hens, humpback whales and mountains? Maybe we should let the ethics of hens be guided by "henology", our ethics towards humpback whales be guided by "humpbackology" and our ethics towards a mountain should be guided by our "mountainology", etc. Maybe we simply don't have to pre-establish the intrinsic value or some other ethical principle before we can treat it "ethically" and maybe ethics is not such a big deal after all, if one is ready to defend the fact that things do have natures in the first place. Maybe the rising importance of ethics that we have experienced over the last couple of hundred years is related to the way that the idea of naturalness has lost ground?

To talk about the intrinsic value of some being in an ordinary way is problematic because the dispositions of things are what they are in relation to the dispositions of other things. They are relational and do not reside inside the being in question (although they *belong* to it – "adherence"). Which dispositions should we respect, then? Any bearer seems to have so many – yes – an endless array. What I have tried to argue in this chapter is that there are no primary essences that are fixed by the necessitation of the essences of the manifesting partners. When we ask ourselves the question "So which dispositions should we respect?", we should look at the relational web of which the dispositions of the being in question are and have been a part. (For further elaboration see Lie and Wickson, 2011.)

What this view gives us is a frame that allows for our *differentiated behaviours*. Humans are parts of this web and *should use nature*, and if we are talking about a 'should' here we should use it in 'the right way'. A farmer, on this account, would be expected to *exploit* the differences of the land that he farmed, because he would explicitly look for and see that every difference has its dispositional fortunes. Her ability to farm, her knowledge and her experience will help her in doing so. It is the knowledge of these dispositions, her ability to learn from them and take them into account, that first and foremost decides whether she is a good farmer or not. Not whether she has the right ethical theory supporting the conduct.

The trouble always starts when our farmer (or the human-made system – i.e., capitalist, etc.) has a fixed preconception of how to farm, what to farm, etc., because it is these fixed preconceptions that require the plasticity and the compossibility of (in this case) the land. In my opinion, it is this fixedness that leads science to *deliver* the compossibility that is demanded and forces scientists to endorse a reductionist account *wherein such compossibility can be found and exploited*.

The normativity necessarily entailed by *use* might be understood differently in the case of use informed and led by possible-N. Closing in on possible-N requires that one's intentions are also guided by 'what is already there', in the same way as they are or should be when we meet other people. That there *is* 'already something there' is therefore crucial to establish. Hence this book. Taking the possible-N dispositions as a benchmark for our use might bring us to realize that what is already there can be seen as opportunities (and not obstacles) that can be the starting point for our further activity and creativity. This means that we allocate more of our attention to perceptive techniques (i.e., to 'the way we do things'), rather than to technology ('how to get things done'). Today we allocate most of our creativity to the manipulation of possible-N as if it were possible-I. The price is the production of environmental problems, massive energy use and resource depletion, which in turn forces us to spend even more of our creative energy on mending the so-called side-effects of this type of *use*. Why could we not spend our creative efforts to come closer to the dispositions that 'are there' and that come for free in the first place?

Environmentalism has a reputation of "gloom and doom", since environmentalists are seldom able to fill the vacancy that occurs in the wake of their many protests *against* the ways that we manipulate nature today. With naturalness as a benchmark and a starting point, one may offer an all-encompassing and systematic strategy that entails a positive alternative and attitude where humans and nature are not in a fundamental conflict. Don't rage against the wind; build yourself a windmill, as they say. Human actions *can* be more or less in agreement with the relationally constituted level-specific dispositions that are already there, and to which we are more or less related in our own nature in the first place.

It also follows from this that the expression 'unnatural', which I have admittedly used at some occasions in this book, is an unfortunate expression. Humans can be seen as one of the manifestation partners bringing about any given joint manifestation. The resulting manifestation might be deemed to be more or less of a deviation from the possible-N, but it should not be deemed as *unnatural* as such. There are no criteria developed in this book that can make us define a partnering action as being unnatural in itself. One may rhetorically say "This seems to be very unnatural" if one means by it "far from possible-N". Crucially for understanding the account developed here therefor is to understand that. Naturalness is a property that describes a scale, not an absolute either/or state.

Notes

1 Quotations from this edition are translated by me.
2 For example, Barrow says that there are at least four different ways that the universe could have developed that would be consistent with all that we currently know about the universe (ibid.).
3 In addition to the factual development there is, of course, the well-known problem with prediction when quantum physics is involved, since any state can only be measured as a 'statistical state'.
4 The reader might think that this conclusion is too hasty, or that the question is too vast, or maybe that this question cannot be answered through science at all. However, I don't think that it hurts to bring arguments from physics into the debate as long as we don't overestimate them.
   A second problem is, of course, that we don't know enough about the development of the universe to say that we know what the initial conditions were, and therefore we don't know the probability of the *de facto* development. According to Barrow (2007), this might be even more complicated. If we factor in postulations about the existence of 'baby and mother universes', we will see that even if we had a theory about everything, it would not even then be possible to determine whether or not the development could have been predicted. At the same time, he later says: "The great unanswered question is whether there exists some undiscovered organizing principle which complements the known laws of nature and *dictates* the overall evolution of the universe" (188). Taking all this into consideration, we should recall our newly acquired ontological argument (section 4.6), according to which the "categorical level does not necessitate the dispositional one". If that is correct, we would be virtually unable to claim that the history of the universe must have developed deterministically.
5 "That there is carbon in the universe is not only made possible by the age and size of the universe, but also by a *staggering* coincidence between the constants that determine the energy level of the atomic nuclei" (Barrow 1996, 138, my italics).
6 We are not up against essentialist thinking wherein we typically find the individual up against society, or man vs nature, etc.
7 Marx would probably have called them the productive forces of the labor-atory.

8 However, this does not mean that the system necessarily returns to the same state that existed previously. Since there are far more non-manifesting than constantly manifesting dispositions in the world, this normal situation is not a static situation. A simple example: if I drop a glass bottle on the ground, the glass will not return to being a bottle again just because the force of my hand has disappeared.

9 For example, the Cartagena protocol defines contained use of genetically modified organisms (GMOs) in the following way: "any operation, undertaken within a facility, installation or other physical structures, which involves living modified organisms that are controlled by specific measures that effectively limit their contact with, and impact on, the external environment" (Article 3 (b)).

10 One may compare the vocabulary used here with Nancy Cartwright's expression 'nomological machines' (Cartwright 1999, 50). Nomological machines are produced in the laboratory, but are also sometimes found outside the lab according to Cartwright.

11 At this point it should be apparent why I had to put so much emphasis on refuting the contingency-thesis. Without that we would have had no way to justify the phrase 'for possible-N to work'. Nothing works well or poorly in a world of total contingency.

12 I.e. problems related to CO_2 emissions, bad air quality in densely populated areas, land use, the expelling of wildlife, etc.

13 I sometimes actually have a hard time explaining to scientists that science today does not really accept naturalness into scientific descriptions. When I sometimes succeed in explaining this to the scientist, I then turn around to convince the scientist that he or she *should* accept naturalness as a part of a scientific *description*. If he or she is convinced by this second turn, for instance through the asymmetry argument above, I sometimes hear: 'Well everyone knows this, especially after a long period with environmental attention'. Answering that I now seem to be stating the obvious *again*, it is tempting to say: 'No, this is having it both ways. That you find this argument convincing should also make you convinced that science should accept naturalness *in general*. If you are really convinced that naturalness should be a part of a scientific world view I should find you protesting against the naïve employment of nanotechnology, GMOs, synthetic biology, the way we medically treat illness today, and not least, the way in which possible-I products are tested. Understanding the asymmetry allows you as a scientist to have an opinion on this.' If naturalness is accepted, one also needs to acknowledge that a whole different understanding of how reality works is required, and one needs to understand how this affects the way we do, and should be doing, science today.

14 Humeans in the sense of believing that the property X is contingently related, and therefore independently related, to everything else.

15 It is today less controversial to say that 'the environment' has a vast impact on the regulation of genetic processes, for instance through epigenetic regulation processes (see also Lewontin 2000).

16 The reader has to keep in mind two different debates. I am not saying that the concept of naturalness is not deployed in general debates. It might often be, simply for the reason that it is legitimate! But that's different from saying that it is accepted as a legitimate concept (by scientists, philosophers, and others) in its own right, or that it is consistently and clearly defined or used.

17 Location effect is the effect that location has on the chromosome chain. The same gene can code for different enzymes depending upon where it is placed on the chromosome.

18 http://en.wikipedia.org/wiki/Substantial_equivalence (last accessed July 2015). See also Millstone et al. (1999) and Levidow et al. (2007).

19 That is, Lockean essentialism, which means: biochemically equivalent and not genetically equivalent. Genetically, they are of course not equivalent since the GMO has new genes inserted into it.

20 For those who think that this is of little relevance, it might be useful to remind ourselves of the name of the official report from the US "National Science and Technology

Council on Nanotechnology", namely: *Nanotechnology; Shaping the World Atom by Atom*. The prospects for how this technology will change the world, as we know it, are, according to this report, next to limitless, and the future for those nations and unions that do not 'understand the significance' of this technology will, according to the report, be devastating.

So, the idea that this passivist ontology will shape the world as we know it into "a better world" is no doubt still going strong, *despite* the many ways 'the reductionist account' has been criticized over the years.

21 Integrity is a problematic concept. Integrity stems etymologically from *integer*, meaning whole, or completeness. To assume that someone or something has (the possibility of) integrity is to assume that the being in question makes up a whole that is not a contingent assembly that accidentally works together, and that is somehow self-sufficient (and maybe independent?). The concept is, however, very complex, as I said (e.g., people can have low and high integrity, etc.), and I definitely don't regard it as a scientifically useful concept. But again: naturalness makes a difference also in this case. Ontologies denying naturalness will not accept the ascription of integrity either. On the integrity of ecosystems see Westra 1994.

22 Kekook Lee uses the expression 'deep technology' (1999; 2003).

23 We should here remind ourselves about the importance of scientific testing. According to Ulrich Beck, 'scientific testing' is the very basis for how we *manage* the autopoetic risks generated by our technoscientific manipulations in modern societies (1988).

24 To take naturalness into account in this way might also turn out to be more rewarding (see Lipinsky and Hopkins 2004).

25 But nature is also forgiving. One type of plasticity is through so-called downward causation, wherein certain effects that would otherwise be adverse are alleviated. I.e., the flexibility of the organism (shown in the case of the eyeless-gene, or in other cases where, e.g., the organism has the capacity to metabolize poisonous substances) plays an important role in sometimes saving the possible-I and the liable parties from bringing about too-adverse effects on the possible-N. It is, however, outside the scope of this book to go further into this issue.

26 'Sinking' was done in the old days to make the wooden piece easy to bend and adjust.

27 The 'activeness' that comes with the theory of dispositions is underlined, as we have seen, by, for example, Ellis and Mumford and others. My argument throughout this book has followed the exact same intuition, but I have perhaps not been fully satisfied with the way that this activeness was *established*.

28 By saying that it is reminiscent of Aristotelian teleology I mean that the requirements that Aristotle made for something to be *qualified* as something active (teleology) are too strong.

29 As I asserted in subsection 1.4.2. A, I think that the criteria of distinction route emerged from the question: If non-human nature is passive, what makes it possible for humans to be free and able to constitute a '*Reich der Zwecke*'? There must be some *traits* distinguishing humans from the rest of nature. My claim is then that this route of justification has been taken over by the environmental ethicists, implicitly accepting the historical situation that created this human-centred ethics route in the first place. The ontological showdown that would be required for something to be truly a non-human-centred ethic has therefore never occurred.

30 Instrumental rationality in the context of a passivist ontology has been described (as highly problematic) by Heidegger, Adorno and Horkheimer, Marcuse, Jacques Ellul and Habermas. Since they did not see clearly that the problem also had something to do with ontology, their solution was to somehow put up a barrier against this rationality (in terms of protecting the rationality of aesthetics, communicative rationality, etc.).

31 One of the main principles in what is called 'permaculture' is that 'the problem is the solution'. This sounds like an empty phrase from a business lecture, but it actually has some value beyond this. In this particular setting it means that in encountering problems

one would be better off if one used the dispositions that are there instead of "problems". (Problems will never disappear!) A farmer who wants to move a big stone in his field might be better off leaving the stone in place and using it as e.g., heating storage for particular plants. By using the different dispositions that just 'lack some partners to be useful' we may trade upon the different heterogenic fortunes that are already there instead of shaping everything in accordance with a preconceived plan or systems requirements.

32 See O'Neill 2003, 136.

33 Taylor (1986).

34 O'Neill's widely acknowledged thesis that: "The defender of nature's intrinsic value still needs to show that such value contributes to the well being of human agents" (2003, 131) is therefore superfluous. To treat something in accordance with its nature is not in a basic conflict with human well-being, especially if such treatment relates efficiency and naturalness in its very foundation.

References

Barrow, J. (1996) *Universets opprinnelse*, Universitetsforlaget.

——— (2007) *New Theories of Everything*, Oxford University Press.

Beck, U. (1988) *The Risk Society: Towards a New Modernity*, Sage.

Cartwright, N. (1999) *The Dappled World: A Study of the Boundaries of Science*, Cambridge University Press.

Ellul, J. (1964) *The Technological Society*, Random House.

Greene, B. (2004) *The Fabric of the Cosmos*, Penguin.

Laubichler, M.D. and Wagner, G.P. (2001) "How Molecular is Molecular Developmental Biology", *Biology and Philosophy*, vol. 16.

Lee, K. (1999) *The Natural and The Artefactual*, Lexington Books.

——— (2003) "The Source and Locus of Intrinsic Value", in A. Light and H. Rolston III (eds.) *Environmental Ethics: An Anthology*, Blackwell.

Levidow, L. et al. (2007) "Recasting 'Substantial Equivalence': Transatlantic Governance of GM Food", *Science, Technology and Human Values*, vol. 32.

Lewontin, R. (2000) *The Triple Helix: Gene, Organism and Environment*, Harvard University Press.

Lie, S.A. and Wickson, F. (2011) "The Relational Ontology of Deep Ecology: A Dispositional Alternative to Intrinsic Value?", in A. Aaro and J. Servan (eds.) *Environment, Embodiment & History*, Hermes Texts.

Lipinsky, C. and Hopkins, A. (2004) "Navigating Chemical Space for Biology and Medicine", *Nature*, 16 December.

Mill, J.S. (1843/2002) *A System of Logic*, University Press of the Pacific, Honolulu.

Millstone, E. et al. (1999) "Beyond 'Substantial Equivalence', *Nature*, 7 Oct.

Moore, G.E. (1903/2004) *Principia Ethica*, Dover Publications.

Mumford, S. (1998) *Dispositions*, Oxford University Press.

——— (2004) *Laws in Nature*, Routledge.

O'Neill, J. (2003) "The Varieties of Intrinsic Value", in A. Light and H. Rolston III (eds.) *Environmental Ethics: An Anthology*, Blackwell.

Singer, P. (1975) *Animal Liberation*, Harper Collins Publishers.

Taylor, P. (1986) *Respect for Nature*, Princeton University Press.

Westra, L. (1994) *An Environmental Proposal for Ethics: The Principle of Integrity*, Rowman & Littlefield.

Winner, L. (1977) *Autonomous Technology*, MIT Press.

6 Naturalness in ecology and wilderness stewardship

6.0 Introduction

My attention in this book has so far been more or less explicitly focused upon how we may or may not employ different science-based technologies in relation to our manipulations of nature.

The purpose of this chapter is to show how the philosophical issues dealt with in the book so far pertain to what one might call 'macro-level-related' topics such as ecosystem management and wilderness area stewardship. How does the discussion of naturalness tap into issues such as conservation policy for wilderness areas, the restoration and general management of ecosystems, etc.? This issue seems increasingly important in the age that many have started to call the *Anthropocene*.

The framework for the thrust of the argument in this chapter is the distinction that can be made between functional and "natural" approaches to ecosystem management and wilderness stewardship. In subsection 6.1.2, I provide a historical picture that is intended to explain the background for this distinction and to explain why I think that a (new) concept of naturalness can be fruitfully employed rather than generally rejected. The last part contains a discussion of whether naturalness should be left out of ecosystem management and wilderness stewardship in general.

6.1 Naturalness, ecology and wilderness

A particularly interesting, difficult and debated issue is how naturalness relates to our understanding and treatment of wilderness areas. Related to this concern are scientific subjects such as conservation biology and restoration ecology.

This issue is of straightforward importance. Ecosystem management and park and wilderness stewardship are some of the last few subject areas in relation to which we could say that the term 'naturalness' still plays a direct and indirect role as a common reference and "guiding principle". However, recent developments have questioned the viability of this concept even within these subject areas. Alternatives to 'naturalness' in these specific areas are not easy to define and make operable, but different varieties of a "functional" concept of wilderness stewardship and ecosystem management seem to have gained ground. With respect to the criticism of the role that naturalness has played, it is often suggested that park and ecosystem managers *de facto* have to make *choices* and that the inevitability of this "fact" should be acknowledged. What does this mean? In reality and in the long run it would mean that we should acknowledge that it is we (humans) who decide what nature should look like in the future. Do we want (in a certain landscape area) a nature that is "pristine", a nature that provides us with monetary value, a nature that has an appeal to tourists – or do we even want to make choices such as this at all?

Proposing a goal-oriented management of "nature" in general, and in protected wilderness areas in particular, means that we have decided to incorporate non-human nature into a functional world. In Aristotelian terms, we would start to make what exists by nature into something that works by technè; in Heideggerian terms, such a proposal implies that we have started to think about the non-human natural world as an immanent realm of *Zeug* (equipment) where the parts in the system stand in a *functional* relationship to each other. For example, we regard certain elements (herbivore w, y, z, q, etc.; decomposer f, l, r, c, etc.; predator a, b, c, etc.) as necessary for achieving goal X. To positively (and not only defensively) change orientation from naturalness to functional views is not a small step, therefore. This is a major, perhaps *the* major, conceptual shift that has occurred in our relationship to nature in this century, and that will potentially be exacerbated in centuries to come. It is a shift that, to my mind, may potentially be "just as destructive to nature as bulldozers and chain saws" (Soule and Lease 1995, xvi).

The account developed here is one in which the concept of naturalness does not imply that we should leave nature alone. We may "use nature" on this account. But "use" means something completely different, as we have seen, if one holds on to a concept of 'naturalness' (as e.g. developed in this book). Use that is articulated to naturalness does not imply a sheer instrumental use (see section 5.7). Proponents of the evolving functional accounts (section 6.3) that have been developed as an alternative to an account based on naturalness need to understand this, and to see that *their* account therefore comes with a price. What this means is that to *use nature* under these two regimes is substantially different. I embrace the idea that we should use nature, but not if this use is based upon a functional approach, wherein "to use" means 'to use as an instrument' and wherein the underlying ontology is a passivist ontology.

Some may answer this by saying, "Well, we know that non-human nature puts limits on our decisions, and that we cannot make decisions that are not in line with these limitations anyway. Passivism or not, I do not care so long as it works." The question is: 'How would you characterize these limits, if not in terms of naturalness?' The functional paradigm is developed as an alternative to an unsatisfying paradigm wherein "naturalness" has been the guiding principle. Since I, however, believe that (possible-N) naturalness describes what these "limitations" really are, I believe naturalness to be an inevitable part of ecosystem management in the first place. My solution is therefore to show that a *different* concept of naturalness is a better alternative than to reject naturalness altogether and then eventually go for an "empty" functional guiding principle that has vast and possibly detrimental consequences.

6.1.1 Constructivism and ecology

Noel Castree distinguishes between four different meanings/narratives of the word 'nature' "and its collateral concepts" (2014, 16): (1) the entire physical world; (2) the non-human world; (3) the essence of something; and (4) an inherent force. As I said in subsection 1.3.1, to be a constructivist is to accept that one cannot go beyond the process of *identifying* and structuring different meanings of a word (which also often means debunking and deconstruction along the way). There is no privileged meaning. The idea of a privileged meaning is vacuous for a constructivist since a privileged meaning can never be more than *yet another* (constructed) meaning. The conclusion is of course that nature is not natural, but *social* (ibid., 105). What we think is natural are socially constructed beliefs that cannot and should not be privileged over any other belief. Why do the constructivists think like this?

Most constructivists do not defend radical or strong constructivism, which would be to say that there is no such thing as "the real external world". In Kurt Jax's words:

> While a few constructivists would really argue that language and social processes are the only "real" things, preceding any physical reality, most constructivists, as the quote from Latour demonstrates, do not deny the existence of some kind of reality existing independently of us, even though they strongly question how much we can really know about it in terms of "objective knowledge".
>
> (2010, 115)

Constructivism is a reaction directed against the naïve realist, according to whom there is a simple correspondence between signs and the world. For this and other reasons, it is difficult to pin down what the constructivist *positively* means.

Castree says, along with many of his associates, that this "is not to say that this 'nature' is constructed by us without ontological reminder" (2014, 137) and further that: "representation is never *sui generis*, never something fashioned out of whole cloth: there are ontological limits to the process of construction" (ibid., 139). What is this ontological reminder? What are the ontological limits to the process of construction? A constructivist has of course closed him or herself off from saying anything about this. Nevertheless she may ask: can anything be said about this ontological realm? Previously in subsection 2.5.1 and Chapter 1, note 4, I argued with the help of Hacking that constructivists have a hidden affinity with "Humeanism". Castree, for instance, admits to what I will call a "flux-of-nature" paradigm when he willingly or not displays his ontological favourite: "... the world is composed not of things but of myriad relations" (ibid.). This unspecified relational ontology is typical for several constructivists, for instance for Latour.[1] Latour's anti-essentialist and anti-reductionist ontology typically rests on a similar relationalist pluralist "flux-of-nature" paradigm, wherein any actant, placed in a network, is as real as any other, and wherein the actant *is* its concrete relation (see e.g. Harman 2009, 11ff. and 151ff.[2]).

What we encounter here is the old idea of nominalism. The nominalist believes in a reality (after all) that is too plural and "crossbred" to fit the neat and perfect boundaries of our nominal systems. What this "reality" is, is famously difficult to pin down, since such an attempt would more or less demand a reality that *could* fit our strict concepts and nominal systems. What, then, can proponents of this 'after all ontology' say about nature? Maybe nothing more than: 'Nature is rather a complex meshwork of complex relations that floats in both time and space', or something like that. In one sense, doesn't it seem as though it is obviously true that constructivists do have an idea of nature that supersedes all narratives after all? Yes and no. This flux-of-nature account is presupposed rather than strictly formulated as an ontology in its own right. It is an ontology that, for the reasons given above, is not explicitly stated and discussed. It is a 'gesturing ontology', one that puts too much trust in a benevolent reader who 'feels the same about the world'. The problem with this 'after all ontology' is when we end up saying, in the end, and together with the Humeans, that there is nothing more to be said about nature than what we find to be possible-I. The problem is, of course, that we will not be able to distinguish between alterations of nature that are "good" or "bad" in a meaningful way. Any alteration will be as good as any other. If 'everything floats' in a way that we are unwilling to formulate more specifically, or that is allegedly impossible to formulate, we are making it impossible to combine theory with action. If proponents of this 'after all ontology' are really saying that nature has no specific natural course, doing so adds an extra dimension to the claim that naturalness is a social construction. It makes it even more obvious that we cannot really distinguish between a good and a bad management of, e.g., a protected wilderness area in the first place – and, accordingly, that a functional approach will be the evident way forward in any case.

The discussion that follows will show that the history of ecology has brought us to the point at which 'the ecology of natural disturbance and patch dynamics' is the prevailing paradigm in today's ecology. This is a paradigm that in many aspects presents essentialism in the same way as constructivism does. Essentialism in ecology, if there is any, has historically been represented by those who think that there exists an ecological balance in nature: the state that nature "tries" to reach (climax community) in a way that in some aspects resembles how, as we have seen, Aristotle was thinking about development and essence. The fact that the majority of ecologists have now come to the conclusion that there is 'no balance' has been interpreted by many as evidence for the idea that nature has no nature – not even at the ecological level. This conclusion combines well with the position of the philosophical constructivists, although I would not say that those who interpret the ecology of natural disturbance and patch dynamics in this way are all constructivists.

However, since we are not talking about just having a free-floating *opinion* on these subjects, but also about how theory should be combined with action (cf. e.g. wilderness area *stewardship*), we are in need of guiding principles that say more than 'Do whatever is possible-I'. Herein lies the deeper alliance between constructivism and 'the ecology of natural disturbance and patch dynamics': namely, they have no *theoretical resources* to say anything more than 'do whatever is possible-I'. To my understanding, this is wherefrom the functional guiding principle yields meaning. Everyone understands that 'Do whatever is possible-I' is highly inadequate as a guiding principle that will work in practice. And if naturalness is not available as a guiding principle, where should we look for one? In the 'flux of nature' that we cannot really say anything about? What about 'a functional approach'? That *sounds* like a solution.

6.1.2 A brief history of ecology as a science in light of naturalness

A. Introduction

Ecology as a scientific field has close bonds to environmental issues. One may say that environmentalism and ecology have common aspects that share a destiny. 'Ecology' and 'ecological' are often used as normative concepts. To have an ecological lifestyle is taken to mean that one lives one's life in 'agreement with nature'. Ecological housing means building houses that are "nature friendly". 'Eco' is put in front of a lot of activities and products these days.

The science of ecology, however, deals with other questions. When we talk about ecology as a science, we are of course pointing to a subject area that is descriptive in kind. The history of ecology shows, however – as is the case with many other sciences – that the line between the normative and the descriptive interests is not very thick after all. In "Environmentalism: Death and Resurrection", Mark Sagoff writes: "Once Forbes and Clements posited the existence of communal bonds or 'community', linking organisms within ecosystems, ecologists saw in this bond a moral good worth preserving" (2007, 4). This is one citation out of many that provide an example of what I think most ecologists and others have already recognized: how we understand ecology (as science) immediately evokes 'normative emotions'. The way we understand 'ecology' is in many ways decisive for how we understand nature and our role in nature in a broader sense.

Ecology is a science in which passivism does not predominate, and wherein naturalness at least could be said to play an indirect role in certain ways. This seems to be a situation that is welcomed by people engaged in environmental questions. One exception (out of several), however, is Mark Sagoff (2003; 2007), who thinks that environmental policy should be based on something other than the science of ecology. He gives two reasons for this.

1   Ecology is a science that cannot provide guidance or a scientifically strong enough basis for environmental engagement and decisions. In "The Plaza and Pendulum: Two concepts of Ecological science" (2003) Sagoff strongly criticizes ecology for having a dubious status as a science. An underlying claim that runs through many of his other writings, a claim that is in line with a more general criticism of ecology, is that ecology has had an underlying normative idea about balance and purpose in nature that has distorted its scientific vision and merit. He asserts:

In the 1970s, legislators relied on ecologists like E. P. Odum to secularize the hidden order of nature and the essential wrongness of humanity. Today, however, ecologists are not sure that ecosystems demonstrate a strategy of development: biologists debate whether ecological communities possess a hidden order that excludes humanity. Amid this uncertainty, ecology as a kind of priestcraft may be doing more harm than good.

(2007, 7; see also Sagoff 1988/2008)

2   The other reason he gives for why we should reject the close bonds between ecology as science and environmental ethics and politics is that he simply thinks that environmental policy should be based on *people's values* rather than prescriptions from a (un)scientific field (ibid., 6).

Sagoff, as we have seen, is worried about the role of values in ecology as a science. Many who want to secure the scientific status of ecology have reacted to this worry by simply saying that there is 'no order' in nature, accentuating the idea that ecological systems are chaotic, randomly organized, patchy and dominated by disturbance, etc. And as we shall see, many have reacted by supporting a "reductive" paradigm of ecology. By making this move they think that ecology as a science will be less value-laden and more scientific. The debate today takes the following shape: a certain paradigm of ecology that we might call Clementsian 'ecosystem ecology' is seen to have hidden values that are smuggled, through it, into the political and ethical debate. Some or quite many ('un-enlightened non-scientific partakers') think of this as good. Others, like Sagoff and Daniel Botkin, think of this as something bad. They see "any" description of patterns and ecosystem as suspicious properties and possible candidates of transformed values. We should therefore, according to them, reject these "descriptions" (this paradigm), change tack and simply decide which values we would like to govern nature with *directly*. I am worried that Sagoff's and Botkin's thinking is no more than an antithetical result of what they deny. 'Patterns, balance and order in nature are the product of the (normative) human mind. *Therefore*: no patterns, balance or order in nature.' To understand this better however, we need to take a closer look at the history of the science of ecology.

While e.g. Botkin and Sagoff says that this is about value-ladenness in ecology, I think that this is and always has been about naturalness, and that bringing this to the forefront enlightens this debate. The concept developed here does not imply improper value-ladenness, as I have argued previously at length. To search for an understanding of naturalness in ecology is not to search for values. As I have argued throughout this book, naturalness belongs to the is-side, not to the ought-side. To talk about naturalness is therefore not a dangerous undertaking 'for an already vulnerable science' (such as ecology), because naturalness is something that we can find at all levels of reality and hence in all types of sciences – including in chemistry and physics!

B. Paradigms in ecology

In keeping with the central disagreements that we find within most sciences, there are also typically two traditions that are dominant in the contemporary debate of ecology, traditions with their own histories of the development of concepts, theories and methodologies (Loreau 2010). Although it is generally unrecognized, we see that these paradigms divide into two camps that, according to the full neutral monist view (presented in section 4.6), should be united. We see that one of the traditions focuses on the components that make up the ecosystem (community/population ecology), while the other focuses on the properties of the ecosystem itself (ecosystem ecology). I will hereafter call the two traditions the "ecosystem ecology tradition" and "population ecology tradition".[3] Typically, proponents of these two traditions have quarrelled over what they believe to be the same subject, although it may be that they are talking about two subject areas that overlap and complement each other (in line with the revised neutral monist view).

This is not a groundless suspicion since there have been many recent attempts to merge the two traditions (Loreau 2010, x–xii). I basically agree with Loreau's synthesizing attempt, which he says will *not* come in the form of a single unified theory (ibid., xii and see section 5.6 here). Currently, however, we are not interested in the synthesis of these two traditions as a topic of its own; the point is only to keep it in the back of our minds. What captures our attention is the kind of understanding of naturalness that can be carved out in relation to the two traditions. To the degree that their proponents have an opinion on the question of naturalness, do they have different understandings of naturalness or do they have the same understanding? To investigate this question we also need to look at the historical development of these two traditions. This is of utmost importance, because it might be the case that the reason for someone to argue against 'the viability of naturalness' in this context is motivated by a particular understanding of ecology that is incorrect.

The most general definition of ecology that one could imagine would be something like: the study of "[A]n assemblage of organisms together with their abiotic environment" (Jax 2010, 59). This definition clearly points to the fact that the elements in the ecosystem are connected somehow, but not in what way and to what degree. We should understand the historical development of ecology as a scientific field with an ongoing process that aims at answering this question. How are the elements of ecosystems connected?

When Ernst Haeckel coined the notion of ecology it was defined from the perspective of the organism that Darwin a few years earlier had described as the agent of evolution. Haeckel wrote:

> By ecology we mean the body of knowledge concerning the economy of nature
> – the investigation of the total relations of the animal both to its inorganic
> and to its organic environment; including above all, its friendly and inimical
> relation to those animals and plants with which it comes directly or indirectly

into contact – in a word, ecology is the study of all the complex interrelations referred to by Darwin as the conditions of the struggle for existence.

(1866, 3)

In hindsight, one may see Haeckel as a representative of the population ecology tradition, seeing the ecosystem from the perspective of the parts that constitute the system (populations, communities). However, one can already grasp a different perspective in its inception in his choice of the concept: 'ecology' (*nature's* "economy"). The point is that nature as a whole can be described as being able to have its "own economy" (Worster 1992, 291).

C. *Directedness in nature?*

In the late nineteenth century there was an agreement that the relationships in ecology could not be understood in terms of mechanistic and passivist conceptions and theories. Ecosystems ("nature") were not conceived of as an aggregated result of their constituent parts, but rather had to be understood as realms governed by "self-activating and self-realizing powers" (McIntosh 1985, 69) (a general idea with which Haeckel also agreed). The overarching and dominating idea was that there was "a balance in nature", and that this balance somehow worked on the parts as much as the parts worked on the whole. An early and telling example of this was Stephen Forbes's writings. "Forbes saw … beneficent laws and forces at work tending towards a healthful and 'just equilibrium'" (McIntosh 1985, 74). He had the idea that each element in the system "exercised prudent self-interest" by not overexploiting its own resources – for instance, by producing enough food for the herbivores to eat, etc. According to Forbes, this was not in conflict with Darwinian thinking. Rather the opposite. He thought that natural selection was the engine that had developed and selected the properties of the populations that were enforcing the balance of the system as a whole. He also emphasized that we should see what was later called ecosystem as a single organism, a metaphor that Friedrich Clements, the dominating figure and main founding father of ecosystem ecology, famously used later on (see McIntosh 1985, 77).

Although Clements did not think about the system as exercising "prudent self-interest", he was eager to promote the idea of what has later been called a 'superorganism' (Simberloff 1980, 13) (at least so the story goes[4]). And even though Clements and others such as Arthur Tansley focused on communities (plant communities), we may in hindsight definitely characterize them as ecosystem ecologists in the sense that they focused on the properties of the whole and not on the constituent parts.

To characterize an ecosystem as kind of superorganism implies a claim about the unity of such systems. Clements and Tansley discussed how different systems were *open* or *closed*. The crux of the matter was whether the system was "vulnerable" to change or not. "[O]pen communities were incomplete, unstable and heterogeneous, closed communities more uniform and stable" (McIntosh 1985, 82). To be a system with an inside and an outside seems therefore to be an important characteristic. A system or a community could even be described as "so closed in itself that it must be called an organism in itself of the highest order" (Thienemann, cited in McIntosh 1985, 124). For a system to be closed in some degree there needs to be something that *integrates* the parts. It would be meaningless to ascribe closedness/openness to an accidental assembly of elements that simply aggregates "wholes".

There are different ways to view this "integratedness". One may see it as a top-down causal situation wherein the parts are somehow regulated by the whole. An organism such as a human being obviously has "parts" that are regulated by the whole. Fleeing from danger, for instance, involves the regulation of numerous processes in the different parts of our bodies, to save the organism as a whole. Gene regulation is more and more thought of as a process that is initiated and coordinated by the organism as a whole (e.g. Strohman 2002). Could this be said about an ecosystem? This is of course a very contentious and difficult question, and it is, for instance, the most debated part of James Lovelock's Gaia theory. (In the case of the Gaia theory there is a host of answers available. James Lovelock himself has been notoriously unclear whether we can talk about downward causation or not, making his hypothesis open to interpretations ranging from religious readings to ways of understanding the self-regulation as a result of feedback systems that can be simulated as normal *causal* processes on a computer (i.e. the Daisyworld simulations).)

Immanuel Kant operates with a distinction between the way in which we should explain physical objects versus objects that have a natural purpose (*Naturzweck*), i.e. biological phenomena. Aristotle and the Greeks called the parts of the body "organs" (i.e. tools) exactly because they thought that the organs were *tools* for the organism qua organism (i.e., downward causation). Kant has a similar (but different) view in *Kritik der Urteilskraft*. Here, Kant argues that something has a natural purpose when: (1) it has a unity, wherein the whole determines the place and function of each part; and (2) that the unity is self-organizing and self-generating in the way in which all parts are reciprocally the cause of one another, and have no outside cause (1987, 251ff.).[5] What Kant is saying here is that an integrated being that is deemed to be something more than the aggregated result of the parts must display some kind of goal-directed behaviour (see also subsection 1.4.2 B). *Integration* comes from the goal-directed behaviour of the being in question. In contrast to Aristotle, Kant is not willing to say that this is anything more than a so-called regulative idea. When we want to explain biological phenomena we need to explain it *as if* it is goal directed. We don't really know if it really is goal directed. All we know is that it does not make sense to explain such phenomena in a causal-mechanical and reductionist way.

This underlying assumption puts Fredric Clements's idea about succession at the heart of the debate.[6] It is a debate that still goes on, although with a more limited scope (Jax 2010, 75). If ecosystems are integrated in this way, we need to understand and take the properties of the *system* into account when we want to understand and explain the role of the parts. In other words, if it can be shown that the system as a whole displays some goal-directed behaviour, then this will have a profound and defining effect on the science of ecology.

Proponents of the theory of succession famously propose that the development of plant societies eventually ends in a 'stable situation' wherein this development comes to rest in what Clements calls a climax society. In an area wherein for some reason there is no vegetation (e.g. an area left "open" by the retraction of a glacier), we will see that the vegetation will change according to a fairly predictable pattern, starting with a pioneer community of lichens (where there is no soil) and "weeds" (later called r-selected species) and *ending* with species that are perennial, grow slower, and are more competitive (later called K-selected species), etc. (i.e. climax community).[7] The main external force acting on this society is the climate. Clements thought that we will, with some degree of accuracy, get a certain climax state that is in accord with the climate in the zone (e.g. the tropical grassland zone, etc.) – accepting a lot of *ceteris paribus* clauses – wherein the plant society is situated. It has been pointed out by many that Clements also sees this development as an analogy of the ontogeny of an organism.

> The unit of vegetation, the climax formation, is an organic entity... The climax formation is an adult organism, the fully developed community, of which all initial and medial stages are but stages of development. Succession is the process of the reproduction of a formation and this reproductive process can no more fail to terminate in the adult form in vegetation that it can in the case of an individual plant.
>
> (1916, 106)

This metaphor again underlines the fact that Clements looked at an ecosystem as a closed and strongly integrated system, and it underlines of course that the *change* in the vegetation that we can see is not contingent or without patterns, but rather has a direction that at least *seems* goal directed. The metaphor also suggests that succession is not a sequence of different systems, but rather *the same system changing the content of its constituents*, much in the same way as the organism changes the individual cells and partly the way they are manifestly organized. The plant society seems to have "reproductive ability" even, and its development is a development that is a *definite* process (ibid., 3).

Although Christopher Elliot (2007) has modified the common interpretation of Clements's ideas given here, we can easily see why his statements were interpreted as expressing the idea of directionality and therefore also of goal-directed behaviour – in keeping with what Kant would ascribe to phenomena that would need to be explained in a way that was consistent with an integrated unit being governed by *Zweckmässigkeit*, and not by what Kant saw as the only alternative: an external source of causal agency operating causally on the being in question. Clements's bold and falsifiable hypothesis soon received criticism that falls into different stages.

Henry Gleason is known to be the first critic of Clements's ideas. Gleason, who initially agreed with Clements, published "The Structure and the Development of Plant Associations" in 1917, one year after Clements's *Plant Succession: An Analysis of the Development of Vegetation*. The critique found in this publication was confirmed and advanced in his *The Individualistic Concept of Plant Association* from

1926 (Elliot 2007). The manner in which Gleason criticizes and crystallizes Clements's position has been widely cited. He characterizes his own position as "*An Individualistic Concept of Ecology*", in contraposition to what would have been seen at the time as a 'collective concept of ecology'. Gleason clearly establishes the perspective that later will be referred to as the population ecology tradition, wherein the "perspective of the parts" is emphasized.

More specifically, he addresses a list of concerns that he has with the organism metaphor and succession in general (Elliot 2007, 18). From Clements's account one might get the idea that species occur together because they belong to a certain super-organism. If one opens a human body, one can be pretty sure to find liver in togetherness with kidneys, heart, lungs, etc. Is this functional unity something that we can expect to find in ecosystems? Not in terms of species, according to Gleason. Gleason noted that the composition of plants in a certain landscape area is not given in the way of concurrence: i.e. if one finds a species F, one will also (certainly) find species G. Gleason stressed that they occur together because they have certain (abiotic) niche requirements that randomly fit together. The distribution of species is individualistic.

According to Christopher Elliot, one of the major differences between the two is related to the way in which they view how the environment selects the potential immigrating populations that belong to the community (2007, 20). Clements puts the emphasis on the environment, while Gleason puts the emphasis on the immigrants. Gleason's point is that 'there are different immigrant populations offered', which means that the species composition is also to a large extent the result of the species that incidentally were and are in the neighborhood while succession and change take place. This contingent factor, in turn, determines the development of the succession that takes place in the landscape area in question.

In general, we see that Gleason seeks explanations that put more emphasis on contingency, stochastic processes and the "agency" of individual contributors. He also directs (seemingly) more attention to what goes on at a smaller scale than that of the ecosystem. It is for this reason that a view like Gleason's later position has been associated with a more *empiricist approach*. In Elliot's article referred to above, we find an attempt to downplay the differences between Gleason and Clements. Elliot's point is that Clements was much more nuanced than he is cast as being within the standard narrative, one in which Clements is put into the corner that Gleason had made ready for him. His commitments stem less from metaphysical ideas and more from empirical findings on the ground than has been claimed in the past, according to Elliot. Elliot argues that the ideas of progressive change towards stability, harmony and predictive behaviour do not apply to Clements, specifically because Clements takes these concepts to represent *ideal types* that function as heuristics (cf. Kant's concept of a regulative idea) for the ecologist in the field and not a representation that corresponds perfectly with reality itself.

Even though Elliot is probably correct in his interpretation, it is difficult for Clements to escape his place in the more overarching metaphysical and lay narrative in which properties such as balance, order, harmony and directedness are ascribed to nature in general.[8]

Eugene Odum is caught up in this same narrative. What is new in Odum's contributions is his *express* emphasis on the ecosystem as a whole. I have previously pointed to the well-known distinction between ecosystem ecology and population ecology. In the case of Clements and his associates it was not an explicitly stated view that an ecologist should study the *properties* of the system qua system. Despite the differences between the two camps (typically represented by Clements and Gleason) there was, before Odum, less of a bifurcation between those who implicitly talked about the ecosystem as a whole and those who were more focused on the parts. With Odum's explicit focus on the properties of the system as such, its "structure and function", it became more transparent that there was really a reason to disagree about what the subject matter of ecology is.

D. Ecosystem ecology

The term 'ecosystem' was coined by Tansley[9] and Roy Clapham, but it was given the extra momentum by Odum who strongly and continuously emphasized the connection between ecosystem ecology and a holist perspective in science (1971). Odum was in this sense a more *self-aware* ecologist (McIntosh 1985, 21ff.).

> Odum's recognition of the distinction between holistic and reductionist approaches to ecology is not the first but it marked a division which is still evident. Moreover, Odum associated the new "systems ecology" with holism and described the ecosystem as "the basic unit of structure and function" around which "ecologists can rally".
>
> (ibid., 201)

Odum associates holism in ecology with the idea that ecosystems are integrated 'superorganism-like units' (1964). The fact that Odum associated holism, ecosystem ecology with the super-organism metaphor is an important element of the explanation for why many, also today, generally think that they must buy into some kind of holistic teleological understanding of nature in order to be ecosystem ecologists.

Odum called his position *New Ecology*, and his focus came as a result of previous developments in ecology – in particular, the attention that was directed towards the *trophic levels* of ecosystems. August Thienemann was the first to assign terms to the functional "roles" that constitute what we today call an ecosystem: decomposers, producers, consumers and "reducers". Thienemann's contribution was further developed by Charles Elton, who studied these roles in relation to the nature of the whole food chain (Worster 1992, 296ff.). An advancement of the development in the ecosystem model came with Raymond Lindeman, who offered an integrated view of an ecosystem as a place wherein *energy* is transferred through the trophic levels (McIntosh 1985, 196; see also Worster 1992, 306). Lindeman's perspective made it possible to see the whole system as a unit wherein the flow of energy and materials through functional compartments of the ecosystem can take place. Lindeman says, according to McIntosh, that he adopted the ecosystem concept because he saw no way to distinguish the living from the non-living parts of the system (ibid., 196). This leap was, according to Worster, "[T]he key that opened the gate to the economic approach". And further: "Without thermodynamics ecologists might still be shuffling around" (1992, 311).

One of the main research fields within this new ecology therefore came to be the *general* understanding of how, where and when the different components of a system were able to exchange and transform energy and nutrient resources (see e.g. Raffaelli and Frid 2010, 9). How, for instance, are the primary producers able to catch the energy from the sun, and how is this energy distributed throughout the system? Some researchers took this view to its logical endpoint by "black boxing" the concrete content of system, measuring and studying only the inputs and outputs of the system (in the same vein in which a proper behaviourist would see the consciousness as the black box, and would focus rather on stimuli inputs and response outputs). From a perspective such as this, a lake such as the man-made Deep Creek Lake in Maryland shows *no structural difference* from "one that evolved or self-assembled over millennia" (Sagoff 2003, 544). This black box approach is surely one in which the researcher is expected to be occupied with the system as a whole, but more important in this story: the focus is not on how the particular and *uniquely evolved system* develops and maintains itself. The focus is rather on the functionality of the system, a functionality that is universal and independent of the particular and historically evolved relations of the parts co-constituting the system as a whole. This is also the main point in Donald Worster's narrative: the ecosystem perspective is mainly focused on the opportunity to study the ecological systems as "economical" production units, which also gave these researchers their important role to play in the "modern society" (1992, 312f.).

Odum (and others) also adopted the assumption (underlying A.J. Lotkas's mathematical models) that evolution had provided organisms with a maximum ability to exploit their resources. Odum (and others) transferred this assumption to the ecosystem as a whole by developing the bold idea that a mature ecosystem (climax) would also have a maximized efficiency in uptake and transfer of energy and that this was somehow the *goal* –if any goal at all – of the climax state of an ecosystem. In contradistinction to a thermodynamic equilibrium wherein the distribution of energy *is* just even, a system such as an ecosystem needs to 'do things' in order to reach and maintain an equilibrium state wherein the efficiency in uptake and transfer of energy is maximized through an increase in the complexity and organization of the components (see also Loreau 2010, 253ff.).

Odum was also inspired by cybernetics, wherein causal chains are parts of feedback loops that contribute further properties that lead to ecosystem stability (Patten and Odum 1981; McIntosh 1985, 210). The focus on cybernetic properties suggested the use of advanced mathematical methods. Moreover, this idea implies the assumption that the study of ecosystems and their functional properties can be done with quantitative methods alone. For instance, the first university course in systems ecology (with the purpose of working as a guide to a new ecology) focused on three aspects: (1) appreciation for the affinities between ecology and mathematics; (2) familiarity with systems analysis; and (3) skills in using computers (McIntosh 1985, 222). In other words, an ecosystem ecologist is not focused upon the qualities of a certain ecosystem. Neither does s/he care about beautiful rivers or old forests, but rather properties that require a lot of formal competence in mathematics and computer modelling in order to be understood. This sparked the complaint that ecology had become a mathematical subdiscipline, and that 'nature' had totally left the scene (ibid.).

It is said that the ecosystem ecology paradigm had its breakthrough and peak in the 1960s–1970s, and that this was accentuated by a research programme "The International Biology Program" (IBP) (McIntosh 1985, 213; Simberloff 1980, 28; Raffaelli and Frid 2010, 5). This programme had a duration of ten years, from 1964 to 1974, and was one of the biggest research programmes that had ever been granted at that time in the US. The program was partly instigated by the "recognition following World War II of the need to feed a growing world … a need which in turn demanded a clear scientific understanding of the functioning of ecological systems and the limits to their production" (Raffaelli and Frid 2010, 5). The upshot was "[A]n ambitious series of site specific studies [that] was established across the world, covering a great diversity of ecosystems types in over 50 countries" (ibid.).

The ecosystem ecology perspective established by Odum and others contains, as we have seen, the idea of what Simberloff calls the belief in well-behaved ecosystems (i.e. predictable successions, ending in a climax state). According to Simberloff, this perception had an appeal to those who were attracted to quantitative and *deterministic* models of ecosystems, i.e. to those who believed in describing processes in nature by modal necessity. Since proponents of this research programme tried to "assess human impacts and predict the effects of natural change" (1980, 7), the programme favoured an ecology according to which one would in fact be able to do this. In other words, with the ecosystem ecology there also came what Worster calls a *managerial ethos* (1992, 313): viz. the belief that ecosystems could be fully managed and even engineered by humans. Assessment of the programme showed, however, that this ambition failed (ibid.).

E. Population ecology, disturbance and patch dynamics

As previously emphasized, when we talk about population ecology in contradistinction to ecosystem ecology, we talk about a view according to which one argues that it is the populations and the other parts that *constitute* the system that also determine how the system works. A population ecologist would first and foremost see the ecosystem as a result of evolutionary changes wherein individuals (or, some would say, 'populations') capable of DNA replication are the primary driving force. Cases in which the ecosystem functioning is in conflict with the fitness of the individuals (or the populations) that make up the system are therefore not possible, from this perspective. One could think of an optimal way for the ecosystem to work, but if there were systems that came close to such optimization it would be due to the *random* ways in which organisms can have the evolutionary advantage of such functioning. We would never see organisms 'sacrifice themselves for the system' in such a case, since to do so would be in serious conflict with the way in which evolution by natural selection works. This fact seems to counter ideas claiming that the ecosystem itself is – or could be – an agent, or that it has a direction, in a similar way as Dawkins's idea about selfish genes takes away the idea that the organism has any agency of its own. Unless one can show that some type of group or system selection takes place, one will have to explain the properties of an ecosystem by ordinary natural selection principles (e.g. Loureau 2010, 228ff. and 254–255). A phenomenon like succession, if it exists, must be in agreement with what can be explained by natural selection (which may also be granted; see e.g. MacArthur and Wilson 1967). There are, of course, also studies and models that show that regular ecosystem properties can emerge from selection on an individual level (De Laplante and Odenbaugh 2006, 11).

A population ecologist would for this reason not have any illusions about the agency of the system as such, and would be more prone to focus on disturbance, randomness, and singularities, rather than on patterns and general principles of the system as a whole. We saw this already in Gleason's rejection of Clements's views. In other words, this view is not a recent view that developed as a reaction towards ecosystem ecology; it is a view that has lived its own life alongside the more dominating ecosystem-view throughout the history of ecology.

However, a more systematic and consistent view whose proponents could challenge the ecosystem ecology view on its own pitch did not emerge before the 1970s. This view is often specifically called "ecology of natural disturbance and patch dynamics". McIntosh (1985) claims that the ecosystem ecology paradigm was not accepted or understood by many ecologists as late as 1975 (despite the IBP). Yet its "counterpart" – the paradigm of natural disturbance and patch dynamics – started its vibrant story in the first part of the 1970s (e.g. Levin and Paine 1974). It is not clear, therefore, that this "new" paradigm was consciously created in opposition to the ecosystem ecology view, although it was ignited by those who were dissatisfied with the idea that ecosystems could be understood as deterministic systems.

In terms of mathematics, one could say that the one emerged from the other in the way that the obsession with trying to apply mathematics to the dynamics of ecosystems forced the ecologists of the time into more and more complicated equations and finally into "non-linear systems of equations" (Wu and Loucks 1995, 444). Already here we may notice that non-linear equations will not predict a single development towards a singular equilibrium, but rather towards states such as a "mosaic of equilibrium patches" (Levin 1976). According to Wu and Loucks, Stanley Holling, already in 1973, "discussed a number of empirical examples from aquatic to terrestrial systems that seemed to corroborate the [mathematical] hypothesis of multiple domains of attraction" (1995, 445).

The focus on equilibria and disturbance that emerged in the 1970s came partly out of the concern for how human action might impact ecological systems. As we have seen, the way Odum described ecosystems opened the way for the interpretation that an ecosystem will be determined to revert back to its climax state despite nearly "all" kinds of disturbances. This understanding was challenged by researchers such as Robert May and Stanley Holling, who started to focus more specifically upon topics such as resilience, tipping points, relative stability and multiple/alternative equilibrium states. One may say that the ecology of disturbance and patch dynamics came as a result of this line of thinking.

The notion 'Ecology of Natural Disturbance and Patch Dynamics' was not fully introduced before 1985 (by Pickett and White). The idea is that natural disturbances, like hurricanes, fire, lava flows, rare insect outbreaks, etc. (see ibid., 10), create patches in ecosystems that eventually create a dynamic that dominates the system as a whole. Patchiness brings heterogeneity into the system, which often creates further heterogeneity. Such disturbances are defined as discrete and "individual" events (ibid., 7), and consequently they are important in co-creating the historical uniqueness of each and every system. An ecosystem is not a neat and uniform stable state wherein one can be sure to find a "well-behaved" uniformity of organisms, but rather a heterogeneous "patchwork differing in successional stages" (Wu and Loucks 1995).

To understand this view further, it is important to ask whether or not the ecology of natural disturbance and patch dynamics *really* denies the existence of some type of equilibrium state or the process of succession as such. We may first note that the very notion "disturbance" points to the existence of something that can be characterized as "disturbable", and therefore suggests that there is some kind of directed development of ecosystems in the first place. In the introduction to *The Ecology of Natural Disturbance and Patch Dynamics*, White and Pickett state that "This narrow definition permits the traditional interpretation, namely, that disturbance acts to 'reset' the successional clock of the ecosystem" (1985, 9). One may take this as an indication of the fact that very few, if any, ecologists deny succession as such (see e.g. Begon et al. 1990, 629). It would therefore be a misrepresentation to say that "the ecology of natural disturbance and patch dynamics" implies the idea that ecosystems are systems that have no patterns or regularities. What proponents of "the ecology of natural disturbance and patch dynamics" do is to take disturbance seriously, and not just as a deviating factor in an otherwise neat and directed developmental process towards a stable state (Pickett and White 1985, 373).[10]

This has led to alternative descriptions of stable states that are dynamic rather than static (which hardly anyone argued for in the first place), but not to alternatives that are *radically* opposed to the idea of "balance" as such. We have 'multi-equilibrium states' (Levin 1976), the 'shifting mosaic steady state' (Borman and Likens 1979), 'quasi equilibrium at higher levels' (Wu and Loucks 1995), punctuated equilibrium states (Gould and Eldredge 1977), and we have ideas proposing that ecosystems go through periods of stability and collapse (Holling, 1995; see also Begon et al. 1990, 646). Researchers today do not reject the ideas of stability and equilibrium states therefore, but they are rather more interested in where we find such states and for what reasons. The hypothesis that biodiversity leads to stability is not an outdated issue, for instance, which it would be if the idea of stability and equilibrium was outdated. A lot of the research that is taking place today is related to concepts such as resilience, robustness, resistance, etc., which presuppose *some kind* of stability or equilibrium state as a starting point (see Loreau 2010, ch. 5). To conclude:

> [W]hile there is considerable evidence that many communities are not the well-ordered, clearly-delineated equilibrium structures that the tradition associates with Clements, there has never been any dispute that phenomenological regularities exist at community and ecosystem levels: ecology journals and textbooks are full of graphs and charts depicting such regularities. The issue that is debated concerns the scope and generality of such regularities, and the mechanisms that explain them, not their existence.
>
> (De Laplante and Odenbaugh 2006, 11)

I am stressing this here because there are several authors who construe the situation as if the alternative to the alleged 'balance in nature image' of ecosystem ecology is an ecology that describes nature as being driven by stochastic and random processes (see e.g. Simberloff 1980 and the way in which the modal dualism between necessity and contingency underlies his argument).

We should also note that there is a logical limit to how "patchy" an ecology can be. If "everything is a patch", then 'patch' works *de facto* as a proxy for 'ecosystem' – and if so, then to call something a patch instead of an ecosystem leaves us *less* well-off than we would be, I would think, since 'patch' has very little meaning in itself beyond pointing out a sectioned "sample" of space.[11] "Patchy" must be a description of an ecosystem and not the ecosystem itself, which means that a patchy system is something that deviates from something that is not patchy. Whether this is a "real system" or an ideal type might not be of great importance. It is, however, important that there exists a description of a system that is "not patchy", since the word 'patchy' semantically depends upon such a description.

One could say that Clements and Odum did not really take disturbance seriously, but if we go to the other extreme and say that disturbance and patch dynamics are all there is (with the aim of stressing that we are *now* talking about a *completely new* way to see and understand ecosystems) we will, if nothing else, get into conceptual trouble.

A last thing to be noted here, if only in a few words, concerns the matter of scale in ecology. (See e.g. McIntosh 1985, 233.) An issue that runs through the population ecology perspective, presently and also historically, is that it is said to be "empirical" and inductive. Gleason was thought to be an empiricist, and his critique of Clements is often viewed as being a critique that comes from a perspective grounded in empirical studies (Elliot 2007). Likewise, according to Simberloff, the publications of Egler, Cain and Mason in the 1940s were also considered to form a critique that came from "simple empirical studies", refuting the more metaphysical ideas of Clements. Simberloff (1980, 16) calls this 'the materialistic turn', referring to the focus on empirical studies and inductive theory-making. Sagoff also emphasizes the difference between, on the one hand, a science that is based on inductive inferences, and, on the other, a deductive and 'theoretical science' (2003, 547).

It is obvious that one cannot observe an ecosystem directly, minimally because one cannot observe relations as such (as Hume famously proposed). It is also obvious that one cannot *observe* what is going on as a *whole* in an ecosystem. From a strict empiricist viewpoint, we would therefore be right in denying that something like an ecosystem really exists. And even though there are few strict empiricists in the field, we may nevertheless see how a more empirically oriented researcher and fieldworker would be sceptical towards ecosystem ecology just for the simple reason that the ecosystem ecologist operates on a *scale* that is not "directly observable". This is interesting because we are right when we say that the way that ecosystems "are" depends upon the scale on which we choose to describe them. If we cut an area (call it an ecosystem) into $1m^2$ sections and put together the information from all of these pieces, we will get a description of *the whole system* that would differ from a description gained from sections that were $1km^2$. Furthermore, seen as a whole, the system might look "harmonious", uniform and stable. Seen from the perspective of 1,000 different patches, the system might look heterogeneous and imbalanced – or look to be a system that should be described as being in a "multi-equilibrium" state, rather than being in an ordered state of mono-equilibrium.

We should also note that if scale is important, it is also important to acknowledge the limits of the inductive method, since one would need "theory" to distinguish the scale on which one's *observations* are based. How do I know that this is a patch and not just a random landscape area? I need a theory to define an ecosystem, but I also need a theory to be able to observe a patch, a population, a habitat, etc.

'Scale' in other words, is relevant for the two opposing paradigms considered here. If you are studying density-regulating mechanisms in populations, then you are not studying the ecosystem as a whole, and there is therefore a limit to how much you can extrapolate from this scale to the scale that you face when you want to say something about the system as a whole. Disturbance and instable oscillation on a local population level might not be disturbance and instability for the system as such (see e.g. Tilman 1996; De Laplante and Odenbaugh 2006, 19f.). And as we noted in the introduction of this chapter, this might give us the opportunity to underline the fact that the disagreement that we are considering here is not necessarily a disagreement between two incompatible paradigms but could just as well be an instance of conflicting perspectives born of different scale and level-orientations.

6.2 Botkin and balance in nature

One may or may not draw strong conclusions from the ecology of natural disturbance and patch dynamics, but one may also see it, as I have pointed out above, as a complementary and moderately critical perspective to the ecosystem ecology perspective.

I think that we can safely say that Botkin comes from the ecology of natural disturbance and patch dynamics tradition and that in his book *Discordant Harmonies* (1990) he is trying to draw radical, far-reaching and definitely interesting conclusions from what he sees as a completely novel way to view nature.

Although Botkin's publication is from 1990, I will use his book as an example of how I think that the view that for some time now has increasingly become the dominant one in public discussion and among ecologists and others is based on some deceptive and hasty inferences. The fact that this view is gaining ground now is of course also due to the influence that Botkin's book has gained from 1990 to now.

The basic idea of *Discordant Harmonies* is that we are thinking erroneously about ecology and nature in the present because we are sons and daughters of a long tradition of thinking that nature is in *balance*, either because of a metaphysically established order (Greek thinking), or a divine power (Christianity), or because we think of nature as a machine in balance ('the machine metaphor', i.e. ecosystem ecology). Botkin's concern is 'balance in nature', and since Botkin associates the *ecosystem ecology perspective* of Clements and Odum in particular with this ancient idea, he thinks that these thinkers are wrong in their claims altogether and that the new paradigm ('New Ecology', *sic*) represents a completely new way of thinking about nature altogether, one for which there has been both a need and a demand. He also thinks that this is important in practice, since he has seen many examples of ecosystem management and human action in general that have involved deficient management models, leading to crashes in marine fisheries, misguided conservation practices and other things (Botkin 1990, 41). Botkin sees an important connection between (*his*) "New" Ecology and a new and more general view emerging in the twenty-first century. The machine technology of the nineteenth century required only surveillance and pushing buttons; New Ecology requires *active* management and choice, and therefore also a technology that can help measure, monitor and provide dynamic "answers" to questions that involve complex causality and feedback. The new information technologies make it possible to monitor and manage "nature" on a new and massive scale, in his view.

Botkin's specific starting point as a population ecologist is the logistic growth equation of Lotka and Volterra, which ideally assumed that population growth had a deterministic course (given certain antecedent parameters), leading to a regime wherein it would be possible to manage the particular resources of nature in keeping with this course (cf. 'MSY'). However, later research has shown that populations vary and fluctuate more randomly; these findings are allegedly a blow to the idea of a stable nature in harmonious equilibrium (ibid., 47).

When models such as this fail in their predictions (and we find examples of instability, randomness and variation in populations in "undisturbed" ecosystems), it is, according to Botkin, because nature is in a "disturbed", chaotic and discordant-harmony state in the first place. In other words, cases such as this show that nature is *not* in perfect stable harmony when left undisturbed by humans in the first place, and that disturbances made by humans therefore cannot really be seen as a problem. An ecosystem does not have any developmental direction or any "preferred" state. This means, in Botkin's eyes, that any disturbance is as good as any other – in principle.

What seems to be going on here, however, is that Botkin is resting his argument on the view that he denies: what he is really saying is that a system would have to conform to the thinking of the ecosystem ecologists of the 1960s in order to be "disturbable". In other words, we are wrong in ascribing any "naturalness" to these systems so long as they show instability, random population dynamics and unstable equilibrium states. The ecosystem ecologists *tried* to ascribe "naturalness" to the system in terms of succession, stable population dynamics and stable climax states, and since they did not succeed, we are right in asserting that there is no (other) way to ascribe naturalness to the system. No 'balance in nature', hence naturalness is a meaningless concept.

There are at least two problems with Botkin's main reasoning here.

The first problem is that Botkin seems to *performatively* overlook the fact that biology is an ideographic science. The object studied in biology is a field that is historical in nature. Again, this is related to what Botkin *requires* when he "looks for" balance and predictability in nature. Inasmuch as biology is an ideographic science, it is contradictory to expect that counter-examples represent full falsifications of a theory. It is therefore "un-biological" to infer from the occurrence of counter-examples to the conclusion that there is no order, no patterns or balance.

Take the intermediate disturbance hypothesis (IDH), according to which species diversity is maximized in systems wherein disturbance occurs at an intermediate rate. Systems wherein there are few disturbances and systems wherein disturbances occur frequently would, according to this hypothesis, be systems that have a lower biodiversity level than do systems with an intermediate disturbance rate. This seems logical, but is it correct when compared to empirical data? *Not always* say critics (see e.g. Mackey and Currey 2001; Fox 2013).

Take the theory according to which interspecific competition will lead to niche differentiation by virtue of the competitive exclusion principle. Such differentiation may not occur under circumstances in which there is strong predator pressure or for other reasons. (See e.g. Strong 1982; Shmida and Ellner 1984.) A third example is r- and K-selection theory, which was proposed by MacArthur and Wilson in 1967 and contained the hypothesis that

> [T]he great variety of mortality mechanisms present in nature (natural disturbance, predation, disruptive impacts of agriculture) could, by acting at various frequencies and severity, generate sufficient habitat diversity and living conditions to select and accommodate a wealth of different organisms.
>
> (Grime and Pierce 2012, 11)

Basically, the theory is that when the conditions are such that the chance of mortality is high, we will find r-selected species, and when the chances are low we will see K-selected species. The theory has attracted a lot of criticism (Stearns 1992). The theory has not been *falsified* by this criticism, however; rather, it has typically been incorporated into new theories (i.e. '*Adaptive Cycle*') wherein it still has validity and through which it has still found its way into the ecology textbooks.

Almost everyone within the scientific community agrees that, e.g., the species, the populations, the ecosystems and the complex connections between the relata in an ecosystem that we find in nature are the result of a *historical process*, and not instantiations of a divinely created order. And for the same reason that theories within ecology are full of exceptions, we could never "hope" to find a full static 'balance in nature' in the first place (*contra* what Botkin indirectly expects). To expect this would run counter to the very essence of biology as a science, therefore (see also De Laplante and Odenbaugh 2006, 15). ('Balance in nature' does not exist, but that does not mean that "balance" does not exist.)

The second problem with Botkin's conclusion is, as I have previously pointed out, that he seems to see balance in nature as the only premise for the possible ascription of naturalness. But as I have indicated in the introduction of this chapter, 'balance in nature' is not the only possible candidate for a criterion for the ascriptability of naturalness. An alternative not considered by Botkin and many others is the obvious non-teleological 'evolutionary developed connectedness' that we find in ecosystems.

When we find systems that are in a stable state, as we do in deepsea waters, for instance, it is not the stability in itself that is important but rather the relational web of *adaptions* that exists within the system. In other words, *it is the historically developed web of interactions and adaptions that is important, not whether or not the system is stable, self-organizing or chaotic, or whatever.* For this reason one may of course also find stable, unstable and even unstable unstable systems – and, correspondingly, a natural state of *adaptive* strategies related to these conditions.

The main problem with the *ecosystem perspective* is therefore not that it involves talks about properties of ecosystems, end-oriented processes or 'balance in nature', as Botkin emphasizes. The problem is rather that from this perspective it is difficult to acknowledge that ecosystems are not what they are in virtue of general principles, but rather because of a specific historical trajectory constituted by an evolution-based, developed web of co-developed adaptions.

The real problem with the idea of 'balance in nature' is therefore that one is liable to see the parts as functional units that are there to do the work of maintaining the balance. From a shallow assessment of the role that *function* plays in the ecosystem ecology perspective, one may be inclined to think that *anything can fill the role* as long as it is able to 'do the job' (i.e. *'black boxing'*; See also Jax 2010, 96f.). This means that one would be inclined to see, for instance, a 'fox as a predator' and to think that foxes generally can be used to 'recover the balance' of a certain "disturbed" system. It is at this point that we need the population ecology perspective in order to challenge and modify the *hubris* that the ecosystem perspective is liable to foster. Evolution plays a crucial role in population ecology. It is the more or less contingent steps of evolution that create each and every ecosystem. Function and "balance" *cannot therefore be defined independently* of the specific web of interconnectedness that occurs in each and every system. If there is some sort of balance, then 'balance' is nothing beyond this relationally constituted web of mutual connections.

The important element in this narrative is that it is a huge misunderstanding to take 'balance in nature' as a starting point for describing the role that we as humans can and should play vis-à-vis non-human nature. Botkin falls prey to the idea that if it is the case that there is no balance in nature, *then* we need to re-define everything. Balance in nature is seen as the one and only premise that *could* define an independent role for non-human nature, probably because this is associated with the idea that a 'nature in balance should be left alone', undisturbed. Accordingly, since nature does not display such a balance *as such*, and since it has the habit of "disturbing itself", there is nothing *there* that we need to take into account when we as humans want to make decisions about our activity towards nature.

A last point about Botkin's *Discordant Harmonies*: despite the fact that his ecology emerges from a rejection of the ecosystem-ecology perspective which also, according to Worster, entailed 'managerial ethos', Botkin seems as we have seen, to hold on to the idea that 'non-human nature should be fully managed by man'. This appears idiosyncratic, since the 'managerial ethos' was connected to the idea of mathematical predictability of ecosystems – an idea which is denied by the tradition that Botkin comes from. Botkin, however, thinks that the lack of predictability can be overcome by managing nature through advanced cybernetic monitoring systems (1990, 192). One may, however, ask why one would need to have these omnipresent, advanced, digitally based monitoring systems providing detailed information to policy-based decision-makers determining the "state of nature" (ibid., 197), if the system is such that it can be "anything you may like it to be" in the first place.

The reasoning that we find in *Discordant Harmonies* is even more explicitly expressed in some of Mark Sagoff's writings. Sagoff is similarly occupied by the fact that (ecosystem) ecology cannot authorize the exceptionless predictions that its proponents (according to him) say that it should be able to make. (Sagoff portrays ecosystem ecology as a mathematical science with Newtonian aspirations, and sides with the population ecology view. Sagoff 2003, 2007. See also De Laplante and Odenbaugh 2006, 12). His reasoning is that since modern biology and ecology contradict the theories of "Odum and Clements based in a secularized idea of a hidden order", it follows that the environmental movement is dying because it expects science to maintain our faith "in the rightness of nature and the wrongness of humanity" (Sagoff 2007, 7), which it evidently does not.

In other words: (1) The only way to secure the independence of non-human nature *was* through the idea of balance in nature. (2) This idea would have enabled us to argue that nature should be protected by leaving it undisturbed. (3) This has proved wrong. (4) We should therefore control our interference with nature via the self-interest of "hunters, anglers, backpackers, birders and other sportspeople" (Sagoff 2007, 8). Science can tell us nothing about 'how to disturb nature' because science only tells us that nature is already in a 'disturbed state'.

It would seem intuitively right, especially seen from the background of the Western tradition, to take 'balance in nature' as the basis for our understanding of naturalness, and to take instances of 'unbalanced nature' as indicators of the "unnatural" ways in which humans disturb nature. We should learn from this history that the idea of an (absolute) balance is not sound, but we should also learn to go beyond the modal bifurcation between necessity and contingency. That a system does not conform to the "necessity ideas" of the ecosystem ecology of the 1960s does not mean, as we have seen, that there is no type of balance or successive development in ecosystems. However, the regularities that we may find in certain ecosystems are not there because of some kind of telos inherent in the system;

rather, regularity is a state of affairs that has a historical explanation. The rationality of naturalness does not depend, as we have seen throughout this book, on the existence of a balance driven by teleological forces, but rather (in the case of ecology) on the fact that each and every ecosystem has a unique ecology, based on interwoven dispositional adaptions that are historically developed in each and every system (cf. HEDFs). It is the uniqueness of this interconnected system that we may or may not disturb. This suggests that ecology and a revised version of *natural history* studies should come together and make up the basis for ecosystem management, (see e.g. Burry 2006).

6.3 Wilderness stewardship

We have seen from the history of ecology that different ontologies underlying scientific research may or may not favour naturalness as a framework for our dealings with the ecosystems that we are a part of. We have also seen that different ontologies may lead their proponents to favour *different* concepts of naturalness or to reject the concept altogether. The current situation today is, as we have seen, dominated by a deep scepticism towards the concept of naturalness as such, mainly due to the historical development of ecology wherein naturalness is and was associated with Clements's organismic view and the ecosystem ecology of the 1960s.

Wilderness stewardship is a topic that evokes a whole range of questions that have an impact on how we think about naturalness and our relationship to non-human nature in general. The most interesting, compelling and thoroughgoing publication on the role of naturalness in wilderness stewardship is, to my mind, *Beyond Naturalness: Rethinking Park and Wilderness Stewardship in an Era of Rapid Change* (2010), edited by D.N. Cole and L. Yung.

The main claim in this book is that we should go beyond naturalness and find other references for our stewardship (see also Cole et al. 2008 and Jax 2010). The authors base this conclusion on at least five different arguments (that may not be completely new to the reader of this book). First, they claim ecological theory tells us that there is no natural state of an ecosystem that can be seen as a completion or a type of "natural state". By this they mean that the science of ecology cannot, as we have seen, underwrite reports that there is a state of balance to which we can refer when we want to restore, conserve or steward landscapes and ecosystems. Second, the history of wilderness management shows, in some established examples, that the protection of certain nature types in national parks changes the ecology inside the parks. The attempt to keep these areas pristine is itself affecting the "pristineness" of the protected area, and such attempts are typically related to the idea of 'balance in nature'. Third, there are many areas inhabited by indigenous peoples that are not regarded as unnatural or disturbed. What could possibly be the principal difference between the interventions and activities of indigenous peoples as opposed to the activities of modern technological humans? Fourth, there are no areas on the globe today that can be said to be untouched by man. Fifth, 'naturalness' relies upon the strong separation between man and nature. If this fundamental idea does not hold in practice or in theory, then naturalness must go.

The alternative to naturalness that these authors see is a functional approach (see also Cole et al. 2008, appendix). This orientation is merged with an argument calling for the steward/stewardess to make *choices*. We need to set goals and choose (changeable) strategies (Cole and Yung 2010, 255, 257). Kurt Jax argues that a functional approach necessarily involves choices (2010, 111). In other words, a functional approach entails that we humans need to decide "*what kind of nature we want to have*", which is similar to the conclusion that Botkin reaches (and which I suspect might be one of several sources that directly or indirectly has inspired this line of reasoning).

In section 6.1 I stated that this change in perspective is not a small step, but instead is something that should attract broad attention. It is a shift that requires that we are able to see what we are venturing into. My worry is that we are not anticipating the wide-ranging consequences of this shift.

All of the "wise advice" typically given (see e.g. ibid., 255ff.; Cole et al. 2008; Levin 1999) in addition to the functional orientation might create the impression that 'the functional' perspective based on human choice is harmless, since it does not necessarily exclude the focus on elements such as diversity, resilience, robustness, etc. The authors even think that this shift in perspective is not in conflict with goals such as "respecting nature's autonomy, the emphasis on ecological integrity, and historical fidelity" (Cole and Yung 2010, 255). Features like this are something that we apparently can *choose* to emphasize. But is this not a philosophically incongruent position so long as choices such as this inevitably require that one can count on the fact that there is a nature (in this nature) that can be respected? If one has discarded naturalness, how can one respect 'nature's autonomy' or the 'ecological integrity' of a certain ecosystem? Moreover is it possible to respect the autonomy of "nature" if we are the ones who are choosing what kind of "nature" we want? What is *there* to be respected if what is *there* is a question of human choice in the first place? Maybe we cannot have it both ways? If one thinks, as I do, that we should have naturalness as a benchmark for our dealings with nature, we will not be *choosing* to follow the autonomy of nature, since the premise for that choice is not on the same (theoretical) level as 'all the other choices' that we would be making on the basis of a functional approach. As I have argued previously, I think that naturalness is what enables us to operate with concepts such as 'nature's autonomy' and 'ecological integrity' in the first place. Abandoning naturalness as a *framework* renders the choice of values such as 'nature's autonomy' vacuous.

In 1999 the prominent ecologist Simon Levin said something that resonates even more widely today.

> The essential constant is change ... One may argue about the universality of any of these perspectives and the degree to which evolutionary forces might modify them; but it has become well accepted among ecologists that classical equilibrium theories are woefully inadequate. Slowly, perhaps too slowly, this acceptance has begun to affect the management of natural resources – for example, in the recognition of the ecological role of fire in renewing limiting resources, or in the advent of metapopulation models in conservation science.
>
> (Levin 1999)

The content of this citation has been interpreted as an argument against 'naturalness as a touchstone' in wilderness area management (p. 26) since naturalness is equated with 'classical equilibrium theories'. I have argued that this criticism is a failure in the sense that its proponents have been excessively focused on 'the balance of nature'. Besides the fact that not even the ecology of natural disturbance and patch dynamics requires a denial of some type of succession concept and some type of (heterogeneous) equilibrium concept, the real problem with ecosystem ecology is, as I have argued, not its proponents' tendency to favour balance, but rather that it fosters *a tendency to overlook the unique web of historically and mutually evolved adaptions that characterize each and every system that exists on this planet.* It is the uniqueness of the historically evolved web of individual and systemic properties that calls for our attention. I argued that to protect the *naturalness* of certain areas does not mean protecting a state in undisturbed balance, but protecting the *specific* processes, organisms, populations and adaptive-dynamic relations that we find in a given ecosystem. The co-adapted "process web" that we find might be in a state of great "unbalance", but that does not mean that there is a nature there that cannot be distorted, crushed or destroyed. The problem here, connected to the characteristic ideas that we find in *Beyond Naturalness*, is again that the wrong concept of naturalness is attacked on the basis of a misconceived criticism of an ecological paradigm, which criticism is eventually adapted as a *starting point* for what the contributors to *Beyond Naturalness* see as the right way forward.

There are two specific reasons to criticize the ecosystem perspective of Odum and others. The first, mentioned above, is that it involves a functional understanding of ecosystems, which makes its proponents prone to overlook the uniqueness of ecosystems and therefore the elements that make a *particular* ecosystem work in the way that it does. The second is that it inclines its proponents to accept deterministic models and therefore to believe that ecosystem processes can be predicted. We saw this in practice with the large IBP programme, in relation to which the optimism directed towards prospects for predictive ecosystem models reached a peak. It is an optimism that in many aspects ignited the criticism that we today find consistently formulated in the ecology of natural disturbance and patch dynamics paradigm.

These two criticisms are the very criticisms that are now passed over in the general and motivating picture described in *Beyond Naturalness*. To discard the idea of balance in nature is in one sense appropriate; the problem is when one proposes to adopt the deceitful functional approach of ecosystem ecology and on top of this "suggests" exchanging the "teleology" of nature for *human intentions* and decision-making. To argue this way is to argue that the lack of teleology in nature prescribes the necessary rightness of human decision-making. Again, this is an indication that one sees teleological ontologies as the only possible candidate that can underpin the property of naturalness that can be ascribed to the being in question (see 1.4.2 B).

To be able to make choices, one has to believe that the choice that one makes may lead to what is intended by the choice (see e.g. Anjum et al. 2013), and from this it follows that we will have to justify a belief in a strong modus of ecosystem predictability. The same issue pertains to the functional approach. A functional approach presupposes that it is possible to predict and plan for whatever purpose the function is a function for. There are different reasons why we should reject the possibility of predicting systems like this. First, I have already argued at length that we cannot determine the higher-level properties by changing the lower-level properties. To choose ecosystem X means that we would need to assume that we can change the system in a predictable way by manipulating the manifesting partners (on the level below). This requires predictability, which is not possible to achieve in the first place because of the 'relational effects' that I have argued are ontologically inescapable of any system (see sections 3.5, 4.2, 4.4, 4.6, 5.2, and 5.6). Second, we saw in subsection 6.1.2 E that the population ecologists criticized the ecosystem ecologists for their deterministic models. The irony is therefore once again that the predictability anticipated in a functional approach is exactly what some of the "extreme" ("black box") proponents of the ecosystem perspective believed in, but that later (and up to this day) received overwhelming criticism from the perspective of ecology of natural disturbance and patch dynamics – *from which, moreover, their own rejection of naturalness owes its appeal and influence!* Thus, what we are facing seems to be a model that involves rejecting (a sound concept of) naturalness for the benefit and advancement of a functional strategy of ecosystem management and wilderness stewardship based on an outdated ecology view facilitating a deterministic and functionalist understanding of ecosystems and ecosystem development. This is not a good deal!

A last word has to be said about the idea that there are many areas inhabited by indigenous people that are not regarded as unnatural or disturbed (Cole and Yung 2010, 18). As argued in the last paragraph of section 5.7, I see it as inconsistent to talk about something being *unnatural* as such. Conversely, one may argue correctly that a certain state or an action leading to a certain state of affairs *deviates* more or less strongly from possible-N. Deviation is not the same as what we mean when we say that something is unnatural. What this means is that we may view indigenous people's actions from the same viewpoint as we would view any other human action. Their actions may and will deviate more or less from possible-N in the same way as any other human actions do, although there are many reasons (also given here) to believe that our modern culture leads to actions that are hazardously further away from the possible-N state than others have been or are. This does not mean, however, that our modern Western culture cannot change attitudes and actions such that our conduct would be less in conflict with the possible-N nature (i.e., in contradistinction to the idea that our modern Western culture is one in which we are bound to act in the ways that we do today, and that indigenous people must act "naturally" in 'order to be indigenous'). In fact, and not surprisingly, I think that the way forward may well be bright if we are able to change our understanding of the real nature of nature and are able to act on those realizations. If we "are" post-modern today, we may venture into a different age tomorrow.

6.4 Ecology, dispositions and naturalness

Since I myself am inclined to argue that we ethically *should* let ourselves be guided by what is natural (although I have not displayed these arguments in this volume), it has been difficult to hold on to the intention of this book – which has been merely to instigate and underpin an *awareness* of the fact that 'naturalness' can be a serious point of reference in debates in which the concept *could be* taken into consideration. The problem that I have with the main authors of *Beyond Naturalness* is therefore not that they have a different concept of nature or naturalness, but rather that "their" account of nature and naturalness leads them to reject the very existence of a possible referent for this concept. This also means that I am not principally against a functional approach in ecosystem management and protected areas stewardship. It is only that I think that a *functional approach without* naturalness as a benchmark will not work and will be a harmful approach in the long run.

Kurt Jax writes:

> While "ecosystem functioning" is frequently (although by no means always) merely meant as descriptively denoting some set processes occurring in an ecosystem, the "functioning" in "functioning ecosystem" almost always denotes *proper* functioning. Otherwise it would mean only something completely trivial and tautological: there are always some processes going on in an ecosystem, even on the basis of the most general definitions of an ecosystem.
>
> (2010, 74)

His idea is that since we cannot assume that ecosystems have a teleological direction, we will have to assume that 'proper functioning' refers to a social construction (what in this context he calls "external purposiveness", ibid., 82).

The idea in this book has been to replace the empty space that he and many with him have no choice but to fill with a social constructivist account. This replacement is given by the dispositional account described in chapters 4, 5 and 6. I have also argued there that dispositions give us *enough* ontological background to ascribe a nature to something, meaning that we don't need to hold to a teleological account of nature in order to "secure" naturalness as a viable and compelling concept.

If we take a closer look at, for instance, Kurt Jax's eminent book cited above, we will see that he, despite his express "dismissal of naturalness", (e.g. 91ff.), uses – and moreover is in need of using – some kind of reference to what might be called the natural. He talks about ecosystems that are slightly degraded (224), about restoring/destroying ecosystems (84), about 'allowing natural dynamics' (100), ecosystem health, disturbance, etc. He thinks that he can "safeguard" these expressions by saying that they are normative and socially constructed. I don't think so. I would say that this reveals a problem that is not in any sense unique to his work. The problem is simply that he and his associates have to accept a passivist ontology of nature in order to underpin their point of view (namely, that there is nothing *there* that can be disturbed, restored or degraded in the first place). All that we would find if we were to examine the reference for these concepts would be a possible-I nature that is compossible within those (physical) limits. One may not see this as a problem, since our values – and especially the values of ecologists, protected area managers, restoration biologists and others – share the similar understanding that secures the same conclusion: that we should more or less 'keep the systems as they are'. But what kind of "defence" is this?

What kind of standing does this 'common understanding' have when interests, especially economic interests, are up against these values when they have nothing to refer to except their own socially constructed private opinions? Besides, management based on conscious reference to a possible-N state will have a better starting point than management in which everything is based on deliberation and agreement between conflicting values. I also think that we should all be worried about the possibility that the downside of the functional approach will develop. For instance, a functional approach allows us to ask the question: "Can species be redundant?" (ibid., 80). The possible-N concept of naturalness that I applied to ecology in section 6.2 would never authorize such a question, since what is natural would be based on the HEDFs of the system. There is nothing good or bad, redundant or important with these systems or parts of the systems in themselves. They are what they are.

There is actually not very much that is needed for an ecosystem to function. If we take away naturalness, what do we then mean by function? A fish bowl with water, oxygen and food supply is a functioning ecosystem. Why should we not be seduced by the idea that we can make every system on Earth into the simplest system possible as long as it functions and provides us with the services that we *value*? There seems to be nothing in this approach that deters us from doing that.

This brings us to another issue that raises the question of whether or not it is possible to escape the nature of things altogether. We have seen why proponents of the functional approach are inspired to go beyond naturalness. Is doing so possible at all? In sections 5.4–5.7, I argued that there is a price for deviating from possible-N. The goldfish bowl example shows, again, that one price is that this system requires substantial maintenance and external energy supplies. But this does not mean that the system has gone beyond what is natural. *The very reason we put the conditions in place for the goldfish is that we cannot escape the relational nature of the goldfish.* And to repeat what I said in Chapter 5: this is already an admission of naturalness. To go beyond naturalness is therefore a strange type of enterprise and we may *therefore* wonder where this strategy would really take us.

A better strategy, from the perspective of the account developed in this book, would be to say that ecology is a subject area that can discover these natures. The question is what this means.

In the first place, it does not mean that I am able to say anything more about these natures than ecologists already do – claims that they also quarrel over. What I can say something about is how I think this research should be ontologically guided. Such an intervention means first of all that I will refer to and reawaken some elements of the modified neutral monist account that was set out in full in section 4.6. What I will say in the following is not necessarily controversial or something that ecologists have never heard before.

The first thing to notice in this context is how an 'ecosystem' should be understood in the first place. Many ecologists as well as non-ecologists have made an easy case out of the fact that it is not an easy task to define what an ecosystem really is. Where does one system end and a new system begin, for instance (see e.g. Sagoff 2003, 537ff.)? Ecologists will in general have no problem with a relational account of objects. One may, despite this, ask whether or not the "relationality of ecosystems" is *really* recognized after all. As argued at length in Chapter 4, anyone who defends a relational account of objects will have to deal with the fact that objects stretch beyond themselves. Where does the object *human* start, and where does it end? This is not only a question that refers to our *de facto* dependency upon food in our surroundings, oxygen in the air and micro-organisms in our stomach, but also that our dispositional properties *are what they are* in relation to these partners. No object is distinct in the first place. In our effort to try to define or reject ecosystem objects, we must therefore not take an essentialist ontology as a starting point for the definition. Conversely, we often see that an essentialist ontology is taken for granted when asking where the ecosystem starts and where it ends.

The criticism raised against the super-organism metaphor of Clements and Odum is, to my mind, well founded. However, I do not think that this makes ecosystems into a false unit. If dispositions that cannot be ascribed to the parts making up the system can be ascribed to the ecosystem as a whole, we may also say that this is a unit that *has dispositions*. Very few, if any, would claim that the level-specific dispositions described in ecology textbooks (such as having trophic levels, being "able" to distribute the flux of energy and matter in a particular way, having a certain kind of biodiversity, having thresholds, some kind of successional development, more or less stability, etc.) are dispositions that can be ascribed to the parts on lower levels. One may view these properties as difficult to define and to specify, but to overlook them will be highly problematic for any account.

The second thing to notice is that a modified neutral monist view underscores the independence between the levels. Neither an inductive approach nor a deductive approach will allow its proponents to describe the relationship between the whole and parts in an ecosystem. In fact one cannot expect to find a single unifying theory of ecosystems (as argued in sections 6.1 and 6.2; see also Loreau 2010). Ecosystems have level-specific dispositions, and they consist of manifesting partners that make up the "base" for further dispositional properties but do not determine what these dispositions are. Conversely, the higher-level properties may restrict or facilitate the manifesting partners but they do not determine their behaviour. (At least, this would be the case for those who think that the super-organism metaphor is misleading.) A theory of ecosystems needs to describe these manifesting partners, as well as the partners "faced" by the ecosystem as a whole (obviously such elements as climate, energy from the sun, nutrients, etc.), in order to provide a well-founded description.

The third thing to notice is how we should view the integratedness of ecosystems. In previous chapters I have underlined the importance of the fact that the relational character of dispositions is historically constituted in general, and how we should understand the integratedness of ecosystems as being historically constituted in particular. This fact means that there is a limit to how far-reaching our *general* descriptions and theories in ecology can be, since the relatedness in ecosystems (and elsewhere) is unique (see section 6.2). For instance, we may describe the dynamics of prey–predator relationships in general terms, but these dynamics will not extend fully to the ecosystem in question. This *does not* mean that ecosystems are chaotic and contingently related; it means that there is *another type of order there*, one that is not fully graspable via universal theories (pace Botkin). Ecology is an ideographic science. To understand this thoroughly one must realize that the tools developed by those working in ecosystem ecology in the 1960s and 1970s can be dangerous tools. We cannot simply substitute one part (having a function) with another that can be generally described as having the same function. This is simply not how ecosystems are related. The real order and nature of ecosystems is simply not the order and nature that informs this functional understanding. Unless one is aligned with reductionism, one will need to acknowledge and understand the unique nature of the ecosystem in order to know what would be a good way to manipulate the manifesting partners that constitute the ecosystem as a whole. In its overall aim, the ecosystem function approach seems to lean on reductionism in that its proponents would (in a more or less naïve way) use the parts in order to manage the function of the whole. This is not a promising approach, especially when naturalness, the nature of the system and its parts are not seen as real properties to take into consideration.

This brings us to the fourth point that I want to underline. Throughout Chapter 5 I described the importance of differentiating between possible-I and possible-N. Entities such as objects, processes and systems have an endless array of dispositions (possible-I). There are restrictions to what kind of dispositions entities might have ("given" by the manifestation aspect/"categorical base"), but there is no counterpart to a *finite* description of these dispositions. This means, as I have argued in Chapter 5, that there is an endless (but restricted) array of possible-I ways in which we *could* physically manipulate ecosystems. These dispositions are, however, *not* the dispositions that describe a *natural ecosystem*. The dispositions of a natural system are specific and historically developed (possible-N), and quite often they depend for their existence upon their different manifestations. One may even describe them as essential, albeit not in a classical universal-kind-intrinsic way. It is essential for ecosystem F to be surrounded by climate Z^{12} in order to be what it is, for instance. This does not mean that this is a good state as such – only that the specific relational web of uniquely adapted dispositions that we find within this system depends upon this fact. From the perspective of the account developed here, it is simply a fact that the parts in the system depend upon their relations to other parts for their *identity* and further existence, in addition to depending upon the ecosystem as a whole.

But even more important in the current context, we do have a benchmark, a point of reference that is not socially constructed. Nature changes all the time, but not in fully contingent ways. I am not saying that it is easy to determine and define what this benchmark state is, but it is nevertheless something from which our manipulations and side-effect-producing actions can deviate more or less. There will be effects on humans also, if we deviate from possible-N! There will be effects because humans, of course, have HEDFs that are what they are in relation to these systems.

In many ways I am not saying anything new here. I am only stating the obvious in a way that *entails* a lot more than is usually acknowledged. Among that which is entailed is the worry that if we don't realize this fully, we will be going in a direction wherein we might have "functional ecosystems", but ones that are functional in a way that requires a lot of human dependent external energy and effort to maintain (see sections 5.5. and 5.6). We may end up in a situation in which, like it or not, we will try to blindly manipulate the parts of the system in order to gain the result that we wanted on the ecosystem level – rejecting the nature of the system as a whole. An ecosystem will not die or go extinct from mismanagement as would a hen or a population. But a management system might turn into a regime wherein the management requires further management, which requires further management, etc. (see also Aronson et al. 2007, 7). I fear that a functional approach, deprived of naturalness as a benchmark, combined with a general passivist ontology of science and technology that is additionally situated within a capitalist economy, will come to mutually manifest a management regime such as that. Caught in the vicious circle of a 'managerial ethos' where further management is the only answer to problems created by management in the first place.

Notes

1 We cannot interpret Latour as a traditional constructivist unless we argue that he is failing in his project to overcome the realist/constructivist distinction and the man/nature distinction in general, and I am not fully competent to make judgments about that. The fact that Latour is engaged in a meta-discussion about this distinction while purposively talking phenomenologically from the *inside* of his "ontology" is not, to my mind, enough to transcend this distinction. As I have argued, ontology got us into this distinction and ontology is the only way out. To my mind this requires that we are willing to say more *substantive* things about an alternative ontology than Latour does.

2 In a suggestive ontology such as this one would typically and elegantly jump over "mundane" problems such as the problem of the relata disappearing into the relation (cf. section 4.5).

3 The two traditions have had many names. George Hutchinson (1964) called these two perspectives holological and mereological. Eugene Odum calls the two perspectives holistic and reductionistic (which I think is misguided). I follow Loreau (2010) here.

4 We will see below that Clements is not such an easy figure to characterize as he is often thought to be.

5 Kant's philosophy on this subject is regarded as one of the main sources of philosophical romanticism, especially of Friedrich Schelling's philosophy, which in turn can be seen as a forerunner of the more romanticist concept of nature that dominated ecology as a science in this first part of the development of the field (Beiser 2006).

6 This idea was first formulated by the Danish botany professor Eugenius Warming (1895), and was picked up by Henry Cowles and later by Clements himself.

7 *Ending* would *strictly* speaking mean that "the individuals which die are replaced on a one-to-one basis by young of the same species" (Begon et al. 1990, 646).

8 There are many non-philosophers who refer to Greek metaphysics in this instance (e.g. Simberloff 1980; Botkin 1990). I have not been able to trace back the main reference for this somewhat inaccurate understanding. The simple idea that seems to guide this understanding is that the Greeks were generally known to understand nature as ordered and harmonious. Centuries of empiricism, positivism and philosophy of science have taught us that there is no pre-order in nature, and that claims about such order are

"metaphysical" as such. By placing the Clementsian claim that there is order and some kind of "harmony" in the category of 'Greek metaphysics' one does not only achieve a "helpful" categorization. One also (indirectly) asserts that these views are metaphysically guided (as opposed to being 'guided by science'). From this perspective it is easy to describe 'Clementsian ecology' as outdated and not in keeping with doing science. Since ecology is amongst the softest of the natural sciences, scientists doing ecology would seem to be extra vulnerable to implicit arguments to the effect that their views are *a priori* unscientific, and that they do not have anything better to do than to seek what seems to be 'an empirical ground' for their research. However: *If we were to really find metaphysical inspiration here I think it would be more* (historically) accurate to trace this back to Kant and the philosophical romanticists (see above and Elliot 2007).

9 O'Neill et al. define the following features to characterize an ecosystem: (i) ecosystems exist independently of specific components; (ii) its components are interdependent; (iii) an ecosystem has a function (e.g. the component parts each have functions that together produce a function of the whole); (iv) it is active; something dynamic, past or present is implied; (v) a sliding scale of organization exists. Quoted in Kormondy 1996, 8.

10 One may, however, also understand the opposite view where:

> Catastrophic destruction whether by natural agencies or whether by man, does, I think, remove the phenomenon from the field of proper connotation of succession, because catastrophes are *unrelated* to the causes of the vegetational changes involved in the actual process of succession. They are only initiating causes, as Clements rightly insists: They clear the field so to speak, for a new succession.
>
> (Tansley 1935, 289, my emphasis)

11 [N] This seems to be the case in Wu and Loucks' article referred to above when they say:

> In contrast to traditional approaches in which the individual organism, population, community or ecosystem is treated as the basic ecological unit of study, the emerging hierarchical patch dynamics paradigm takes a natural spatial unit, the patch, as a fundamental structural and functional unit.
>
> (1995, 450)

12 [N] A climate is of course not an exact entity, but we may define the variability of a "certain climate" within a particular range.

References

Anjum, R.L., Mumford, S., and Lie, S.A. (2013) "Dispositions and Ethics", in Groff, R. and Greco, J. (eds.) *Powers and Capacities in Philosophy: The New Aristotelianism*, Routledge.

Aronson, J. et al. (2007) "Restoring Natural Capital: Definitions and Rationale", in J. Aronson, S.J. Milton, and J.N. Blignaut (eds.) *Restoring Natural Capital: Science, Business, and Practice*, Island Press.

Begon, M., Harper, J. and Townsend, C. (1990) *Ecology*, Blackwell.

Beiser, F. (2006) "The Paradox of Romantic Metaphysics", in N. Kompridis (ed.) *Philosophical Romanticism*, Routledge.

Borman, F. and Likens, G. (1979) "Catastrophic Disturbance and the Steady-State in Northern Hardwood Forests", *American Science*, vol. 67.

Botkin, D. (1990) *Discordant Harmonies*, Oxford University Press.

Burry, B. (2006) "Natural History, Filed Ecology, Conservation Biology and Wildlife Management: Time to Connect the Dots", *Herpetological Conservation and Biology*, vol. 1, no. 1.

Castree, N. (2014) *Making Sense of Nature*, Routledge.

Clements, F. (1916) *Plant Succession: An Analysis of the Development of Vegetation*, Washington DC: Carnegie Institution of Washington.

Cole, A. et al. (2008) "Naturalness and Beyond", *The Georg Wright Forum*, vol. 25, no. 1.

Cole, D.N. and Yung, L. (2010) *Beyond Naturalness: Rethinking Park and Wilderness Stewardship in an Era of Rapid Change*, Island Press.

De Laplante, K. and Odenbaugh, J. (2006) "What isn't Wrong with Ecosystem Ecology", *Philosophy and the Life Sciences*, MIT Press.

Elliot, C. (2007) "Method and Metaphysics in Clements's and Gleason's Ecological Explanations", *Studies in History and Philosophy of Biological and Biomedical Sciences*, vol. 38, no. 1.

Fox, J.W. (2013). "The Intermediate Disturbance Hypothesis Should be Abandoned", *Trends in Ecology & Evolution*, vol. 28, no. 2.

Gleason, H.A. (1917) "The Structure and Development of the Plant Association", *Bulletin of the Torrey Botanical Club*, vol. 44.

—— (1926) "The Individualistic Concept of the Plant Association", *Bulletin of the Torrey Botanical Club*, vol. 53.

Gould, S.J., and Eldredge, N. (1977) "Punctuated Equilibria: The Tempo and Mode of Evolution Reconsidered", *Paleobiology* 3.

Grime, P. and Pierce, C. (2012) *The Evolutionary Strategies that Shape Ecosystems*, Wiley-Blackwell.

Haeckel, E. (1866) *Generelle Morphologie der Organismen*, Reimer.

Harman, G. (2009) *Prince of Networks: Bruno Latour and Metaphysics*, Re-Press.

Holling, C.S. (1995) "What Barriers? What Bridges?", in L.H. Gunderson, C.S. Holling and S.S. Light (eds.) *Barriers and Bridges to the Renewal of Ecosystems and Institutions*, Columbia University Press.

Hutchinson, G. (1964) "The Lacustrine Microcosm Reconsidered", *American Scientist*, 52.

Jax, K. (2010) *Ecosystem Functioning*, Cambridge University Press.

Kant, I. (1790/1987) *Critique of Judgement*, trans. W. Pluhar, Hackett Publishing Co.

Kormondy, E. (1996) *Concepts of Ecology* (fourth ed.), Prentice Hall.

Levin, S.A. (1976) "Population Dynamics Models in Heterogeneous Environments", *Annual Review of Ecology and Systematics*, vol. 7.

—— (1999) "Towards a Science of Ecological Management", *Conservation Ecology*, vol. 3, no. 2.

Levin, S.A. and Paine, R.T. (1974) "Disturbance, Patch Formation and Community Structure", *Proc. Nat. Acad. Sci.*, vol. 71.

Loreau, M. (2010) *From Populations to Ecosystems: Theoretical Foundations for a New Ecological Synthesis*, Princeton University Press.

MacArthur, R. and Wilson, E.O. (1967) *The Theory of Island Biogeography*, Princeton University Press.

McIntosh, R.P. (1985) *The Background of Ecology Concept and Theory*, Cambridge University Press.

Mackey, Robin L., Currie, David J. (2001) "The Diversity–Disturbance Relationship: Is it Generally Strong and Peaked?", *Ecology*, vol. 82, no. 12.

Odum, E. (1953/1971) *Fundamentals of Ecology*, 3rd edn, Saunders.

—— (1964) "The New Ecology", *BioScience*, vol. 14.

Patten, B. and Odum, E. (1981) "The Cybernetic Nature of Ecosystems", *Am. Nat.* 118.

Pickett, Steward T.A. and White, P.S. (1985) *The Ecology of Natural Disturbance and Patch Dynamics*, Academic Press.

Raffaelli, D. and Frid, C. (2010) "The Evolution of Ecosystem Ecology", in D. Raffaelli and C. Frid (eds.) *Ecosystem Ecology: A New Synthesis*, Cambridge University Press.

Sagoff, M. (1988/2008) *The Economy of the Earth* (second edition), Cambridge University Press.

—— (2003) "The Plaza and the Pendulum: Two Concepts of Ecological Science", *Biology and Philosophy*, vol. 18.

—— (2007) "Environmentalism: Death and Resurrection", *Philosophy and Public Policy Quarterly*, vol. 27, nos. 3/4.

Shmida, A. and Ellner, S. (1984) "Coexistence of Plant Species with Similar Niches", *Vegetatio*, vol. 58.

Simberloff, D. (1980) "A Succession of Paradigms in Ecology: Essentialism to Materialism and Probabilism", *Synthese*, vol. 43.

Soule, M. and Lease, G. (eds.) (1995) *Reinventing Nature: Responses to Postmodern Deconstruction*, Island Press.

Stearns, S. (1992) *The Evolution of Life Histories*, Oxford University Press.

Strohman, R. (2002) "Manoeuvring in the Complex Path from Genotype to Phenotype", *Science Magazine*, vol. 296, no. 5568.

Strong, D.R.J. (1982) "Harmonious Coexistence of Hispine Beetles on Heliconia in Experimental and Natural Communities", *Ecology*, vol. 63, no. 4.

Tansley, A. (1935) "The Use and Abuse of Vegetational Terms and Concepts", *Ecology*, 16 July.

Tilman, D. (1996) "Biodiversity: Population versus Ecosystem Stability", *Ecology*, vol. 77.

Warming, E. (1895) *Plantesamfund – Grundtræk af den Økologiske Plantegeografi*, P.G. Philipsens Forlag.

Worster, D. (1977/1992) *Nature's Economy*, Cambridge University Press.

Wu, J. and Loucks, O. (1995) "From Balance of Nature to Hierarchical Patch Dynamics: A Paradigm Shift in Ecology", *The Quarterly Review of Biology*, vol. 70, no. 4.

Index

Printed in the United States
by Baker & Taylor Publisher Services